Second Edition

Coaching Quarterbacks:
By the Experts

D1611304

Edited by
Earl Browning

COACHES
CHOICE™

ISBN: 978-1-58518--079-0
Library of Congress Control Number: 2007941279
Book layout: Bean Creek Studio
Cover design: Bean Creek Studio
Front cover photo: ©2007 Getty Images

Coaches Choice
P.O. Box 1828
Monterey, CA 93942
www.coacheschoice.com

Contents

1

Coaching the Quarterback

Ken Anderson
Cincinnati Bengals
2000

What I want to do is to talk about things I feel are important in coaching a quarterback. I will not get into the X's and O's so much. When you talk about the plays you run this is my feeling: we know every play is good, if it is executed well. I have a thousand plays drawn up on my computer. If the line blocks, the quarterback executes well, and the backs do their job, they are good plays. If they don't, they are not good plays.

I want to talk about a couple of things. First, is how to throw the football and how to drop back away from the center. Second, is how you get your quarterback ready for the season, and then how to give your quarterback a chance to be successful. That is the way I am going to start.

A lot of high school coaches get afraid when they get involved in a talk about coaching the quarterback. "I never played quarterback," some of you may say. Or, "I do not have anyone on my staff that has played quarterback at any level." You do not have to be afraid of those situations. Look at Bill Walsh, perhaps one of the greatest quarterback coaches of all times. He may have played quarterback in high school, but he did not play quarterback in college, and yet he was a master at coaching quarterbacks. He became a great quarterback coach because he studied football and he studied the position. He became a great teacher by studying the fundamentals and how to play the position. So don't feel that you can't get it done because you or someone on your staff has not played quarterback.

Another important point as a high school coach is this: do not feel that you must have a Division I prospect playing quarterback to be successful. On the college level, you do not have to have a pro prospect playing quarterback to be successful. As Bill Walsh said in his book, "The sum of the whole is better than its parts." A classic example is to look at Joe Montana. He is one of the best quarterbacks to ever play the game. He was a third-round draft choice out of Notre Dame. No one thought he was going to be a great player. He was not big enough, he was not strong enough, and his arm was not very strong as compared to some of the other quarterbacks who were coming out that year. But Joe Montana turned out to be a great quarterback. He developed because he was smart, and he had great fundamentals. He had a great awareness for the game. So the point I am trying to make is this: don't think you can't be successful if you do not have a quarterback that the Division I schools are recruiting.

Next, I want to talk about some general things. This is what I talk to my quarterbacks about. First, the quarterback is not going to win the game by himself. Now, your quarterback needs to play well to give you a chance to win. But he is probably not going to win the game by himself. But he can lose the game by himself. If he goes out and throws four interceptions, or if he gets hit in the pocket and he fumbles and they pick it up and run it back for a touchdown. The quarterback can devastate your team.

We talk a lot about our quarterbacks being fundamentally sound. We talk about them being consistent. We talk to them about doing their job. We are not concerned with them making the big play, but we want them to do their job. We tell them to give us a chance to win. We ask them to give our other players a chance to make our team successful. So, we do not try to put the whole ball of wax on our quarterback. We want our quarterback to do his part of the offense, nothing more and nothing less. We want them to blend in and make their share of plays, but not to make plays that kill us. If they can do that, then we have a chance to win. Your quarterback must be consistent and blend in with your offense.

I have been reading Bill Walsh's book, Finding the Winning Edge. In the book he talks about football organization. He is talking about the players in general when he makes this comment. "For a coach, what you have to do is to determine what skills and abilities are essential for a player, and then take the progressive steps to develop the player." That is one of the things I want to talk about. I want to cover what you need for your quarterback to be successful. Then, you must have a plan to accomplish that. The big thing I try to do is get our quarterbacks to think about the things they have to practice to make them successful.

A lot of the things I will talk about may not apply to you. I was trying to think back to the days when I was a high school quarterback in Batavia, Illinois. I can't think back that far. I can't remember much when I was playing quarterback in college. I can't even remember much about my first year in pro football. But I think the things I am going to discuss here will apply to everyone in terms of how you are going to get your quarterback ready to play. A lot of this is what you do to develop your plan to get your quarterback ready to play. You must develop a plan to develop your quarterback.

First, I want to talk about the proper throwing motion. This is how to throw the ball. The first thing is the grip. I have seen a hundred different grips of the football. Terry Bradshaw had his finger on the top point of the ball and he had a lot of success throwing the football. Joe Kapp gripped the ball right in the middle. I think the most important thing about the grip is the fact that it is predicated by the size of the hand of the individual. If it is a smaller hand, it must come up closer to the point of the ball. This is so he can get a feel for the football. I am not so concerned about where the grip is on the ball as much as I am about it being a fingertip grip. You want the ball in your fingertips and not in the palm of your hand. There should be a space between the ball and the palm when he grips the ball.

I talk to my quarterbacks about taking a firm grip on the ball, but you do not want it to be a death grip. Again, I am not so concerned with where his hand is on the ball as I am about the fingertip grip and the space between the palm and the ball. I do feel the grip is very important.

The next area that I am big on is pushing the ball back. This is putting the ball into the throwing position. We talk in terms of pushing the ball back with the left hand. I do not want them to drop and wind up. We do not want to allow the point of the ball to drop below the waist. First, if I drop the ball and wind up, it takes too long to get the ball off. Second, when you do all of those big motions it tends to lead into long strides. When they become big you become inefficient and you become inaccurate. So we talk about pushing the ball back. A lot of the quarterbacks coming out of college today carry the ball high as they drop back. They have the ball high where they can push the ball back when they are ready to throw. They do this so they do not have to drop the ball down below the belt when they get ready to throw. We do not want the quarterback to drop the ball below the waist and wind up when he throws it. Pushing the ball back is a big deal. It is important in getting the ball back into the throwing position.

Next is the release. Here is my thinking about throwing the football: either you can do it or you can't—to a certain extent. If he can't throw the ball, you are not going to make him a good passer. He either has a natural ability to throw or he doesn't. I wrote a book in 1982 entitled, The Art of Quarterbacking. I was working with a friend of Paul Brown's in writing the book. When we got to the chapter on throwing, they asked me how I threw the ball. I said, "I don't know, I just do it." We took a lot of film and studied my throwing motion and tried to describe it from pictures. I did not know how I threw the football. I feel to a certain extent, a kid has to be a natural thrower to be able to pass the football. A lot of the times either you can do it, or you can't. That is one of the things I look for in a quarterback: either he can throw it, or he can't.

Look at Sonny Jurgensen. He could throw the ball where he wanted it to go regardless of how he gripped it. Now, I am not saying you can't make a quarterback better with the things you do. But as far as teaching them a throwing motion, by the time you get them in high school, or certainly by the time you get them in college, you have no chance of changing a quarterback's throwing motion. A lot of it is natural ability.

It is important to let the quarterback use his natural throwing motion. Don't try to change it too much. To take someone and try to change the throwing motion is going to be more trouble than it is worth. If you take a very young kid and you tell him to throw a certain way, then you have a chance. When a kid comes to you in high school he must use his natural throwing motion.

We want them to release the ball somewhere above the shoulder. You do not want the sidearm motion. It is tough to follow through throwing sidearm. It is tough to get a consistent spiral on the ball. So if I am looking for a quarterback, the first thing I want to see is for him to push the ball back, have a natural throwing motion, and then release the ball above the shoulder. If you get that, you can be effective.

If you are talking about a pro quarterback that drops and winds up, we are not interested in him. We want consistent mechanics with our quarterback. We want a decent release, but we do not try to change it too much.

The next point is to use your whole body when you are throwing the football. You must make sure the arm strength does not come just from the arm. It must come from using your whole body in conjunction with the throw. Your legs give you balance and power. A lot of your power comes from the lower body. We want to be able to push off the back foot and step into the throw. This is what changes the momentum to get power on the ball. It is like a golf swing. Just watch Tiger Woods. It is getting the weight from the back foot to the front side. It is the same with the quarterback. You have to start it with the step into the throw. We want to push off the back foot and step into the throw. Then it is a combination of rotating the hips and shoulders. Everything has to work together. How do you do that? I am not so sure. It is timing, number one. It is a throwing motion. It is the rotation, clearing the hip, driving with the hip, and getting the shoulders through the football. It all has to happen in a sequence. A lot of this comes back to a natural throwing motion.

Another thing you see with the good quarterback is pulling the non-throwing arm down. For the right-hand passer it is the left arm. As you get through the throwing motion the left arm is coming down to the side as you drive through the throw. That is what happens in the throwing motion. You drive the left arm down and you come through with the release.

Next I want to discuss the follow-through. We do not want to kick the front leg. If we do that we have no chance to be accurate with the pass. You have to have a throwing motion with the knees flexed. As you come through, the knee has to lock. If you try to do it at the beginning of the throw, you have no chance to throw the ball accurately. You do not want to have the front leg locked when you are throwing the football. On the follow-through, the throwing arm goes to the opposite hip.

The thing I talk a lot about with our quarterbacks is the wrist snap. This is part of the reason you want to grip the ball firmly, but you want your wrist to be loose. When you throw a football the tightness of the spiral comes from the snap of your wrist. I just tell our quarterbacks to see how fast they can snap their wrist straight down. We just stand in place and work on snapping our wrist down. When you get a good wrist snap you do not have to have a great arm motion with the throw to get the tight-spiral work on snapping the wrist down. When you throw the football, you must understand the shape of the ball a little. If you watch the way the ball comes out of your hand, it is just like throwing a screwball. That is the motion. If you try to throw it like a screwball, you can't do it. So we work a lot on the wrist snap.

If I had to pick one trait that I look for in a quarterback, first I want a quick release, and then I want to know if the passer is accurate when he is throwing. You can make him a little more accurate with better body balance, and with a little more anticipation, but you are not going to make a 40-percent passer into a 60-percent passer. It comes down to this: either you can throw it, or you can't. You have to find a quarterback that gives you a chance and then work on his fundamentals and try to make him more consistent.

Next, I want to get into some drops for the quarterbacks. One of the things you need to do is to identify the things your quarterback needs to work on. What am I going to work on to get our quarterback ready to play next season? We are going to have a three-step drop, a quick five-step drop, a five-step drop, and a quick seven-step drop. Then we are going to have our play–action passes, which are all different drops for the quarterback. We will have our out-of-the-pocket drops, which all have different set points. They all have different footwork and different mechanics on how they are going to come away from the center. Also, we are going to work on the shotgun. You need to identify what you need to work on and what is in your offense. What kind of drops do you have in your offense? What are you going to ask your quarterback to do? Make sure you cover those things in an organized manner and then drill the hell out of it. You must be consistent with it. That is what we do and those are our drops.

Next, I want to talk about a five-step drop. About 90 percent of the passes in our offense are out of a five-step drop. We do not have a seven-step drop in our offense.

We have a quick seven-step drop, but the mechanics of the quarterback is more like a good five-step drop.

On the five-step drop, the first thing we start with is the stance. We want to be in an athletic position. The feet are about shoulder-width apart and you are balanced. You want to have most of the weight on the balls of your feet. The weight should kind of be evenly distributed, but it should be a little toward the balls of your feet. We want the knees flexed. You want to be able to move once you get the ball from the center. You can't move if your legs are straight. How much you flex your knees depends on how big your center is. The shorter the center, the more you have to flex the knees. You want the arms bent slightly under the center. If you tighten up your muscles before you take the snap you can't be fluid. Part of playing quarterback is being fluid. By flexing the arms it allows you to ride the center on the snap.

I always talk to our quarterbacks about having the weight evenly balanced. But I tell them to think mentally that the weight is on the left foot. The reason I say that is because I want to push off with the left foot when I am dropping back. We try to eliminate false steps. I do not want our quarterback to step in and then back. We want to eliminate the wasted motion coming away from the center.

I am real big on the first step. Every day my quarterbacks hear, "First step – kick step." The first step away from the center is the most critical step. You want to drive away from the center. It is an explosion away from the center. We should be going about 90 percent when we are coming away from the center. But the first step should be a drive away. You are pushing and extending. When you do that your left shoulder comes up. As our quarterbacks come back on the first step, I want to see the left shoulder come up as they come away from the center. That means they are getting a good first step. Your separation is going to come on your first step away from the center. If it is a five-step drop, I talk about depth on the first three steps and transition on the last two steps. You want a good step on the first step. You want to lengthen it out and get the shoulder up in the air. That tells me you are pushing away from the center.

Everything we do with our quarterbacks, we are working on a line. As we are coming back we want to work down the line. We want the first step to be behind our left foot. If the quarterbacks are not extending enough on that first step, I will put a towel down and tell them to step over the towel on the first step. I force them to step over the towel to get depth on the first step. It is important to work on a line because I want to see where their first step is. It should be just inside the line.

After the first step we concentrate on the crossover steps. Again, you should be straddling the line on steps two and three. As we come back the left foot is on one side of the line and the right step is on the other side of the line. The line is not over the left guard or right guard. It is expected to be straight back. We have the quarterbacks drop back for 20 yards just to get the feel of keeping the line between the legs as they drop back.

The crossover steps are our transition steps. We have our momentum going back and we have to stop and get into the throw. That is where our transition comes into play. The first three steps are big steps and the last two steps are little steps. Then it is planting the foot.

We want the hips perpendicular to the line of scrimmage or parallel to the line that I am working on. When we are dropping we want the arms to swing naturally. We want the arms chest high and in a natural position. As I drop back the ball should cross my shoulders. If I try to drop back fast my arms must flow across my chest. Let the arms swing across the body as you come back. We want two hands on the ball as we drop.

In the transition portion, we want two shorter control steps. After three good steps, the other steps have to be shorter. We must get our weight shifted back toward the line of scrimmage into our throw. I tell the quarterbacks to let their left shoulder dip. If the shoulder dips down he will have a chance to plant. We want the shoulder down when we are making our transition. We want to stick the back foot and make our transition back to the line. When that foot hits it should be on the insole of the shoe. If the weight is on the balls of the feet, the weight is still going back. We want them to stick the foot in the ground, plant, and come off the foot.

We do not throw off our back foot. There is going to be some type of hitch step to get our balance. It is tough to throw off the back foot and be successful. Most of our passes are thrown with a hitch step coming forward. There are two big things with a hitch step: number one is not to cross the feet, and number two is not to bring the feet together.

You heard me talk about the first step being a *kick step*. This brings into play the going to the left and the right. When you are throwing the football you want your hips pointed toward the target so you can step into the throw. If I am throwing to my right and when I plant, basically my hips are already pointed toward my target. It is easy to the right. What we work hard on in the kick step is throwing to the left. Again, we work on the line. The point is we are trying to get our hips turned so we can face our target as quickly as we can. As we come back on the drop, as we get to the last step, we want the quarterback to kick step across the line that will open the hips toward the target going to the left. To get my hips turned I have to swing my leg open. If we do not swing the leg far enough we end up throwing the ball across the body. We are trying to preset our hips toward our target. You must be working on a line to do this. It all comes down to teaching techniques.

Now I want to talk about some *drills* we use with our quarterbacks. First, we put all of our quarterbacks together. We are all on a line. We may be working on a three-step or a five-step drop. I will tell one of the quarterbacks that he has the cadence. We are all going to drop back together, but no one is going to throw. I can stand there and look at their first step. I can see if they are all getting the same depth, or if their first step is on the line. I can see if the rhythm of our drop is the same. The depths of the routes tie in with the depth of the drop. They all take their drops on one quarterback's cadence, but they do not throw the ball.

The other thing we do is to have the quarterbacks work in pairs. I will put two quarterbacks here and two over there. They throw to each other. Now, I can watch two quarterbacks on their drops and their releases.

Next we have them throw routes to stationary receivers, and that is usually me. I have them throw it to certain spots on my body. One time it will be at my head, the next time it will be at my knees. I will go to the left and then the right. We try to get them to think about the plays we are running that day and what they have to do on their drops.

One of the things we have fun with is throwing between two defenders. We put two defenders in front of the receiver and have the quarterback throw the ball between the defenders. We are trying to get the quarterback to focus with his eyes on where he wants the ball to go. I tell our guys the accuracy does not come from the arm, or lower body, it comes from the eyes. You have to focus where you want to throw the ball. It is just like shooting at the bull's eye. You want to aim at the bull's eye of the target so the shot will be as close to the center as possible. It is the same thing with the quarterback. We want him to focus to a specific spot. We want them to pick out a spot they want to throw to. We want him to be able to throw into a tight spot so he has to focus in with his eyes.

Another drill that we like is what we call *two to the head, and one to the body*. We have two quarterbacks playing together. They are dropping back. If they throw the pass and it is at the receiver's head, it counts two points. If the pass is in the framework of the upper body, he gets one point. The first man to get 10 points wins.

Next, I want to talk about *pocket movement*. Nothing ever happens like you want it to happen. How many times is everything perfect in a game? We stress to our quarterbacks to *make the routine plays – routine*. When they drop back and the protection is good, and the receiver is open, they have to complete the pass. When everything happens like it is supposed to, we have to make the play. But things do not always happen the way we want it. So you have to be able to move in the pocket. First, we want two hands on the ball. I threaten the quarterbacks when I see one hand on the ball. I tell them I will take duct tape and tape their other hand to the ball if I see it again.

We want to always maintain the throwing position. Now, we are talking within the framework of the pocket. I am not talking about breaking containment or about scrambling. If I have to avoid one man, I have to slide in the pocket. We must always stay in a throwing position. As soon as I get out of throwing position that receiver will get open and I can't make the play. We stress the point of relaxing before throwing.

Some of the drills we use are what we call *slide left* and *slide right*. We have them set in the pocket and then slide one man to the left or right and make the throw. We want to maintain the throwing position. Then we throw it to one of the other quarterbacks. We work to one side and then to the other side.

Another drill we call *step up quickly*. We get to the set point and see the defender has beaten the blocker. I realize that I have to step up quickly to get the pass off. He steps up and maintains his throwing position and makes the throw downfield.

Another drill is called *hit them with the dummy*. We do not hit our quarterbacks in practice. So when we are in drills, we have them set to throw. As they throw the ball I take a hand dummy, or a shield, and hit them with the dummy. I do not hit them in the head or on the throwing arm. I will hit them in the butt, or in the legs, just to help them to get use to things happening around them.

We still use the old wave drill. The quarterback drops and then I motion for him to come up, or go back, go left, or go right. As the quarterback is doing the wave he has the ball in position to make the throw. He has two hands on the ball. He is ready to throw the ball when I raise my hands. This is a way for us to work on pocket movement. We try to simulate things that are going to happen in a game. If we run a skeleton-pass drill, we will make him move in the pocket at times before he makes his throw. We do not want to make the seven-on-seven drill perfect for the quarterback all of the time.

The other thing is progression footwork. We have four receivers, and we have the quarterback work through the progression to the receivers. We always talk about letting the feet lead the way. We want them light on their feet. It is almost a tiptoe action. We tell them to let their feet take them to where they want to throw. Unless the feet are there they can't throw it. We do not want hopping motions.

Some Odds and Ends: This all goes back to what you have to do to have your quarterback ready to play when the season starts. You want to cover all of your basics. We make a list of all of the things in our playbook that I want to cover. This is just a partial list.

First, make sure your quarterbacks work with a wet ball. If you practice in the rain one day you can mark that one off. If we do not get rain we will take one practice and wet down some balls so the quarterback and center get a chance to work with a wet ball.

We do not want our quarterbacks to take hits. We work on sliding. We have too much invested in our guys to have them take the hit. So, we work on them sliding instead of taking that hit. We wait for a rainy day and we look for a puddle and have them slide into the puddle. If we do not get rain, we go to where they have the sprinklers going and work on the slide.

We work on recovering a fumbled snap. We try to simulate this and have the quarterback and center covering the fumble. Then we work on fumbles between a back and the quarterback. We show them how to cradle the ball and how to recover it. These are things that are going to happen during the season.

Next we work on interceptions. We work on playing off the blockers. Everyone comes after the quarterback first. He has to learn to play off the blockers to buy time for the rest of our team. Also, we teach them how to use the sideline for help. We show them how to prevent the guy that intercepts the ball from cutting back. We want him to use the sideline to push him out of bounds.

We also have some tackling drills for our quarterbacks. It is a matter of putting the head in front and wrapping the arms. We do this just so they can get ready for the season.

We work on the *hot throws*. They may have to throw off balance. We work on our scramble throws. You can script some of those in practice. You must be sure you cover that in getting ready for the season.

We work on throwing long. We call it *drop in the basket*. We want them to throw it at a 45-degree angle. For us, it should be completed 42 yards from the line and 5 yards from the sideline. I put a laundry basket down there. The quarterbacks take their drop and hitch step and try to throw it in the basket. We use the goalpost to give the quarterbacks a touch on throwing the ball. They have to throw the ball over the goalpost to me after they take their drop. If they throw it over my head they have to go get it. This is used when we want to drop the ball over a linebacker's head to a receiver. We work on our *keeper* action, and when they get to the goalpost they dump the ball to me on the other side of the goalpost. This helps them develop a little touch on the ball.

The other thing we use is what we call the *throw of the day*. We pick out special situations that happen during the season that we have in on our training tapes. We script this so we will have to make a certain type of throw for the *Throw of the day*.

Finding the time is always a big factor with coaches. How can I find the time to work on everything? First is off-season. Hopefully, you can find some time during the off-season to work with the quarterbacks on some of these points. The big thing for us is prepractice. We have a 15-minute special teams period. Our quarterbacks know they must be loose before that period. They are not involved with special teams so I am working with them during that time. When the team goes to stretch the quarterbacks continue to work on individual work for another 15 minutes. So, before our practice starts, I get one-half hour with our quarterbacks. Then we start our practice with a

30-minute *individual period*. A lot of that may be group work. I may send two quarterbacks to the tight ends and take two with me with the other receivers. The other thing is postpractice. If we do not get enough work during the regular practice we stay out and work after practice.

My final session is how to give your quarterback a chance to be successful. My feeling is this: *plays are plays*. You have to do the things that are in your offense, but do the same things over and over for your quarterback. You may want to mix up the looks, change the personnel, and change protections, but let the quarterback do the same things over and over again. I am talking about mixing up the play but making it the same for the quarterback. It is a different look for the defense.

One of the first plays I learned from Bill Walsh was *76 Exit*. It is a play with our X receiver doing a shallow crossing route. First we are throwing to the X man on the shallow cross. The number 2 man is the Y on the route over the ball. The H back is on a scat and the fullback is on a swing route and is our number 4 man. The protection is this: if the Sam linebacker blitzes we have to throw it to the tight end. That is the route, 76 Exit. We call this *formation weak right*.

76 EXIT

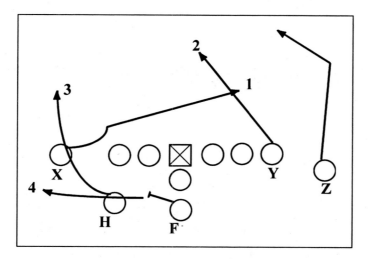

To change it up we may call *weak right, Y right*. Now we motion the tight end across. We change the strength of the formation. It is still the same read for the quarterback. We may call *strong right, mum across*. Now we flutter the halfback across the formation. We will also have some runs that tie in with this. We may call *strong right, hum left*. We can go *far double wing right*. Now we have the halfback break the formation and put him out wide. He gets to the same spot from a different formation. All of this is a different look for the defense, but it is the same read for the quarterback.

We could *tag* the Z and call *Z out*. If the defense is camping on our crossing route, we can tag it. Now the quarterback reads the Z as number one. The things you can do are unlimited. The whole idea is to have the same read for the quarterback.

You can take the same play and go with two tight ends, two wide receivers, and one running back. It is the same routes as before, but with different receivers.

2 TE'S / 2 WO'S / 1 RB

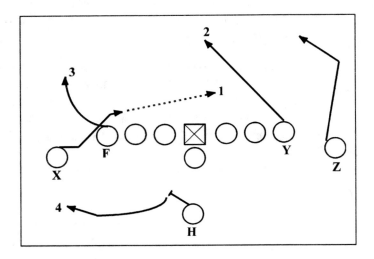

You can go with two tight ends, one wideout, and two running backs. Now you just have your extra tight end run the shallow.

2 TE'S / 1 WO / 2 RB'S

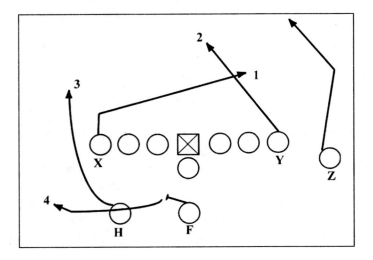

You can do the same thing with three tight ends. You can give them a trips look with a man in motion and run the same patterns. It is the same play with different personnel. It is a different look but it is the same read for the quarterback.

3 TIGHT ENDS

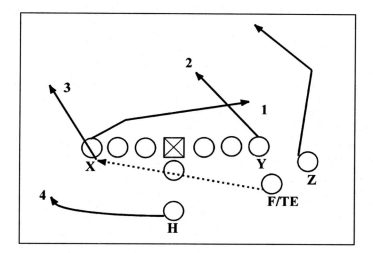

We can run it with three wide receivers. We can put the X receiver in either position and run the same route.

3 WIDEOUTS

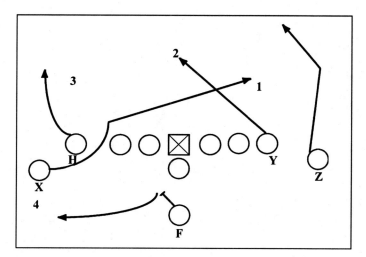

We can run the same play with four wideouts. The play is the same. It is the same read for the quarterback.

4 WIDEOUTS

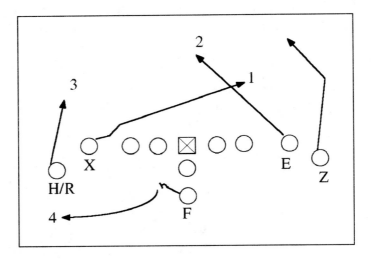

The protection is the same. The read for the quarterback is the same. But it is a different look with four wide receivers.

We can change up the pass protection. We are concerned about one linebacker making the quarterback throw the ball. We will run the same play but change the protection. Instead of having one back scat and one back blocking weak, we will block both backs on the outside linebacker. It is our *solid protection*. We then call *84 Exit*. It is still Exit to all of the wide receivers, but now we tag our backs. They change up a little to take care of the linebacker.

SOLID PROTECTION – TAG BACKS LEFT

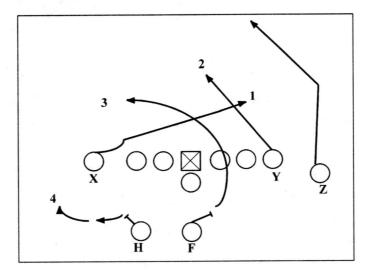

We can get real fancy and give the defense a *five-wideout* look and run it off *hot protection* and tag the fullback on a *wheel*. Again, it is the same play. Now, we have a hot receiver, but it is the same read for the quarterback.

HOT PROTECTION – TAG FB WHEEL

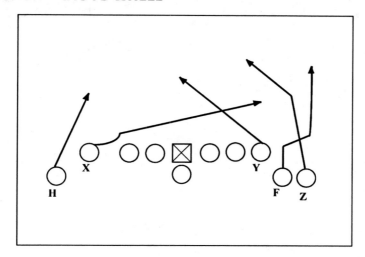

We go into a game with about 30 passes. That is our base game plan. We have another 15 in our *third-down package*. Most of those are converted from our *first-down package*. We will put in two or three plays for special situations. But the key is this: we do a number of things over and over again from different looks so our quarterback has a chance to be successful.

2

Developing High School Quarterbacks

George Curry
Berwick High School (PA)
1997

My topic today is developing high school quarterbacks. Before I talk about the X's and O's, I want you to know that we are not a big high school, but we compete against big high schools. Some of you may say that we get a lot of talent at our school. That is true, but we handpick our quarterback. We have 350 boys in our school. Our whole schedule was against 4A schools. I am not going to bullcrap with you. I will tell you how we approach quarterbacks and how we teach them, and I will take you through the things we do with our quarterbacks.

I have had 13 Division I quarterbacks since 1971. I think it all has something to do with the way we approach the quarterback position. It has to do with the way we pick the quarterback and how we work with the quarterback.

There are two things that I feel are important in developing the quarterback. Number one is mechanics. You can coach the hell out of mechanics, which we do. Number two is the decision making. We have 210 players in our program from seventh grade to 12th grade. Every kid in Berwick plays football unless you are handicapped or an oddball. We tell them we will teach them the quarterback mechanics, and we also do a segment on making decisions. I have had some great quarterbacks. I had Ron Powlus, Kelchner, and Orlando, who is now with the Cincinnati Bengals. Those quarterbacks were decision makers. I do not give a darn how far a kid can throw the football. I do not want to hear that. There are kids that look good in the punt, pass, and kick contest, but we want the player who can make decisions. A quarterback is a decision maker under duress. When the pressure is on the quarterback, he must make a quick decision. That is the kind of kid we want. We have a way of training those players.

We start with the *mechanics*. We break the mechanics down into two areas: *passing mechanics and running mechanics*. First, I want to go over the passing mechanics. There are three things you must look at when you are trying to develop a quarterback as far as passing mechanics:

- Developing the hands.
- Developing from the waist up.
- Developing from the waist down.

We take the body and break it down into three areas. We spend a lot of time on the last two—from the waist up and from the waist down.

Some of you may wonder what I am talking about in regard to the hands. I have been in coaching 30 years, and I can tell you that you do not want a kid in your program who has bad hands. We want a player with good hands to handle the ball on every down. That includes games when the field is wet and muddy. How many of you ever looked at the hands of your quarterbacks when you picked him? Have you ever looked at his hands? I have 21 quarterback candidates in my junior high program. I look at everything about them. I check their feet and their hands. I want to know what my quarterback is all about. I want a kid with hands that are big enough so he can handle and throw the football.

We start off with a couple of hand drills. First, we do the palm drill. We just take the ball and hold it out palm down. Then we do the *around-the-waist drill*. We just pass the ball around our waist. Next, we do the *figure-8 drill*.

I got a great drill from Paul Hackett. It simulates the center snap. We want the quarterback to be aware of the snap at all times. When you do these hand drills, you are strengthening your fingers and hands as you grasp the ball. The kids get down in position, bounce the ball off the ground, and grasp it like a snap. This develops the hands. We do a series of these drills every day. We do those drills every day in the weight room. When our players get through lifting weights, they are going to do those hand drills.

Next, we do a *seat drill*. Then, we do a one-hand snap and have the quarterback take the snap and try to curl the football. Everything is done with the hands. I want to make the kids aware of the hands. If we are playing a game in front of 12,000 people, I do not want the ball on the ground.

In the hand drills we are trying to simulate the snap, and we are trying to strengthen the fingers and hands. We want to make him aware that they are the most critical part of his body.

Next is the area above the waist. The most important thing about passing the football is the release. I will ask those of you in the audience this question: did anyone ever show you how to throw the football? If so, you were lucky! I run quarterback camps. I see over 1,000 quarterbacks. Those quarterbacks had no idea what I was talking about. Most coaches teach their quarterbacks the X's and O's, and they teach them how to read defenses, but they never show them how to play quarterback.

I want to talk to you about five major points involved in the release of the football. We start on this when the quarterbacks are in the fourth grade. I do not want them to get screwed up when they get to the high school level. It is too late to change their release at that age. If you get them early, you can teach this. First, we get them in a pre-throwing position.

Step 1: We want the ball in a trigger position. The ball is between the earlobe and the armpit. I do not want it away from his body; I want it here along and parallel to his chest. We call Step 1 the trigger position.

Step 2: Release the ball at the top of his throwing circle. If we took a hula-hoop and placed it in front of the player, it would form his throwing circle. We want the player to release the ball at the top of that circle. This is how you develop overhand releases. We do not want a sidearm quarterback. We want him to release it at the top of the throwing circle. You have to have a slight bend in the elbow because you cannot throw the ball with a stiff arm. We do not want a javelin thrower for a quarterback. We want to keep the elbow at a right angle or perhaps at a little less than a right angle. If you raise your arm up and bend your elbow, you will be at the top of your throwing circle.

Step 3 and Step 4: These two steps go together. Step 3 is transferring the weight from the back foot to the front foot. It is a short step. We do not want to overstride. It is a transfer-of-the-weight step. We want you to get your hips into the step. As you transfer your weight, the ball is going on the top of the throwing circle. You are stepping and hitting that circle all together. As you transfer the weight, you follow through. You should aim your belly button at your target. I want to bring the off arm down and back.

Step 5: As you throw the football, bring the ball up to the top of the circle, bring the opposite arm down to break the plane of the back, and transfer the weight. As you bring the off arm down, your index finger is the last finger off the football. That should put your palm out of the way. If I throw the football, my palm should rotate inside and point away from my body. If the palm is turning over to the side where you can see the palm, you are sidearming the ball. That means you are turning your wrist. I promise you, if the index finger is the last finger off the ball, you will not break your wrist. As you come over the top of that circle, it is a perfect overhand throw.

We need to talk about a couple of side points here. Let me review the five major points of throwing a football: *trigger position, top of the circle, transferring the weight, elbow breaking the plane of the back*, and *palm turned away with the index finger off the ball.*

Now, consider a couple of other points. We emphasize this to our quarterbacks: we do not want them to *patty-cake* the football. A lot of quarterbacks patty-cake the ball as they are holding it. I see them on TV. They patty-cake from the throwing hand to the offside hand—back and forth. Do you know what you are telling the defense when you patty-cake the football? Here it comes! If you do that against a good defensive secondary, they will pick you to death. You do not pat the football! If I see my quarterback pat the ball, he has to run a 40-yard sprint.

When you are standing up and have the football in the trigger position, it is a short release. Have you ever heard a coach talk about shortening the release of a quarterback? If the football is in the trigger position and you come to the top of the circle, you are shortening the release. One thing I take pride in with our quarterbacks is that they have a short release. They are not going to separate and have a big windup. One of the best releases in football is by Dan Marino.

I videotape all of our quarterbacks on their release. I tape other quarterbacks in college and the NFL as well. I am fascinated with the release of the football. I have the kids sit down and look at their release. I show the quarterbacks on the video in slow motion. Some of my players think they are movie stars. I go over the release with each of them, and then I tell them what they need to work on.

Question: What drills do you use to help with the release? We have a couple of drills that we use that I want to discuss with you. We have a drill that we call the *rope drill*. We have the player bring the ball to the top of his circle and have him stop at that point. We take a rope and tie it over his wrist and have another player hold the rope. We make the quarterback throw the ball over the top of the rope. We want them to pretend the rope is not there. Some kids get obsessed with that rope. We tell them not to worry about it. We want them to throw through the rope. It is not going to hurt anyone. We have taken care of sidearm quarterbacks with this drill. We get some kids who want to come under the rope on their release. The rope drill will help them get the ball to the top of the circle. I have seen other coaches who use a volleyball net to force the quarterback to release the ball over. Some coaches use a goalpost for the drill. I use the rope because you get 100 feet of rope for two or three bucks. You can have them work on it in the off-season. This is especially good for your young kids. I love working with those young kids. They will listen to you. They are all eyes. If you can get them going in peewee football, you can teach them good habits.

We put the players in a circle and have them throw the ball over the rope to each other. We want the throwing motion to be natural. What we do at our quarterback camp is to tape every kid when he first comes in. I see all kinds of techniques. Then I show them at the end of the camp, so they can see the progress they have made.

Next, we need two quarterbacks here and two over on the other side to do the *kneel-down drill*. We start with one knee up. Everything is going to be the same. The ball is between the earlobe and the armpit. We still stress all of the points in the release. He still has the circle, he still releases, he brings the left or non-throwing arm down, and he comes off with the index finger last. They play pitch and catch with each other. Next we go to two knees. It is the same thing. This time they pick the ball up and follow through. Everything is from the waist up.

Next, we stand up and put the throwing foot forward. If you are right-handed, we want to put the right foot forward. We have them pick the ball up and do the same as before. It is still from the waist up. We do not want them to use their legs yet. We want them to come to the top of the circle and stop. We want them to come over the top.

Let me bring you up to date at this point. There are five points in the release, and I gave you four drills to improve the release. There are other drills you can do. I have a lot of drills to use on this technique. I give our kids only five or six and have them work on those.

Next is *footwork*. Now, we talk about the quarterback from the waist down. We are assuming your kids will soak all of that in so it becomes a habit with them. They must be able to do the drills naturally. Now footwork. We do what we call *quarterback agilities*. I have talked to the best quarterback coaches in the country. When I go to clinics, I look for different ideas. I pick the minds of the people I come in contact with. I want to know everything I can about quarterbacks. I share this with our kids, and I am sure it helps our kids. Paul Hackett will tell you that no matter what, footwork is the most important thing in being a quarterback. If your feet are not in the right position, you are not going to throw the ball properly. He is correct. Some kids have strong arms and throw the ball improperly, but they get away with it on the high school level. When you get up against a good team, they are not going to get away with it. It is just like a boxer. He can throw a good punch if he has a good stance. If you are a quarterback, you can throw a good pass if you are in a good stance and your feet are in the proper position. When quarterbacks are under pressure, they never get in the right throwing position. This is where footwork comes into play.

Here are some of the things we teach our kids. We work hard on this. The first thing I want our quarterbacks to do is to learn how to *run*. A lot of kids do not know how to run as quarterbacks. We talk about an armpit-to-armpit motion. We run down the field in about three-quarters speed. As we come down the field, I want the ball to come from one armpit across to the other armpit. We want them to come out nice and easy and transfer the ball back and forth. We want the ball up to the chin. Some players will get a little stiff when they run this drill. We do not want too much sway in the motion. It should just come naturally. It is a natural motion, armpit to armpit.

The next thing we teach them to do is *run backward*, looking over the non-throwing shoulder. If they are right-handed, they should look over the left shoulder.

They are just going to run back, taking a crossover step. As they do this, their eyes are focusing down the field. We want them to run as fast as they can. We do not do the carioca. We do that later. We just want to run backward. Why run that drill? That is a quarterback agility. Some kids cannot turn their head around and move their legs at the same time. It is side vision. This is how I work on the drill. I want my quarterbacks to see from sideline to sideline. We have them put the chin down so they can see to both sides. Some players cannot put their chin down and run backward. You are coordinating all things together. If you start with the kids in the seventh and eighth grades, you can develop them to do this drill. If you want to develop a quarterback, work on this drill. Don't just tell the kid he is the quarterback and let him go on his own. Work with him.

After he learns to run backward with his chin down, we have him turn the chin over his shoulder and run backward. Then we have him turn the chin to the opposite shoulder. Next we work on going back and switching the chin from one side to the other side. As they come backward, I will yell, "Switch." They turn from the right side to the left side. They turn the chin and switch. As they are doing this, I want the ball in the trigger position. I want the chin tucked and the head on a swivel. The head stays the same. They must be able to move. They are developing hip flexibility as they switch from one side to the other side. You have to be cool and calm. We want the ball up high on the drop. If you have the ball down low, you tend to fumble the ball. If the ball is up high, you can tuck it away and run. If you do fumble, you have a chance to recover it.

Next, we go to the *carioca drill*. We cross the front foot over the back foot as we back up. It is front-back, front-back, front-back. This is how we work this drill. We work the drill across the field or along the sidelines. You want the kid to do the drill on a straight line. We want him to come back straight on the line. Do it on the sideline or on a line across the field. We may start out on a walk-through. Then we gradually speed it up. We may go to half speed and then to three-quarters speed. We want it nice and smooth. Your kids will develop agility to do this drill. In a week you would be surprised what the kids can do in this drill. This helps develop the feet.

Next is the *backpedal drill*. We want them on the front half of their shoes. It is just like a defensive back on the backpedal. Instead of pumping the arms, the quarterback has a football in his arms. We want the weight distributed over the front of the shoes on the toes. We are looking downfield as we backpedal.

We can take a rolled-up towel, take the quarterback, and do the side-to-side drill for footwork. We want him to step 1-2-3, 1-2-3, 1-2-3, throw. Next we have the quarterback step forward and then backward. We have him step over the towel and then back over the towel. We have him working his feet over the towel.

Now, we want to go to the *drop step*. I assume most of you know about the stance and how to take a snap. We use a power step and two shuffle steps. We always talk about the power step. When you take the football from the center, the power step is a good drive step. On the first step we want to turn the toes on the lead foot at an angle. We want to turn the toes of the back foot toward the sideline. By pointing the second step toward the sideline, it will help the quarterback stop. I got that from Dave Roberts when he was at Notre Dame. He is now the head coach at Baylor University. The second and third steps should stop the quarterback. The feet are the width of the shoulders. The chin is down so they can see the field. We want to take the power step, then two shuffle steps, and then stop.

I am going to give you two more terms. Once we get back on our drop, we have two kinds of steps. First is the *hit*, and the second is the *hitch*. A *hit step* is one step and throw. When we three- and five-step drop, we want a hit step. That is a 1-2-3 step. That is a hit step. Step and throw. We have the ball up ready to throw. We can move the feet 1, 2, 3, and throw. That is a hit step. If we drop back seven steps, we can use what we call a *hitch* step. The quarterback can come back, set up, hitch step, step up, and make the throw. Some of the young quarterbacks use the hitch step. Why? Because they are too weak to throw the ball from the deep position. They have to step up to get anything on the ball.

We make all of our quarterbacks lift weights. All of our quarterbacks can bench-press at least 300 pounds. If you are getting hit, you had better have a body that can take it. The stronger the quarterback, the quicker he is. If a kid is quick, he can control his body. You can control your body when you are stronger. You can go one step and two shuffle steps, and that would be the three-step drop. You can go three power steps and two shuffle steps, and that is the five-step drop. The seven-step drop is five power steps and two shuffle steps. We still want to keep in mind trigger position and five major points in the drop.

We run an *evasion drill*. After we teach them to drop back at five steps, we do what we call a *cross drill*. They go back five steps and stop, slide to the right, slide all the way back to the left, come back to the middle, then a three-step drop, and throw the ball. When do we teach this drill? If the rush comes, we want them to have some agility to avoid the rush. We are teaching them to keep their eyes open. When they move, the ball stays in the trigger position. When they take the five-step drop and they see the rush coming up the middle, they step to the side and throw the ball. You must be able to do that. If the rush comes from the other side, they must be able to avoid them and make the play. You can improvise on the drills. We have all kind of drills we use to teach them to evade the rush.

There is a lot to playing quarterback. I have 10 decision-making drills. We use these drills to help them make their decisions. I have four camps in Pennsylvania. We work the hell out of the kids that come to our camp. We charge them $35 for an eight-hour day.

3

Coaching the Quarterback

Todd Dodge
Carroll High School (TX)
2005

Thanks for inviting my staff and me to speak here today. This invitation came late in our season when we were getting ready for the playoffs. I told the staff if I got the chance to speak at a clinic like this, they were all coming with me. All head coaches know I would not have the opportunity to be on a dais like this, if it were not for our assistant coaches.

This past season, our defensive coordinator passed away nine days before the start of two-a-day practices. It was a great challenge for us to overcome that. We get the credit because of our offense, but we have won two of the last three championships in Texas because of our defense. The old adage, which states, offense may put the fans in the seats, but defense wins championships, is true. My coaches do a tremendous job on both sides of the ball, and I am proud to have them with me.

I am going to discuss our quarterback-training program with you. We have a quarterback-training program that starts in the seventh grade and continues through high school. We have a high school with a population of 2,100 students. Our football program is in Class 5A in the state of Texas. Carroll is a small 5A high school with two feeder schools that have seventh- and eighth-grade campuses. We start those young men when they are in the seventh grade. We have four quarterbacks at each school in our quarterback-training program. We have two teams at the seventh-grade level on each campus.

When they get to the eighth grade, we start to cull the numbers down. By the ninth-grade year, we have three quarterbacks in the training program. When they become sophomores, we reduce the number to two quarterbacks. In our training program in general, we like to start with a large number of quarterbacks.

The thing we try to do is have an efficient well-coached quarterback each year. That way you do not have to say we lost Chase Daniel to graduation, so we are dead for next year. Chase signed with Missouri and was the Texas 5A Player of the Year the last two years. We are not going to have an all-state, All-American, Division I quarterback every year. However, we will have a very efficient quarterback to take over the following year.

I will try to hit on several things in the time alloted for my lecture. There are two areas in dealing with our quarterback-training program. The first thing is to show you how we promote accuracy with the quarterback. They are a series of drills we call splash-down drills. The other thing we do from a teaching standpoint with our quarterbacks is video training. Through this program, we find out if they truly know our offense. We will talk about our series of video tests for the quarterback. It is a simple way to check the knowledge of your quarterbacks throughout the system.

We feel we must have a quarterback who can hit people with passes each year. Three years ago, our school went up to the highest classification in high school football. The last three years we have gone to a no-huddle offense. During that time, we are 47-1 since going into the no-huddle offense. We have been in the spread offense forever, but three years ago, we adopted the no-huddle scheme also.

People think the spread offense is a big-play, pass-happy offense. Last year during our 16-game season, we averaged 27 first downs a game. The spread offense is as efficient an offense as any I have ever seen. I learned this a long time ago from coach Ronny Thompson, who was my high school coach. He is the reason I am in coaching right now. He always talked about "spreading the wealth."

I advise you not to be a coach who relies on one player to carry the offense. Do not let the defensive coordinator say, "If I stop the slot receiver, we can beat them." We want to be able to spread the ball around to our receivers.

Over the course of last year, we averaged 305 yards passing and 237 yards rushing. We spread the ball out to many different people. Our running back and our quarterback both had over 1000 yards rushing. We had six receivers that recorded 30 or more catches during the year.

The reason I am telling you all of this is that we must have a quarterback who is a distributor of the football. We are not a place where we have a big stud year in and year out. Those places have the big running back with 10.5 speed for 100 meters every year. They have the big, tall, and fast wide receivers that every college program wants. We do not have those types of athletes on a yearly basis.

For our program to be successful, we have to spread the ball around to a number of different receivers. That is what we try to do.

Testing

I want to try to paint a picture for you so that you can write down what you need to know. On February 1, we do a pretest. We test them on everything you can imagine, including formations, running plays, and pass plays, and make them draw up the diagrams. We have them draw an offensive line diagram and identify the line techniques assigned to each lineman. It is important in our offense that the quarterback be able to count the number of defenders in the box.

When you deal with the quarterback, do not assume anything. They will sit in the back of the classroom and nod their heads, as if they understand. However, you will find in some cases that they do not have a clue. The way you find that out is to test them on essential information that they should know.

The second day, we reviewed the pretest and went over the quarterback manual. On February 3, we cover the trips package. We begin teaching our trips package by doing several classroom exercises. We then go outside to perform several quarterback drills.

The quarterback-training program starts on February 1, and runs through March 8. We cover the points we want to accomplish with our quarterbacks (i.e., what I need to get across as a quarterbacks coach through that six-week period). I have to be sure we are prepared to go into our skills phase of the off-season program. That has to carry over into spring football that starts in late April.

We give the quarterbacks a video test during the later weeks of the program. When we get to the video test, we have taught the trips, doubles, and empty packages. I have covered our entire running game with them. They should know when they look at video of the Carrol Dragons, what they are looking at. As coaches, we assume that quarterbacks can look at video of our own offense and tell you what the play is.

When I started giving our quarterbacks a video test, I found, in some cases, that they did not know what was going on. On the video test, we pick out 12 to 15 plays from a particular game and put it on the recorder. We meet in a classroom and watch the tape. When the first play comes up, the first thing they write down is our formation. The next thing they write down is what coverage they see the defense playing. We then run the play all the way through and all the way back to the beginning. We repeat the procedure, and I freeze the tape. I ask them what play we just ran. The last thing they write down is how many defenders were in the box.

I want to train them that when they watch game tapes that they should automatically look to see how many defenders are in the box. We go through 12 to 15 plays and do the same thing with each play. They turn it in, and I grade it. If someone is way off in a quarterback's learning process, we give him additional training to bring him up to speed.

We treat this time in the training period just as we treat a student's time in an English class. Too many times, coaches do not get the credit for their teaching duties. Some of the best teachers in North America are sitting in this room right now. Coaches teach in a different venue. We take a lot of pride in the teaching of the things we do. We handle our subject matter the same way the English or Math teacher would.

Quarterback Qualifications

Qualifications are part of our quarterback-training manual. We go over these points with our players in the training program. You must be an accurate passer. That is not necessarily the most important point, but I will take a quarterback who can get the ball into the receiver's hands over one who sprays the ball all over the place. We are asking our quarterback to be more of a duel-threat player than ever before. However, we want to make sure he puts the ball on people.

In Southlake, Texas, the name Chase has become synonymous with quarterbacks. Chase Watson and Chase Daniel were the quarterbacks during our three-year run of championship final games. They averaged 67 percent completion over a three-year period and threw 152 touchdown passes. They put the ball on receivers down the field and in splash-down situations.

Another key attribute for quarterbacks is being a positive leader. He has to be an encourager, not a discourager. Probably the number one thing I talk to quarterbacks about is to be an encourager of other people. I have heard coaches talk about their team having a chance to be good, if only their quarterback had some leadership ability. We teach "leadership" the same way we teach the quarterback to read cover 3 or cover 2. It takes no special ability to be an encourager of his teammates. The quarterback is a player who is looked up to and a person who typically gets much of the glory on your team. If he is constantly encouraging his teammates, he is building respect for himself on the team.

The athlete must be confident and want the responsibility of playing quarterback. I think it is important early in a young quarterback's career to have the whole deal of football explained to him. I think as early as the seventh grade, he needs to learn the quarterback will get too much credit for his team's success. When the team is on a five- or six-game winning streak, everyone will love you and tell you how good you are.

Quarterbacks should not get the big head over that type of praise. Understand that such praise is only the human nature of football fans, moms, dads, and boosters in town. They all want to tell you how good you are.

On the other side of that scenario is the three-game losing streak. When that happens, everyone may call you a bum. In that situation, the quarterback will get more of the blame than he deserves. They have to understand that situation and that all quarterbacks tend to experience such circumstances.

After we go through the training program with regard to the intangibles, I want to find out if an athlete really wants to assume the responsibilities that are inherent in the quarterback position. Fine athletes have come to me and told me they did not want any part of that kind of responsibility. That is fine with me. We can move them to another position, but we do not want someone playing quarterback who does not want the responsibility. The quarterback must be willing to spend endless hours learning the position, and he must be coachable.

The next factor is the preparation involved with a Carroll quarterback. We go over these things with each quarterback. He must know the strength and weakness of each of his teammates.

What coaches want from their quarterback is to be an extension of the coaching staff. They want him to be the coach on the field. I want our quarterbacks to have an opinion of his teammates. If I ask my quarterback who is the best receiver to throw to in a third-and-seven situation, I want him to have an opinion. I may not agree with him, but I want an answer. I want him to have an opinion concerning who the best blocker is and who our clutch receiver is.

A very important point we go over with the quarterback is to know who to encourage. We cover each of these points with the quarterback in our program. As coaches, we know there is a covey of athletes within our program to whom we need to give extra encouragement.

There are some players, who play for us, who do not need us to say anything to them. Most of the time, those guys are the real deal. They do not need anyone to tell him he is good. We ask the quarterback to figure out who on the team needs extra encouragement. The team is never going to be as good as it can be if we have a bunch of players running around with no confidence.

The quarterback has to "convince" his team of victory. When I cover this point with young quarterbacks or quarterbacks who are new to the program, I get that blank stare. They do not have a clue what I am talking about in this area. I give them an example to illustrate what I mean. The example is the quarterback who throws the pick to kill a drive. It happens a lot of times in football—from the pro level all the way to junior high football.

You can see it happening. The quarterback walks off the field and takes his helmet off about the numbers. When he gets to the sideline, he throws the helmet up against the bench. He then walks off by himself, stands by himself, and shows everyone how miserable he is.

That will happen, and he will flat out do it if you do not talk to him about it. We talk to our quarterback about things like that. We tell him to get on the bench, hold his head high, and not pout. We tell him to talk to his teammates and encourage them to keep on blocking and playing hard. Tell them you will do better the next time. When the quarterback does that, he is convincing his team of victory. The quarterback touches the ball on 100 percent of the offensive snaps. If the offense snaps the ball 72 times, the quarterback touches it 72 times. He has a lot of opportunities for success and failure.

We do not want a quarterback who has tremendous swings of emotions. On one series, he is great, and on the next series, he is terrible. We want to coach all of that out of him before he drives us crazy. Playing quarterback has so many small intangible things to handle. He has to gain the respect of his teammates. He has to take the responsibility of a poor play if he was involved in it.

We do not take the snap from underneath the center much. We are probably in the shotgun 99 percent of the time. The point I want to make to the quarterback is to take responsibility for a poor play. It is all right to say it was your fault. Too many times when the quarterback-center exchange hits the ground, the quarterback can blame the fumble on the center, and everyone will believe him. I have played quarterback, coached quarterbacks, and have been around the position all my life. If the quarterback blames the center, it is a mistake.

If the quarterback throws the ball away from the receiver, it was because the receiver ran the wrong route. I tell the quarterback by deflecting all the blame from him, he is killing the respect he has from his teammates.

He has to congratulate his teammates on a good game or practice. Do not be a player who makes excuses; just get the job done. The quarterback has to execute his assignment with precision on every play. Regardless of what offense you run, the quarterback can control about the last 20 minutes of practice. When we get into team offense, if the quarterback is doing his job the proper way, it influences the rest of the team.

When we get into team offense, we do not do exotic things. I simply want completions. I call pass plays that are completed. The quarterback has to complete the pass, carry out his fakes, and handle the audible the right way. Proper quarterback execution can take care of many things.

Training Tips

At this point, I want to give you some tips and thoughts about training the quarterback. There are some simple coaching points on the mechanics that I want to point out. These are quick ways for getting a particular point across to the player.

A right-handed quarterback has three cameras on his body. The first camera is camera A and is located in his left shoulder. The second camera is camera B and is in his belly button. The third camera is camera C and is located in his right shoulder.

When the quarterback is retreating in his three- or five-step drop, camera A is on the target. As the quarterback strides to throw the ball, camera B is on the target. People have told the quarterback to step at his target, when actually he is stepping about four to six inches past his target. If he lines his belly button to the target during the stride, he has lined up correctly. That sequence lets his hips roll through the throw. In the follow-through, camera C should point at the target.

If I have a quarterback throwing with an open chest, especially on sprint-out or bootleg passes, this helps square the throw. When a quarterback throws with an open chest, all I have to tell him is to get camera A to the target. If you have a quarterback who is locking his hips out, all I have to tell him is to get camera B on the target. If I have a quarterback who is pulling the string and not following through, I simply tell him to get camera C to the target.

Another thing you will hear me refer to is the type of ball I want thrown. That factor refers to the trajectory of the football thrown in the passing game. In this area, we talk about a one-ball, two-ball, and a three-ball.

A one-ball is a curl route. It is on a rope with no air under the ball. We are a four-wide team, and the two-ball for us is a pipe route. Such a route involves an inside receiver pushing off to 10 yards and popping right down the pipe or seam of the middle of the field. That pass goes about 25 yards down the field over the top of a retreating linebacker with some nice air under the ball. The two-ball is a pass thrown on a smash route also.

We throw the three-ball on fly routes and take-offs. We want maximum air under the ball. We even talk about a one-and-half ball. It is a quick and easy way of teaching so the quarterback has a mental picture of what type of ball that he needs to throw.

Each day we start out with a warm up drill, with the quarterbacks 10 yards apart. They load the camera and throw the ball. When we finish the warm up, we end on the move. We run, curl the shoulders, throw, and follow through.

We do the second drill on a three-pocket net. It is eight feet in height but adjusts to six or seven feet. When I was a young quarterback, my coach had a contraption that looked like a fence on wheels. I threw the ball from a three-quarter-arm position. The fence was about seven-feet high, and he made me throw over the top of the fence. I do not remember him saying anything about getting my arm up. We set our nets at eight feet. To throw over the top of the net, you have to come over the top with a high release.

We do not want the quarterback to have his elbow surgically attached to his rib cage. We want our quarterbacks to play tall. If they are 5-10, we want them to play as if they were 6-2. If they are 6-2, we want them throwing as if they were 6-5. The net drill helps the quarterback come over the top with the ball. We want them to play big with their release. We train the release to be over the top of the nets. If a quarterback throws side-armed, he cannot get the ball over the net. The closer he gets to the net, the higher his arm has to come up.

The next thing we do in the warm-up is to simply shuffle forward and throw the ball. We emphasize that the quarterback should focus his cameras on the ball in every drill.

The next drill is called "walk away easy or hard." The quarterback walks away from the net, and I then tell him easy or hard. The easy way for a right-hander is to turn to his left. The thing I like about the drill is that I can watch the feet of the quarterback. The common mistake a quarterback will make as he gets the information is transferring the information from his eyes to his arm. That means he has bypassed his feet. We teach the quarterback that the feet precede the arm.

The second part of the drill is to turn the quarterback the hard way. If the quarterback is right-handed, he has to turn to his right. That really requires him to snap his shoulders around and get his feet set. He rolls up on his toe and delivers the football. We can use the net from all different angles. There are three pockets on the net for the quarterback to direct his throws. They can throw crossing patterns into the net. We are emphasizing the cameras, but I am watching the footwork. We have several of the passing nets. All the throws the quarterback makes are at a target.

Another common mistake a quarterback sometimes makes is dropping the ball down below his chest before he throws. I tell them to imagine they have a board around their chest. The elbows must never drop below their chest. The coaching point is to keep the elbows above board.

The next drill involves working on our quick-passing game. We have big red dummies placed as targets for the quarterbacks. The quarterback catches the ball and releases it as quickly as he can. He catches the ball and throws it. He does not adjust to get the laces.

If he throws to the right, we use a term called "turn-toe." He catches the ball, turns his right toe, and releases the ball. When he throws to the left, we use a baseball term called "coming across the bag." The turn is the movement a shortstop makes as he throws to first base. We throw to the dummies to try to promote accuracy. I tell the quarterbacks the red bag will not make a play for them. They have to hit the bag, because it will not go up or down to catch the ball.

You can use your imagination and put the big red dummy anywhere you want on the field. The dummy is about the size of a high school wide receiver.

The next exercise is the pocket drill. Several different things happen in this drill. What I want the quarterback to understand is that there is always something going on around his feet when he is in the pocket. There are things flying at the quarterback. It could be his offensive linemen. In this drill, he tries to work himself into position on a pass set.

A quarterback has to have movement in his feet at all times while he is in the pocket. The foot movement is not a big movement, but is quick and choppy. The movement is not far, but it could be the difference between a sack and a completion. We try to train the quarterback in this drill to be patient in the pocket and move within the pocket and not scramble.

We do this drill into the nets. They start to walk away from the net. I give them a verbal command; they turn their hips around, and set their feet. As they are turning, I roll a big ball at their feet. I want them to shuffle out of the way, step up in the pocket, and throw. They have to step away from pressure and up into the pocket. I have a coach moving around to different spots, and they are required to throw the ball to him.

To build on the drill, I give them a command of "left" or "right" when they throw. They walk away, I call out "hut," and they flip their hips. I roll the ball at them and call "right." They avoid the ball, step up in the pocket, and throw the ball right into a net. As you watch the players in the drill, you see them all looking at the red ball instead of feeling where it is.

We can do the same drill from the drop, but I think this is better because of the unknown direction of the ball. It builds muscle memory in their feet to step away from pressure.

The next part of the drill is the scramble from the pocket. It is the same pocket drill, while adding another part of that progression. At some point in the drop-and-reaction, it is time for the quarterback to leave the pocket and scramble. We have stepped away from the pressure at the feet, stepped up in the pocket, and now it is time to go. It is time to leave the pocket and make something happen.

The first thing the quarterback does is to burst from the pocket with a flash of speed. He scrambles to the left to protect the ball. We put a net about 30 yards away to simulate a receiver who has run an out route and turned his pattern up the sidelines.

I have another net at a shorter distance for a verbal command given to the quarterback. To use that net, I yell "stop," as if the quarterback were contained. The quarterback stops and throws into that net. The factors he must think about, as he starts to scramble, is burst, camera on, and throw.

These three pocket nets are portable and can be moved inside during our off-season workouts. We can put the nets anywhere we want to practice our throws. In this drill, the quarterback practices his two-ball into the net. He throws the ball over a retreating linebacker into the net. The next net is set for a hot-route read. We have a quarterback reading a blitz and hitting the receiver on a quick break inside on what we call "hot grass."

On first net, the quarterback is taking a three-step drop and releasing the ball as soon as his plant foot hits the ground. He practices the quick throw with two different ball throws. The first net is a two-ball, and the second net is a one-ball.

The pocket nets save so much time in ball retrieval. We have several of these nets, and they are invaluable in the training of our quarterbacks. They are adjustable up and down and portable from one spot on the field to another. They have three pockets to change the direction of the throw. If I want them to throw a particular pocket, I simply say one, two, or three.

I think you can visualize the possible throws. We work our fade routes into the end zone in these drills also. By placing the nets at various places, and giving the quarterback the situation, we can achieve the desired throw from the quarterback. These are two-ball throws. We position the nets to practice the pipe route, which comes off our four verticals, and the smash route to the corners.

This next exercise is the four-vertical drill. We teach the quarterback to look off the defender and get the safety moved to where he wants him. We set the nets on the seams at 17 yards. If we find a defender cheating one way or the other, the quarterback carries him the way he is cheating with his eyes and drives the ball the other way with a one-and-half ball. It is a one-hitch throw. The quarterback drops three steps, takes one hitch, and throws the ball. That gives you the idea of the seam throws.

When I started this talk, we talked about splash-downs. There are very few throws in football made to stationary targets. We make most of the throws to grass. In this drill, we try to promote accuracy to grass. We work on the fade drill by throwing the ball into trash cans. These are three-ball throws, gauged to come down at a particular spot on the grass.

We throw the ball any way it comes back. Some of our quarterbacks like to find the laces before they throw. It gets them in trouble sometimes on quick throws.

We end each day with a competitive drill. The drill is the same drill we started out throwing in the earlier part of practice. They walk away from the target. When I call "ball," they flip their hips around and deliver the ball to a red dummy. We want to see which quarterback's ball hits the dummy first. We go four quarterbacks at a time and eliminate them one by one on a certain amount of throws.

What you find out happening, in their haste to turn and throw, is that they bypass their feet and become inaccurate. We start the easy way and then go the hard way. We work quick feet, quick release, and accuracy, with a little bit of competitiveness—all in one drill. We continue by doing the cross-field throws with the easy turn and the across the field throws with the hard turn.

On everything we do in the drills, the quarterback throws the ball into a net or at a dummy. We are promoting accuracy with every pass. Accuracy is the one essential skill our quarterbacks must have to play for us. It does us no good to get the match-up you want if the quarterback cannot hit the throw.

The last thing I want to discuss is our video test material. This is part of our quarterback training and our teaching our offense to our young guys. When I start the test, all the quarterbacks have a notebook.

The first thing they write down is the formation in which we align. The next thing they identify is the coverage. We run the play all the way through, then we reverse it all the way back, and then we pause the tape. I ask them to write down the play we ran. The last question is how many defenders are there in the box? They write down the number, and we go to the next play. The smart quarterbacks figure out that we are running the ball every time a certain number of defenders is in the box.

With regard to teaching our quarterbacks, we undergo a ten-day period in which our quarterbacks do the video test every day of that period. The test is the first thing they do and only takes 15 minutes to complete.

Before too long, the quarterbacks are "running" the offense and understand what we are trying to do against certain teams. For example, if I have "five in the box" written down on a particular play and we ran the ball five times, I know we are running at numbers in the box. Eventually, the quarterbacks will recognize certain coverages and notice that the ball goes the same direction every time. They begin to see the things we see.

We appreciate the opportunity to come here and share our thoughts and ideas with you. Thank you so much.

4

Fundamentals of Coaching Quarterbacks

Mike Emendorfer
Hanover College
1995

When I was preparing for this lecture, I prepared it just like many of you have prepared for a lesson plan for your classes. I set down two objectives:

- I want you to come away with some basic fundamentals and ideas on how to drill the quarterback in practice.

- I would like for you to come away with some ideas about developing a game plan in the red zone, and some different ideas on how to prepare your quarterback in the red- zone passing game.

First, let me talk about quarterbacks in general. We have had a strong tradition at Hanover and we have produced a number of All-American quarterbacks. Each quarterback was different. I think you have to coach it that way. There is no one set way on how to approach the quarterback position. There are some basic fundamentals you can stress, but how many of us at the small-college level, or the high school level, have 15 minutes a day to sit on a knee and throw the football. Hopefully, the quarterback will be able to master that technique in the summer camps. I will cover some *do's and don'ts* for the quarterback. Then I will go into some basic fundamentals for the quarterback. Hopefully, I will get into some of the red-zone passing plays at the end.

Let me get to the do's and don'ts for a quarterback. Don't try to turn the quarterback into a robot. I can assure you our quarterback does not adhere to everything that is written in our manual. I take one or two pieces that each quarterback can use each year and try to apply them to that quarterback. The big thing I want with a quarterback is footwork. As far as upper-body work, I think it is natural for a quarterback to throw a little sidearm or overhead, whatever may be the case. Don't make your quarterback into a robot.

Do emphasize the knowledge of the game with the quarterback. Emphasize field awareness, coverage recognition, the width of the field, and rules of the game. One of the things I would encourage high school coaches to do is to send out a small manual to their quarterbacks. Include the basic rules of the game and concepts of the game, and test your quarterbacks. Find out if your quarterbacks know the hash marks divide the field into thirds. He must know if he is in the middle of the field, how many yards it is to throw the out route to the sideline; it is 27 yards. If the ball is on the left hash and the quarterback is looking to throw a speed-out route to the right sideline, it is about 36 yards. That is a tough throw. Teach the quarterbacks field awareness, dimensions of the game, and dimensions of the field.

Don't tear down your quarterback in front of your team. You can't do that and then expect him to be a leader. In August, we put a lot of pressure on our quarterbacks, but when we get into the season, we just basically talk with them.

I try not to criticize the quarterback's decision making. I will ask him *why* he made his decisions. Let the quarterback explain his decision to you. Another *do* is to listen to your quarterback. It is tough as coaches because we all have egos, and we think we have all of the answers, but the players are the ones out there playing. He knows his own ability. He knows what is going on. Listen to him. If he wants to change his drop to a straight backup instead of a crossover, or if he thinks he will do a better job this way, we are going to be flexible. I have been at Hanover College for four years and we have had three different quarterbacks during those four years. Two of those quarterbacks were All-Americans, and the two individuals were quite different. You have to be flexible and you have to listen to your quarterback.

I think it is important to send your quarterbacks to camps especially in their senior year in high school. They need to be exposed to throwing the football and going through the drills for the quarterbacks. They are going to cover a lot of material that you will not be able to cover in August. It would be good if your quarterbacks could go to summer camps all four years. Basically, the camps are covering fundamentals. There are a lot of quality camps around. By the way, we have a summer camp at Hanover.

The first thing I want to cover relates to some basic fundamentals. First is our *stance*:

• Feet—Comfortable spread, about as wide as your shoulders. Keep them staggered, toe to heel. Most important: be consistent. Make necessary adjustments on the snap.

- Knees—Bend comfortably, but not strained.
- Hips—Drop to comfortable position, remaining as tall as center will permit.
- Arms and Shoulders—Bent slightly forward, shoulders even with center's hips.
- Head and Eyes—Straight ahead or from side to side, reading the defense.
- Balance—Remain balanced until last possible instant before snap, then transfer weight to stable foot (push-off) to prevent a false step.
- Poise—Keep relaxed and reflect a confident attitude. Don't hurry the play.

Next, we take a look at our *hand position*:

- Upper Hand—Right hand up, palm parallel to ground. Position wrist deep and flat, arm bent, elbow close to body. Extend and spread fingers strong but not tense. Press firmly against center's crotch for target and follow-through on snap. This is the receiving hand.
- Lower Hand—Left hand thumb to thumb and wrist with right thumb pointing downward toward the feet. Fingers extended and spread similar to the right hand. This is the support hand, used to trap the ball.
- Let's look at the snap:
- Laces—Give laces to center; adjust to fingers after snap.
- Exchange—Ball should be received by upper-right hand, centered in the groove of the palm. Lower hand traps the ball in the support position.
- Follow-through—Both hands must follow the center as he charges forward. Proper hand pressure encourages this.
- Next come the head and eyes:
- Pre-snap—Approaching the line of scrimmage examine the PSL. Continue reading progression through cadence (possible audibles?).
- Look—Upon snap, turn head quickly to locate where the ball will be placed. Keep the eyes fixed.
- Pocket—After follow-through, bring the ball into your body at the belt area, elbows close to your sides. Adjust for the handoff.
- Step—Patterns vary with play called. Generally, step to deliver the ball as deep and/or as quickly as possible. Let your eyes determine the length of your step.
- Fake—Again, it varies with the play. Options include the following handoff to check for fumbles, look to the second option, eyeing the defense to hold secondary.
- Pass—Eyes downfield reading the keys at all times during cadence, snap, drop, and through the release.

Let me get into the *signal-calling process*. The quarterback takes complete command of the huddle. He must assume the Captain status even if he is not the team captain. He must get everyone's attention and follow this progression:

*   Formation

*   Play

*   Snap Count

*   "Ready—-Break". Always encourage a sharp, loud break as this breeds confidence in the team. It all begins here.

As the quarterback comes to the line of scrimmage he must be calm, patient, and most important, confident. He commands signals, not simply calling off numbers. The quarterback follows this progression:

*   Check the defense on the way to the line of scrimmage, allowing the offense to reach a pre-shift position.

*   Place the hands under the center and command "Down" giving signal to shift.

*   Pause to allow initial movement.

*   Call (Fake) audibles in a series.

*   Command "Set."

*   Pause and check alignment.

*   Use non-rhythmic cadence using the words "GO—GO—GO," etc.

Let me talk more about cadence. I think cadence needs to be coached. I think you need to start the first day of teaching your quarterbacks how to use the cadence. Cadence can be a weapon for you—both for the quarterback and for the offensive unit. In our cadence everything has a purpose.

The offensive cadence we use is a very unsophisticated cadence system. We hope the offensive team can better concentrate on *what* and *how*, rather than when they are going to do something. There is no question that concentration is a key to getting off the ball. But once the snap count is called, it must be stored in your mind and your thoughts, and you should switch to assignment recognition and intensity. The snap count must be automatic! The cadence is divided into five phases.

*   *Phase 1*: Quick count or first-sound snap—To keep the defense off balance we use a first sound command as a quick count. The first sound is *down*. The quarterback will merely call the snap as "On the first sound," which means down. Everyone must get up to the line of scrimmage quickly and get set in his stance. No shifting or motion will take place when a play is called on the first sound. Example: "62 - 62 on the first sound."

- *Phase 2*: Color phase—The ball can be snapped on the color if called by the quarterback. He merely calls the play and says, "On the color," and the second color is used as the snap count. No motion or shifting. Good to use versus defenses that stem or jump from defense to defense.

- *Phase 3*: Non-rhythmic snap counts—Go is the term used as our snap count, even though the quarterback will call the count on 1-2-3 or 4 as a huddle call. If called on 1, the quarterback will pause for at least one full second after the set and then shout, "Go!" If the snap count call was on 3, the quarterback will call go three times on the line of scrimmage and the ball is snapped accordingly. This phase of the cadence is *non-rhythmic*.

- *Phase 4*: No play—No snap—Purpose is to try to draw the defense offside. The quarterback will call in the huddle, "No Play—No Snap," unless the defense penetrates across the neutral zone. If there is movement, we run the *quarterback sneak*. If no movement, the quarterback will either take the penalty or call timeout, depending on the situation.

- *Phase 5*: Repeat (second cadence)—Repeat stands for a *dummy cadence*. The quarterback calls the first set and we ignore the calls. If the defense does not jump, the quarterback starts over. Then we go on the first *go* after set. If the quarterback calls *check* after the dummy call, it means he is going to call an audible. This is how we describe it. The quarterback will go trough one cadence; if no one jumps offside he starts the second cadence always on 1. The purpose is to try to draw the defense offside. The purpose is also to help determine fronts and coverages.

Let me get into footwork with the passing game. Balance is more important than speed in dropping back to pass. Passing begins with the proper quarterback stance. Generally speaking, the stance should be such that the passer is capable of pivoting in any direction while maintaining good body control and balance.

The quarterback should *anticipate the count*. This means just before the ball is snapped, the quarterback should begin shifting about 80 to 90 percent of his weight to his pivot foot. Although most of his weight is on his pivot foot when the ball is snapped, he should not appear to be leaning in any particular direction.

Let's look at the actual *drop technique*. The action between the quarterback's stance and the ultimate pass is the *drop* of the quarterback. The following types of drops are listed according to the number of steps required, not including play-action drops.

This is the setup procedure for *dropback passing*:

- Quickness in getting away from the center and sprinting to the set position is one of the most important elements the quarterback can posses to assist the pass protection.

- You must *push* off the left foot and *reach* with the right foot. *Push step*—gives you quickness and power. (Weight is on the push foot. Helps to eliminate false step.) Cock knee inward. *Reach step*—(first step) gives you depth and direction. In executing the reach step, you must anticipate the snap count and reach with the toes touching the ground first. Be careful not to pull away from the center until you have received the ball. This step should be slightly more than 90 degrees so that the hips are open.

- Get away from the line of scrimmage and into the set position as quickly as possible. Technique will vary depending on the drop used. Look over the left shoulder and key the defense. Get the eyes in position. This will enable you to pick up coverages, breakdowns, and complimentary receivers.

- When sprinting to the set position, emphasis should be placed on *body balance* and being able to deliver the ball at all angles and at any depth. Don't shuffle or drag your feet. This causes excessive strain on the groin (pull). Pick up your feet. Make use of moving the ball from side to side to maintain good balance. Run naturally but with the ball raised to the sternum and slightly to the side of the throwing arm. The ball should be relatively motionless.

- Head and eye position: get your eyes *upfield*.

Here are the dropback techniques:

Two-step drop—Inside +10, with fade routes. A right-handed passer will back out from under the center leading with his left foot. The second step is planted and the quarterback is prepared to push off at this time and pass the ball. Also, when the ball is received from the *center it is immediately brought into the passing position.*

Three-step drop—3H, 3T. There are two different techniques for the three-step drop. First there is the three-step drop followed by a hitch step in the direction the pass is to be thrown (3H). This type of three-step drop is used when throwing the 5-yard slant routes. Second, there is the three-step drop where the passer is pushing off the third step to pass (3T, no hitch step). This method is used to obtain a quicker release on timing routes, e.g., when throwing a 6 to 8 yard quick out. When the quick out is being thrown to the right, emphasis is placed on *pointing* the left shoulder to the throw. The second and third steps on the drop are slightly shorter than the first step. We use both an open or straight drop technique, depending on the situation. We encourage a straight drop when throwing the hitch to the left (i.e., R-L-R). When passing to the left, the passer will emphasize cocking (pointing) the front shoulder to the receiver.

Five-Step Drop—There are two types of five-step drops, (5H) five steps plus a hitch, and (5T) five-step drop without a hitch step. The 5T is used on five-step timing throws. (The hitch step is a short step used in moving up into the pocket and is always in the direction the pass is to be thrown.)

The 5H-step drop (plus a hitch step) consists of three steps to obtain maximum acceleration and depth. Your back shoulder should be lower than your front shoulder as you accelerate. Then use two shorter steps to stop your backward motion. At the same time, your front shoulder should be dipping forward and be lower than your back shoulder as you shift your weight forward to aid your legs in stopping. Also, as you complete your fifth step you should be hitching forward without passing after the fifth step. As stated in the description of the three-step drop, the foot on the fifth step should be toe-in or out depending on if the pass is to be thrown to the left or right.

The 5T-step drop (without a hitch step) is used to obtain a quicker release and for timing routes such as the 12-yard out. When throwing the out route to the right, the quarterback will take three steps straight back for maximum depth followed by two shorter steps and the toe-out technique. When throwing the out route to the left, all five steps are approximately the same length. Note again the rocking of the shoulder is evident as you accelerate backward, and again as you shift your weight forward to stop in the 5T drop. But it is more pronounced when using the five-step drop with a hitch step. In comparison, the 5T drop should be executed with the emphasis on body control and smoothness rather than speed and depth.

Using gun formations with dropback techniques—We have the quarterback set 4 yards from the center, then complete his last two steps of his dropback.

Let me cover some passing techniques. You can't be *accurate* without *technique*. In the evaluation of the proper throwing motion, it must be emphasized that not all passers are the same. The skill to throw begins very early in life. Each of us has a style of walking—either good or bad. Each of us has a way of throwing that is either good or bad.

Some gifted players are successful at passing despite some poor mechanics. But most successful throwers have seven basic fundamentals they execute to perfection that separate them from the rest.

At Hanover College, we believe that since throwing is a basic physical skill involving an interrelationship on body parts, you begin evaluating the throwing motion from a kinesiology point of view. (The study of principles of mechanics and anatomy in relation to human movement.)

Naturally we must then consider the major joints or rotation areas (moveable parts) in the throwing motion. We evaluate and coach seven specific areas in the throwing motion beginning with the feet and ending with the index finger.

• Feet (The foundation of the body including feet and ankles.)

• Knees

• Hips

- Shoulders

- Elbow

- Wrist (Hand)

- Fingers (The end result of the seven rotation areas.)

FEET— Set up with the feet closer than the shoulders and stay tall. The weight is on the balls of the feet. Start the throw with most of the weight on the right foot. Point the left shoulder toward the target. The left leg should slide slightly forward as the weight is transferred from back to front. Point the shoulder toward the target. If you lack consistency in throwing, you may be overstriding. Shorten your slide with the left foot; the shorter the better.

The weight transfer is complete with the left foot on the ground as the ball is released just past the head. As the ball is released, the back foot should slowly drag forward to approximately even with the front foot. If the back foot ends up in front of the front foot, then this indicates the weight was transferred too soon from the back foot to the front foot. The effect on the throw is that the passer doesn't get any power from his hips and body. He is throwing with only his upper body. The quarterback's chin should even up over the front foot.

*KNEES—*During the weight transfer phase of the throw, the left leg will lift slightly, indicating a bend in the left leg as the weight begins to transfer from right (back) foot to the left (front) foot. At the end of the follow-through phase of the throw, the right shoulder should be on a line directly inside of a slightly bent left knee.

*HIPS—*The hips are essential to the throwing motion. During the weight transfer of the throw, it is important to check for the proper back-foot position (anchor) in order that the hips can properly rotate. The hips should precede the shoulders and then the ball is delivered with the arm. The hips are the significant source of the passer's weight transfer from the feet to the upper body. Emphasize the right side of the hip, not the belt buckle.

*SHOULDERS—*This is the key element in weight transfer and power. The shoulders should be parallel to the ground and the line of scrimmage. Immediately prior to throwing, the left shoulder should be pointed at the receiver. Sharply twist the upper body when the ball is in pre-pass position. Don't wind up. As the shoulders rotate to bring the arm around to deliver the pass, it should be noted that the rotation is approximately a 45-degree angle, and not side to side. This is because the front shoulder is dropped slightly to allow the back shoulder to *come over the top*. This results in the so-called *high release*. The proper rotation of the shoulders will prevent the passer from *pushing* the ball. For example, the elbow is in an extreme position in front of the hand as the hand is being brought forward. Always cock the left shoulder to the target regardless of the type of pass.

ELBOW—During weight transfer, the *left* elbow and arm move in a direction toward the target. Point to the target and keep them level. The elbow of the throwing arm should be above the shoulders when the ball is released. Slow-motion films of top pro passers show, a pronounced *chest thrust* and the elbow level with the passer's ear. Exaggerate throwing the elbow forward on the delivery so the point of the ball will stay up. During delivery, the right elbow in front of the right hand leads the way as the forward arm motion begins.

WRIST (Hand)—After the snap, control the ball with both hands and immediately bring the ball to the numbers while going to the set position. This is the *pre-passing* position. During the *push phase* (beginning the throwing motion), the throwing motion should always start from the number up to the final point of delivery. You must *force the ball up with the left hand* so that it is high enough to get the proper arm movement for release. As the right hand continues to draw the ball back to pass, he should never rotate the nose of the ball more than 90 degrees in relation to the line of scrimmage. Some quarterbacks have the habit of pointing the nose of the ball in exactly the opposite direction in which it is to be thrown. This erroneous technique many times causes a curveball action with the wrist as the ball is delivered, resulting in a poorly thrown pass.

FINGERS (Passing grip)—The grip is primarily in the fingertips. Hold the ball firmly beyond the middle with the fingers comfortably spread with the fourth and fifth fingers over the lacing. This will vary with the size of the hand. The thumb should be below the ball for support and the first finger about an inch from the tip of the ball. This method will allow daylight between the palm and the ball and will provide you with a delicate feel on the football. Don't lock the wrist; this impedes follow-through. Keep it flexible. The index finger is the last finger to leave the ball and therefore becomes the *control finger*. The control finger forces the front tip of the ball up making it an easier ball to catch. After the release, there must be a *follow-through* with the elbow and the wrist snapping downward with the palm of the passing hand parallel to the ground. Remember the control finger. Exaggerate the follow-through diagonally across the body. The right hand reaches for the knee on the down movement.

Common passing errors to consider are:

- *Poor timing*: Throw the ball as the receiver breaks into the clear, not after he gets in the clear.

- *Underthrown pass*: Poor follow-through, late release, or making weight transfer at wrong time.

- *Lateral inaccuracy*: Sidearm delivery.

- *No spiral*: Wrist twisted on release instead of whipped; keep the wrist locked against the twisting motion.

- *Throwing across* the body: Not stepping toward the target.

- *Poor ball control*: Ball carried too low when setting up; could force you to hitch or wind up.

- *Concentration on intended receiver*: Linebackers and the secondary men are told to key the quarterback; do not telegraph the primary receiver.

- *False step*: Can cost you valuable seconds.

- *Consistently overthrowing and underthrowing*: Check your stride.

- Don't try to throw with men all around you and when an opponent has his arms or hands on any part of your upper body.

- Any time you must run and an end has rushed to the inside, then run to the outside. Once you get outside, you have a better option of running or throwing the ball away.

- *Back foot in front of front foot following release*: Early weight transfer. Upper body throw.

  Common causes of interceptions to consider are:

- Throwing off-balance. Step to throw.

- Throwing behind the receiver.

- Throwing late. Throw when the receiver begins to get open. Hit the *window*.

- Throwing over linebackers. Hit the window.

- Throwing long passes short.

- Throwing short passes long.

- Bunched receivers.

- Receivers running curved routes instead of angles.

- Desperate heaves.

- Deep passes on obvious passing downs.

- Always keep a positive *passing attitude*:

- Have the courage to stand back there and take some occasional punishment.

- Complete concentration on your target.

- Confidence in the system, the receivers, and yourself.

- If you get an interception, stay loose and learn from your mistakes. Do not allow it to throw you off your game. Interceptions can be reduced by a one-target attack; maximum protection; freedom to the receiver.

- Work with the wet ball in an educational frame of mind; you will get better with practice.

- Don't be a thrower; be a passer.

5

Teaching Quarterbacks
to Attack Defenses

Ralph Friedgen
University of Maryland
2002

I want to take you through the teaching process we involve our quarterbacks with in attacking defenses. I will take you through the whole concept of defense that we want to get across to our quarterbacks. We have been doing this since I have been working with quarterbacks. We concentrate on learning about defenses. We teach them how to recognize fronts and how to recognize coverages. We teach them how those things relate and what they can learn about the defense in general.

Quarterback play is about how fast you can react and how accurate your decision can be. In order to do this, you must be able to anticipate certain things the defense will do. We teach the quarterbacks how to recognize certain aspects of the defense so they can anticipate and react and make the proper decision quickly.

When I went to San Diego of the NFL in 1991, I went as the H-back and tight-end coach. I was also the running-game coordinator. We also had a passing game coordinator on the team. Now in my opinion, if you have two offensive coordinators on the team, you are probably going to get them both fired. I think you should go with one coordinator. In 1994, I was elevated to the coordinator position. I did not coach a position then, but I did work directly with the quarterback coach. I was with Coach

Bobby Ross and I had the opportunity to hire the quarterback coach, so philosophically we were on the same page.

In February, we brought in the quarterbacks to meet with the coaches. We had Stan Humphries, John Friesz, and Trent Green. We started teaching them the same things I had taught the quarterbacks when I coached in college. I did not know any better and that is the way I wanted to do it. If you know me, you know I always go back to the fundamentals every year to start out. Those three quarterbacks were not real happy campers to start out with in February.

We worked three to four hours a day for three or four days a week. In the middle of this quarterback fundamentals review, John Friesz was traded to Washington. He was a free agent and signed a nice contract with a bonus. He told me he was going to go with the Redskins. He said, "I really appreciate all the help you have given me. The thing you are doing right now, no one has ever sat me down and taught me those things. It is amazing what I have learned."

Now, those guys did gripe about the meetings, but what he said really opened my eyes. At first, I was a little concerned about the meetings, and I was a little intimidated. Stan Humphries had run the offense for the Redskins for nine years, and I had only been working with the quarterbacks for two years. We did go on to the Super Bowl that year. Stan went on to have his best year and was named all-pro quarterback. So, I am convinced now more than ever that the program I am going to go over with you can help at all levels.

Depending on how much time we have, I will tell you how we train quarterbacks on *vision*. Vision is a big part of playing quarterback. We will start off being very basic, and then we will get more complicated. I will teach you just like I would teach our quarterbacks. You are going to get in one lecture what the quarterbacks get in a month.

First, I want to talk about our *offensive philosophy*. We want to be able to run and pass the football. Let me talk about balance in the two areas. When I came back to the college game from the pros, I could have gone to Detroit, but my family did not want to move to that area. I had some property in South Carolina and some in Atlanta. Coach George O'Leary was at Georgia Tech. He is a good friend of mine. He offered me a job. I talked with George and he said, "Ralph, we are going to be 60-40, right?" I asked what he meant by that statement. He said, "That is our philosophy. We run the ball 60 percent of the time and pass it 40 percent of the time." I told him to get himself another coach. I told him I was not going to get tied down to percentages. I told him the game would dictate how much we run the ball or pass the ball. He agreed to this, and so I stayed with him.

I think you have to do run and pass equally well. You can do both averagely and still be successful. The thing you are going to learn here is how to make the right play at the right time. I believe you train your quarterback, and the moment of truth comes when the ball is snapped. No matter how hard our coaches prepare, the opponent's coaches are preparing as well. You have good coaches on both sides of the ball. If your quarterback can get you in a good play or get you out of a bad play, you are one up on the defense.

You hear coaches make the statement that they are not going to put their job in the hands of a 17- or 18-year-old kid. I am not afraid to do that. It is not because I am a great play caller. It is because about 60 percent of the time our quarterback is going to put us in the right play. That is what I want to cover with you here tonight. So, we want a balance between the run and pass, and I want to have the ability to do both.

In the last six years, I have had four teams that have run the ball for 200 yards per game and have passed for 200 yards per game. This past year, we were only seven yards apart on the average. In some games, we have 300-plus yards passing, and in some games, we have 300-plus yards running the ball. At the end of the year, it always comes out that way. Each of those teams won 9 or 10 games in those four years where we had such a great balanced offense. I think it is a good philosophy to have.

Multiple formations, personnel groups, shifting, and motion are ways we use to create problems for the defense. Formations to me are like weapons. Every formation attacks the defense in a different way. I will tell you how we use these formations to attack defenses. I will tell you what the defense has to do to defend us.

I learned in the NFL that matchups are a big part of winning. If you can get the right matchup, you have a chance to win. Let me give you an example. A few years ago at Georgia Tech, we had two running backs hurt, so we had to go to a spread formation with four wideouts. I put the offense into a tight slot and we were getting nickel-and-dime coverage. We were running the wishbone to the tight slot with four wideouts. That was fun. We could still run the triple option with Joe Hamilton, and yet we could throw the pass too.

I like to look for players who are dual players. I like players who can play either tight end or fullback. I look for players who can play running back or play slot back. If we have these types on the field, we can change the personnel groups and not have to change players on the field. I get some matchups that way.

Sometimes when we use shifting and motion, it is to create movement on the defense. I do not want the defense to sit there and tee off on us when the ball is snapped. I do not want them to line up with all the blood out of their fingers and here they come. I want them to have to think, and I want them to adjust. This takes some of the aggressiveness out of them.

The line coaches will say that it is a headache when our offense is moving around. "We do not know who to block." I will show you how to cover that situation. I will show you how simple it can be.

We prepare for every situation that may arise in a game. We have our four-minute offense when we are ahead. We have a four-minute offense when we are behind. We have a four-minute defense when we are ahead, and when we are behind. We try to cover every situation at least by Friday in the walk-through, but also during the week.

Now, I want to talk about training the quarterback. This is very basic, so hang with me for a while. When we start game planning, the first thing we do is determine what kind of animal we are going against. Defenses to me are different animals. You have the seven-man front with four secondary players. We declare the defense as a seven-man front or an eight-man front. If they have four secondary players, we know they have seven up-front players. Now, does the defense play with four down linemen, or do they play with three down linemen? If they have four down linemen, then they have three linebackers. If they have three down linemen, they have four linebackers.

If it is an eight-man front, it means they only have three secondary people. We see two kinds of eight-man fronts. We see the four down linemen with four linebackers. In high school, you may see five down linemen and three linebackers. That depends on how the ends play. Are they linebackers or are they down linemen?

We do this in determining matchups. *Nickel* to us indicates the defense has five secondary players. You can have a 40-nickel, which is four down linemen with two linebackers. You can have a 30-nickel, which is three down linemen, three linebackers, and five defensive backs. I tell our staff that when we see a 30-nickel defense, a loud siren should go off in their heads. We have problems with this defense. The 30-nickel defense creates problems for us. We have problems in the areas of protection and identification. You must be sound against this defense.

If you see the dime defense, you have six defensive backs. You could have a 40-dime. You have four down linemen and one linebacker. You could have a 30-dime with three down linemen and two linebackers.

Next, I want to talk about naming the defenders. This is very elementary. If we face a four-down-linemen scheme, the two inside men are called tackles and the two outside defenders are ends. If we have a three-down-linemen scheme, the middleman is the nose man, and the two outside men are the two tackles. If we face a five-down-linemen scheme, we have a nose man, two tackles, and two ends. We do this so everyone is on the same page.

If we have a three-linebacker scheme, the Sam linebacker is to the tight-end side, Mike is the middle linebacker, and the Will linebacker is the split end. If we have a four-linebacker scheme, Sam is to the tight-end side, Mike is the inside linebacker, Buck is the weakside inside linebacker, and Will is to the split-end side.

If the defense is in a nickel, you have two linebackers inside Mike and Will. Again, Mike is to the nickel side, and Will is away.

Let me get into reading defenses. What does a quarterback look for in reading a defense? First, let me tell you that we run all of our plays with a 25-second clock. When the quarterback breaks the huddle, the clock is the first thing he should look for. He should look to see how much time he has to deal with. I want our quarterbacks to the line of scrimmage with 18 seconds to go on the clock. This is because we shift, because we motion, and because we *check off*. The quarterback must have time to get all of this action called. If the quarterback is still calling the plays out at 10 seconds, and we are still shifting or in motion, he has a call he makes, and everyone lines up where they are going to end up.

The next thing the quarterback does is to look at the free safety. I am going to tell you how we read coverages. He looks at the free safety and determines where he is. You will hear me use the term *open* or *closed*. Closed means there is a defender in the deep middle of the field. *Open* means there is no defender in the middle of the field deep. The quarterback looks to see where the free safety is lined up. He looks to see the depth of the free safety. If he is at 12 yards, he is a deep back. It could be deep one-half or deep one-third of the field coverage. If the man is lined up less than 10 yards away, the quarterback should be alert because that free safety probably is in a blitz mode.

The second thing the quarterback wants to know about the free safety is where the safety is in relation to the hash mark. If the ball is on that hash mark, where is the free safety in relation to that hash mark?

The next thing the quarterback looks at is the strong safety. Where the strong safety is lined up verifies what the quarterback reads in regards to where the free safety is lined up. The quarterback looks at the strong safety and determines if the defense is man or zone by the way the strongside safety is playing.

Next, the quarterback looks at the front. He determines if the front and secondary are coordinated. So, this is what he looks for. He reads the free safety first, the strong safety second, and the front third.

One year, I had a quarterback that refused, flat refused, to look at the free safety. You know how quarterbacks are when they come out of the huddle. They are thinking of all the pass patterns they have, what the snap count is on, and what the defense is playing. Now, everyone thinks we have the answer to attacking defenses. The closest thing I can give you on this is to read the free safety. This kid I had playing quarterback that one year would never look at the free safety. He would throw the ball into double cover more than a few times. So one day I started calling him *Ray*. "Ray, you have to get the ball to the tight end." He said, "Coach, my name is not Ray. Why do you call me Ray?" I said, "Well, you play quarterback like Ray Charles."

Another day, we came out and we were getting ready to scrimmage. I had a red bandana. I took it to *Ray* and told him I wanted him to wear it over his eyes in the scrimmage. "Coach, how can I play quarterback with that bandana over my eyes?" I said, "You do not use your eyes anyway, so what difference does it make?"

This is how I finally got the kid to read the free safety. I had him come to the line of scrimmage, and I had him call out the coverage to me as he pre-read the coverage. He would come up to the line of scrimmage and call out, "one," "two," or "three." Now, the defensive secondary was really getting nervous. I did not care if the quarterback was wrong on his call, because I was trying to train him to read the free safety first. That is the first man he needed to look at. It all starts from there.

We look at the play clock, the free safety, the strong safety, and then the front. I will tell you how to identify defensive fronts. To the offensive line coaches, this is the simplest method I know. In high school and sometimes in college, the fronts do not always line up where they are supposed to line up. Those are the worst fronts to work against. You get these *bastard fronts*. A defender lines up in the gap between the guard and tackle. The guard thinks he is in a 4technique. The tackle thinks he is in a 3technique. Neither of the blockers picks him up, and he comes free and makes the tackle. The guard tells the coach, "I thought the tackle had him." The tackle responds, "I thought the guard had him." We all have been down that road. So to prevent that, we have what we call *identifying characteristics*. I make everyone on the team learn these characteristics. If there is no one over the guard or if a linebacker is over the guard, it is a 50 defense to us. It is not if the defense has a nose guard. If our guard is uncovered, we call it a 50 defense. Now, everyone should be on the same page. If there is not a playside linebacker over the guard or tackle, it is a 60 defense to us. If we are going to the three-man side and there is a linebacker on the outside of the tackle, it is a 70 defense to us. An 80 defense is four defenders to that three-man side. On a 90 defense, the linebacker is over the guard, or he is in the A gap.

Here is how we call them out: *50—linebacker over the guard. 60—no playside linebacker. 70—three-man side with a linebacker over the tackle. 80—four defenders to the three-man side. 90—to the three-man side with a linebacker inside over the guard*. So, we are talking about the 50 defense, the 60 defense, the 70 defense, the 80 defense, and the 90 defense.

We have a couple of other terms to clarify these fronts. If it is a 50-stack front, then the linebackers have slid one man toward the tight-end side. If it is a solid defense, it means the center is covered, and the two offensive guards are covered. If we called *wide-70 solid*, it means the three-man side is solid and the linebacker is over the tackle.

A bear defense is when you have that 46-bear look, where you have a linebacker inside the tight end and another cover man outside the tight end. A plus front is when the nose guard is shading the center to the tight-end side. A minus front is when the nose guard is shading to the split-end side. You can have a 50-minus or a 50-plus front. A wide front means there is no down lineman over the tackle. If we are going to the three-man side and we have a linebacker over the tackle, it would be a 70-wide front. If the linebacker aligned on the tackle, it would be a 70 tight. It is the same call on an 80 or 90. If the tackle is covered it is tight; if he is uncovered, it is a wide front.

With that in mind, this is how we call our fronts. We call the tight end first, and the split-end side second. If we call a combination, it is a call to each side. For example, we could call, *plus 57-tight*. We could call, *wide 70-wide solid*. We could call, *tight 89-tight*. We use this system in breaking down film and in communicating.

Here is where we tie it all together. When the center comes out of the huddle, he is going to make one of four calls. If he calls *odd*, he is telling the quarterback, the guards, and the tackles that the defensive man is shading him. That is *odd*. If there is a linebacker over the center, he calls it even. If there is no one over the center, he calls out *clear*. If he is covered and the two guards are covered, he calls out *solid*.

This is how it all works. The center calls the separation first. Each side calls out the defender to his side. We are communicating with each other. We may not block it right, but we are all on the same page blocking the defense. The right side will come out and call the front: *odd-50*. They do not need to hear the plus or minus calls. On the backside, we may call out *90*. We know the frontside called an odd defense.

Let me talk about coverage. There are four types of zone coverage. That is all God created. You have a three-deep coverage, a two-deep coverage, quarter coverage, and rotation coverage. I love the word rotation. Ask your quarterbacks what rotation means. They will surprise you. They do not know what you are talking about. What is rotation? Rotation is when a secondary man lines up deep but ends up playing an underneath coverage. He ends up playing one of those short zones.

If we see three-deep zone coverage, we see a free safety 12 yards deep. In our league, he can disguise his position at about two yards off the hash mark. If he gets three yards off the hash mark, he cannot make it back to the other side. On his first step, we expect him to go back to the middle of the coverage. The strong safety is usually lined up outside the tight end in a five-by-five area looking into the backfield. This is a strong rotation because the strongside safety is playing the flat to strongside. If I know it is cover three, I also know my rush-pass ratio. We know there are four deep defenders and seven rush defenders.

Another thing I know about cover three: the strong safety has the flat, the Sam linebacker has the inside hook, the Mike linebacker is going to go weakside, and the Will linebacker has the weakside flat. Why is this important? If I tell the quarterback to read the weakside flat, he needs to know what the coverage is.

We call a cover six a weakside, three-deep coverage. *Fox* means the weak safety rotates to the flat, and *cloud* means the corner comes up and takes the flat. If we say the coverage is a *6 cloud*, it means the rotation has occurred to the weakside corner playing in the weakside flat. Now, the safety is going to be created 12 yards off the hash mark. On the first movement, he is going to get width. Anytime the safety gains depth, I know the cornerback is going to roll up. I do not have to see that corner roll up; I know he is going to roll up. Otherwise, they would have two men in the deep-third area. The free safety is giving you the answer. You do not have to look at the corner to tell what he is going to do. The corners lie. They are deceptive. The free safety is a truth seeker.

Another thing we will see is that the strong safety is a little deeper, and he is going to the middle. Now, when I see the weak safety go to the weakside, I know who has the strong flat. I know the Sam linebacker has to get out covering that strong flat. I like that Sam linebacker covering backs in the strong flat if I have a quarterback that can throw the strong flat route.

The defense still has a three-deep coverage. They have three deep and four underneath. One side is strong rotation, and one side is weak rotation. The Mike linebacker goes strong, and the Will linebacker has the weakside-hook area.

Here is what I preach to the quarterback against three deep: "You should never throw a possession pass for an incompletion against three-deep zone coverage." That is an aggressive statement. The defense had four men underneath on the coverage. Every possession pass route I know has three receivers coming to one side. That gives us a 3-on-2 option against the coverage. The offense should win. It is a fast break. The defense only has two men on each side underneath, so we should win on either side of the ball. It is our three receivers on two of their defenders. We like to throw the ball against three deep.

Now, we take a look at a two-deep zone coverage called cover *two*. Now, we have a bigger challenge on our hands. The rush-pass ratio is this: They are going to rush four men and defend with five men underneath and two deep.

There are a lot of different types of cover two. You must decide which type of cover two you are facing. Is it going to be a cover two that sinks, or is it going to be a collision-type sinking defense? Now, teams are playing the two deep backs closer to the sideline and sending the Mike linebacker down the middle.

There are a lot of variations of cover two. They are in the cover two family. You must attack each type of cover two differently. There are some phony cover twos. You see the two deep, and you release two vertical receivers. They drop with the receivers, and it becomes a cover four. They do not end up in cover three. If you high-low them, it becomes a cover two.

In cover two, here is what we look for: the safety is three yards off our hash mark. He could be on the hash mark in high school. He is 12 yards deep. Where is the strong safety going to be? He is going to be 12 yards deep too, and depending on what the split of the wideout is, he could be on the hash mark or inside the hash mark. But he is deep. He is not down low where the strong safety was before. His first movement is backwards. He is going to back up as soon as the ball is snapped. What do we know when that safety starts backing up as soon as the ball is snapped? What do we know? If we are smart, we will not throw the out route if the quarterback reads the free safety backing up. We are not going to read the corner. We are not going to fall into that trap. We are going to read the safety. Don't read the corner because he lies. That is a weakside cover two.

We also have a strongside cover two. Most of the time, the strongside cover two is played against a slot formation. The weak safety will come all the way across the formation, and the safeties will roll up on the slot. The corners will play half coverage. The safeties' depth will be determined on how good the tight end is. The front is kicked over, but we still have the same ratio of five defenders underneath, with two deep and four men rushing. That would be cover five for us now.

The next coverage we have is quarter coverage. This is the *in* coverage. Woo baby! Teams think they have the world by the tail with this coverage. They have two safeties on run support. They come down on the run. They have four players defending the deep pass. Now, what is the cover ratio on this defense? You have four men rushing. How many underneath men do you have? They have three linebackers underneath. If the offense was good against the defense in four underneath, you should be great against three underneath. This is where we run the possession-pass offense.

In cover two, we wanted to attack the deep thirds. You do not want to attack the underneath with four defenders underneath. In the four-deep look, we want to attack the flat. The defense has Sam and Will covering the flat on the four-deep alignments. If Sam and Will cannot cover the flats, we want to attack the flat. We must know the strengths and weaknesses of the coverage.

We have strongside-quarter coverage. We call this *cover seven*. The strongside safety is going to be the strongside-flat defender. The safeties are lined up about 11 yards deep. If the corners roll up, the safety will cover deep.

Let me tell you how those quarter-coverage people play safety. They play flat-footed. When the ball is snapped, they are hanging in that position, looking at the number two receiver. If the play is a run, the safeties want to come up to support. When they do that, we can throw over their heads. So, if the safety is backing up, it is cover two. If the safety goes into the deep one–third, that indicates cover three. If he is standing flat-footed at 10 yards deep, it indicates cover six. Those are all zone coverages.

Let me talk about man coverage next. First is man free. We call it cover one. It is a strongside coverage. It is like our cover three. Now, I look at the strong safety, and he is sitting *inside* of our number two receiver. He is not outside anymore. He is inside and he is eyeballing the second receiver, who could be a tight end or a slot man. He is not looking at the quarterback. I can confirm this by looking to see how the corners are playing. They are lined up inside the wide receivers, and they are not looking at the quarterback. They may be pressed up on the widest receivers. On cover one, I always assume we are going to get a five-man run. If you run hot routes, the quarterback has to be alert for the six-man rush. If Sam is coming, the quarterback has to dump the ball to the hot receiver. You can tell when Sam is coming on the blitz. How? He lines up like he is on the hood of a car. Right! The quarterback reads the free safety, then the strong safety, and then he looks at Sam. Oh, Sam, how are you doing? The quarterback is anticipating what is coming on the play. He can see if Sam is up on his toes.

Let's say Sam does blitz, and the defense only rushes four men. Now, the quarterback knows they have a free linebacker inside. That means we must watch our crossing routes. If Sam does not come, it is still five underneath, but one of those defenders is free to play ins and outs.

If we go the other way on cover one, it becomes cover eight. Now, the weak safety comes over and takes the second receiver. The strong safety goes back to the middle. Everyone else plays the same, but I know the pressure is coming from the weakside now. Another thing I know is that I have Sam lined up on our second receiver on the other side. It could be a tight end, and it could be a wideout. I like that situation. I like that matchup. When you get a wideout or the tight end covered by the Sam linebacker, you should light the wind. I also know I am 1-on-1 on the strongside. Those are man-free coverages.

Next is pressure-man coverage. We have two of those coverages. If the safeties are lined up less than 10 yards back, but playing over the number two or number three receivers, you are going to get linebacker pressure, and it is going to be a six-man dog. Here they come. How do you tell if they are coming on the blitz? If the safeties are lined up less than 10 yards deep, the linebackers are coming. They are telling you to be alert for your hot receivers. That is cover zero to us. When we see this defense, the Mike linebacker lines up in some really unusual positions to line up on number three.

Next, we have what we call *cover nine*. Cover nine is three secondary players lined up less than 10 yards deep. When that happens, it means we are going to see the safety blitz. If the free safety is all the way over to the strongside, we get the strong-safety blitz. If that free safety is all the way over to the weakside, you get a corner blitz. If the free safety is cheating down on his alignment, and the corner and strong safety are on the same side, you are going to the weakside-corner blitz. I will not get into zone blitzes. Those are all of your coverages.

Let me get into formations and how they affect defense. The big thing you want to know is this: is the middle of the field open, or is it closed? If the middle is open, and the defense is playing cover two, we have a running situation. If the middle is closed, and the cover three defense is called or you have cover three man coverage, you have a passing situation. When we talk about a right or left formation, we are talking about two wideouts, a tight end, and two backs in the backfield. Most defenses are going to play you with eight defenders in the box. If the middle of the field is closed, they are going to play cover four and bring the safety down. You cannot run the ball. You will see at least eight men in the box. If you are really good at running the ball, the defense will bring nine in the box. If the defense plays cover two here, you have a good chance to run the ball.

It all depends on where they are playing you. The number of men in the box will be determined by the way the defense plays you. It is a numbers game as to whether you run the weakside or the strongside against the seven- or eight-man fronts. It will depend on where the ball is in the middle of the field, and if the middle of the field is open or closed. In our open-slot formation, we do not have a tight end. We have two wide receivers and two backs. Now, you look to see if you have a six-man box or a seven-man box. If the defense lines up with the middle of the field open and a two-deep look with six men inside the box and another man outside, where you cannot block him, you have to take advantage of the alignment and throw the football.

The more you spread the offense or reduce the defense, the more they come out of the box. Let's look at a one-back formation with two tight ends, one back, and two wide receivers. Is this a running formation, or is it a passing formation? What would you think? It is a passing formation. How does that stretch the defense? It stretches the defense because you have added another gap. If you have one tight end in the game, you have seven gaps to defend. You have the A, B, C, and the D gap to the tight end. When you put the end on the other side, you force the defense to defend that other gap. You have the same four gaps to both sides. You are going to see cover four where the defense can cut the gaps down or where they can support on either side of the gaps.

The other look you will see is cover one with four defenders to both sides. If you get any coverage other than cover four or cover one, you should *run* the ball. Run it! If you get cover one and cover four, you are 1-on-1 on the outside. Throw the ball!

George O'Leary used to get after me about throwing the ball. "Why are we throwing the ball when we have two big slugs at tight end?" Every Monday, we went in and did our self-scout. Every week, the most productive formation was the two tight ends and two wideouts. The reason for this was that those two slugs at tight end ate up those two safeties. It left our two wide receivers one-on-one on the outside against their corners. We were not throwing the ball to the slug ends. We were throwing the ball to the wide receivers. When the defense came outside to double those wide receivers, we ran the football. We would come out and call *alert-quick-hitch*. If the defense was in cover two, the quarterback would check the play, and we would run the ball.

On doubles, this is what we do: we have three wide receivers and one back. If the middle of the field is open, you have a six-man box. If the middle of the field is closed, you have a seven-man box. In our spread formation, we have four wide receivers. It is a fun formation. You can run the ball with four wide receivers. When the middle of the field is open, the defense cheats the Will linebacker halfway into the boundary, where he can still help on the run. You can run play-action and get the receiver down the middle. You can crack-block on the Will linebacker, and you can run the option. You can do a lot of things and still run the ball. But when the defense closes the middle, you are one-on-one with four wide receivers. Now, you can go to your three-man side, and you should win all of the time on that play.

Next is a three-back formation. We run the double slot. I love that formation. We see how the defense is going to play us, and take what they give us. I just went through our cutups. Every year the defense plays this formation differently. When I was at Georgia Tech, we ran the formation with four wide receivers. We would see quarter coverage. They played a 60 defense with the man in the middle pretty much balanced. This year, we did it with a running back and a wideout in the two slots, with our fullback deep in the middle. The defenses played us with an eight-man front. The coaches thought they did that because of the particular personnel we had at the slots. But, we got eight-man fronts almost the whole year. We use a couple of checks with it, and it has always been good for us.

We have not gotten to the no-backs formation at Maryland yet. But when we get in no-backs, you want to look for linebackers and displace them. If you have a quarterback that can run, you can use all of your one-back plays with the quarterback running the ball. But, you must be ready to handle pressure.

Next, we want to look at understanding how fronts and coverages are coordinated. We talked about rotation. We said that is a secondary defender with underneath coverage. You can have strongside or weakside rotation. We talked about rush-coverage ratio. We said that related to the number of defenders that rushed and the number of defenders deep. We identify the flat defender. The quarterback should know the flat defender, both strong and weak, by reading coverage. He must be able to anticipate pressure by reading the coverages and fronts. It is important to identify the front and coverage and to coordinate them. What do I mean by this? If we have weakside-zone coverage, such as cover two let's say it is a 4-3 defense—the quarterback should know that the Mike linebacker is going to be to the strongside. Against the 4-3, Mike tells you if the defense is undershifted or overshifted.

If we had cover three with the strong safety rotated down, the Mike linebackers should be to the weakside. If we see a 3-4 defense and we have a weakside coverage, the nose man is going to tell you which side is strong or weak.

On cover three with a 4-3 defense, where is Mike? He is weak. That is balanced. You have two rush defenders on each side of the center. Mike has the weakside hook.

Will has the weakside flat. Sam has the strongside hook. The strong safety has the strongside flat.

On cover two, you have a 59 defense. In pro football, the coaches would see this defense and tell me the front is undershifted. That is because they see the line is undershifted. If you count the defense, you have three-and-a-half men to the tight end and only three men to the split end. The strength is where Mike is lined up. Now, the safeties are lined up less than 10 yards deep. Here comes the pressure. When you get man coverage, this does not always hold up. Now look at the 3-4 defensive alignment. The problem with the 3-4 alignment is that you do not know which outside linebacker is going to rush. If we have a weakside coverage, who is going to rush? It will be Will or Buck. If we have a strongside coverage, Sam or Mike is going to rush. It will be one of those two on the rush.

Another thing about the weakside coverage is the nose man should be kicked to the strongside. This is so they are balanced up.

How to understand where to run the football is our next coaching point for the quarterback. We number the defense. This is our two-back set running rules. Everyone can run the ball to the tight-end side. But we do not want to run the ball over there if they have five defenders there. If there are five people to the tight-end side, here is what is happening: the front and the coverage are together. I will guarantee you the weakside flat is open. We have a general rule for the quarterbacks. If the middle of the field is closed and the Will is over the tackle—man or zone coverage, the receiver is 1-on-1 to the weakside. He can check off and go there anytime he wants. If we get the 1-on-1 to the weakside, we will take it. We will throw the ball to that side. If you see the five-man side to the tight end, that is what is happening. We are not going to run the ball to the tight-end side if that is what the defense is going to do. We are going to throw the ball to the split-end side, or we are going to run it over there.

You must be able to run the ball to the split-end side. The defense is going to make you run the ball to the weakside. If you want to be able to run the ball to both sides, you must be able to run the ball to the split-end side first. You must know how to do that.

We have a two-backs-with-a-split-end formation rule. When we have two backs and a split-end formation and we want to run the ball to the split-end side, this is how we do it: each week we group plays, but the rules do not change. If we tell the quarterback we are going to run the sprint draw weak or strong this week, we are going to run it off the two-backs-split-end rule. He knows right now if there are three defenders or less to the split-end side, we are running the play to the split-end side. If there are three-and-a-half or more to the split-end side, we are going to run the play to the tight-end side.

It is simple, right? Let's look at it. How would we attack that defense? The tackle is one-half, the Mike is one, the end is two, and the Will linebacker is three. So we have three-and-a-half defenders to that split-end side. Where would we run the football? We run it to the tight-end side.

Over on the tight-end side, we have a shade to the other side. We do not count that man. He is zero. If we have three or more to that side, we run the ball to the split-end side. The safety man is up close. Why would we want to run the ball? Let's throw the ball. Why run it into pressure? You could run the ball to either side, but the quarterback can throw the ball outside anytime.

Here is a rule you can use with your countergame. It is a rule where you do not want to run the ball to the split-end side if two defenders are hanging over the outside. I call this the split-end-reduction rule. Remember what the 70 defense was? If the defense is in a 70-90 look to the two-man side, we are going to run the ball to the split end. On any other defensive look, we are going to run the ball to the tight end. We are going to run the ball to the split-end side against a 70 defense, a 90 defense, and the stack defense. If we have a 50, 60, or 80 defense, we run the ball to the tight end.

We are going to run counter-gap weak, or we are going to run toss strong. Let me take you through that situation. Is the defense in a 70 or 90 look to the two-man side? No! It is a 50 on the two-man side. So we sweep to the strongside. We do not want to run the two plays into that look on the split-end side. Why do we not want to run the plays into that look? If we block down and kick out, I still do not know if our tackle can get the Will linebacker.

I would prefer to run the sweep to the tight-end side and put the three down linemen on the inside down blocks and use the fullback to kick out at the point of attack. But, when we get a 70 look on the split-end side, we can get a double-team block on the 3-technique. We can kick out or log the end. We can put the tackle or the back on the Will linebacker. I like to run the weakside counter against that look.

We may want to run some of our option game to the split-end side against that defense. That is a reduction defense with three men.

Let me talk about two backs with three wide receivers. Say we have called the spring draw to either side. I tell them if the middle of the field is open, we are going to see a six-man box. We must determine if the Y end can block the Sam linebacker. If he can't make that block, then we have to run the play to the weakside. If the Y end can block Sam, then we only have a two-man side over there, and that is a better way to go. We have a split-end rule, but we have to be careful to see where the reduction takes place.

On a one-back set, we have a rule. On the tight-end side, we never run to the four-man side. We do not like to run into a four-man look. Some teams do run into four men. On the split-end side, we count the men in the box. If the middle of the field is open and it is a six-man box, we run the ball. If you can block the defenders, you do not count them. If you can't block them, you count the numbers. You must look at the depth and the width of the safeties. We split the receivers wide enough to force the safeties to declare. If they are going to cover deep, they must get depth and width.

It is easy to count the number of people in the box. You want to be able to run the ball from the one-back set even though the defense has seven men in the box. We apply the one-back-split-end rule that allows you to run to the split end when there are seven men in the box. Here is the rule: if the center is covered and there are two men to the split-end side, we want to run the ball to the split end; if the center is uncovered and there are three men to the split-end side, run the ball to the split-end side.

If the center is covered and there are three men to the split-end side, run the ball to the tight end or throw the ball. If the center is uncovered and there are four defenders to the split-end side, you have to run the ball to the tight end or throw the ball. That is another rule that can work for you. If we are in a one-back set with four wide receivers and it is strictly a five- or six-man box, we block it straight up.

Let me hit on the spread formation. If the middle is closed and there are six men in the box, we are going to throw the ball. If we get cover two, we are going to run the football.

It is the same thing against quarter coverage. If the safeties are 10 yards deep and flat-footed, you throw the ball, but you can still run it because you have a five-man box.

Let me review the topic of understanding where to throw the football. Know how to read the coverage on a pre-snap look. Know the position of the free safety. We talked about the hash mark and depth they line up. Identify the flat defenders.

I bet a lot of you read progression. I did it for a long time myself. What I mean by progression is say you are running a curl-flat-hook with three receivers, and the quarterback comes back and sets up. He reads the receivers in the order we gave him: curl, flat, and hook. We do not read the play that way now. We read the flat defender now.

I identify the flat defender by reading the coverage. Against a cover three, I am going to look at the strong safety. If he runs to the flat, I am going to look for that linebacker. I am throwing either the curl or the hook route. The strong safety took the flat out of the equation. If the safety went back and played the curl, we do not need to go any further. We go to the flat right now.

When you read the defenders, your decisions are more accurate, and they are faster. The reason for this is that you read the body language of the defender. If that man has his shoulders turned and he is running, and you are looking at a receiver, you do not see that. You throw to the receiver, thinking he is open. But, the defender comes out of nowhere and picks off the pass. If you can see the body of the defender, you can make a better decision.

When the quarterback gets really good, he can start making the defender do what you want him to do. I do not do this with the kids until I feel they are confident. I have the kid take the ball back on the drop and look at the flat. But, he still sees the flat defender. If the safety jumps the flat, he comes back to the curl route. He can look the defender off, but he has to be pretty good before he can do that.

We talked about recognizing man coverage. We talked about all of these things. For example, look at the depth of the secondary. If you see the safety is in the middle of the field, the strong safety is lined up inside, and the corner is pressed up, we are looking for the Sam blitz. If we have a hot on and we have called what we refer to as *press-no deep help*, and I have an X receiver that I think is a good receiver, and the safety is in the middle of the field, we can run the conversion route to the split end anytime we want. If we have a *hot* called, we will throw the ball to him. But, I would rather take a shot throwing the ball up the field than throwing the *hot*.

In man coverage, the defenders are going to look at the receivers and not the quarterback. The alignment of the corners and the body of the linebackers indicate man coverage. The quarterback must know when he is 1-on-1 and take the first open receiver.

I talk to the kids in terms of field zones. I tell them how accurate we should be in each field zone. The first zone we talk about is the *no-cover zone*. We should be 90 percent in that no-cover zone. The no-cover zones are routes such as swings, screens, check downs, and any pattern that is behind or on the line of scrimmage.

On the short game, we should be successful on 60 percent of the passes. I would change this based on the last few years. We are closer to 70 percent now on completions in the short game. If you have the middle of the field close and you are reading the defenders, you should make those completions. They are a pitch-and-catch for us. If we see quarter coverage and we have the hitch and flat routes wide open, we are going to take them. We do not want to turn down a six- to eight-yard gain if it is there. Be patient, and take it. Take it, and then the defense will try to jump the play. When they do, then hit the big play up on top.

The next zone is the intermediate zone. It is about 50 percent for us. These are the play-action passes on normal downs, the third-down-and-seven yards plus. Now, we are going to high-low the safety man. It can be against a two deep or a three deep. If we are throwing a post with a dig route, I want to read the safety. If the safety is going back and we are close and the shoulders of the safety are square, we want to throw to the post. If it is close, we want to throw to the post. If the shoulders of the safety are not square, I tell the quarterback to throw the dig route. So, the body language is involved in the read.

The last zone is the deep zone. I think you have to go deep at least four times per game to let them know you have a chance to hit the long ball. This may be the most underpracticed, yet the most important, skill we do.

At Maryland, we have dotted lines three yards from our sideline on the field. That is for the wideouts to allow for a cushion for the quarterbacks to throw the ball. We run a simple pat-and-go drill. We let them throw the long ball down the sideline. Then we put the defensive backs running with the receivers and make them catch the ball by looking it in. Throwing the deep ball is an art. You need to know where the safety is on the deep throw. If the safety is in the middle of the field, I can put some arc on the ball down the sideline on the deep ball. If the safety is playing too deep, I have to drill the long ball to keep the safety from getting to the ball. Knowing how much air to put under the ball is very important.

I have a test that I give the quarterbacks. I think most of them can pass the test without any problems. I will review some of the items on the test with you. I am going to give you my slide show. At Georgia Tech, I took file-folder-type cards and on the back of the card, I put a formation, a front, and a coverage. On the other side, I listed all of the plays we would run from that formation. Then, I laminated the card. I would make up 10 plays in a set of cards. I used them as my *flash cards*. I would hold up a card and the quarterback would respond to my questions. "What is the coverage? What is the front?" I would call out a pass route. "Who is your read?" Then, I would do another card. The kids were getting good at the end. I was trying to teach them to make quick decisions.

Then, I went to see an eye doctor, and he showed me some interesting things to do with the players. I got PowerPoint on the computer. I emailed the same type of cards to the quarterbacks. They had to complete the cards and email them back to me to let me know they completed the test. I would do this on Sunday night. They were getting part of the game plan then.

I made up the cards and sent the quarterbacks questions that I wanted them to be aware of concerning the plays we selected. We ended up putting the plays in a manual. It is a fun thing to do because you are training the kids to know the routes and the situation, and they have to do this under pressure.

Now, what I am working on is virtual reality, where we put the system into a video where the quarterback can make the same decisions. The difference is that we are seeing it in video. We are getting close to that position and hopefully that will be even better.

I hope you have gotten something out of this tonight. I think there are some values in this for high school coaches, but I realize some of this material is not possible for high schools.

In closing, I encourage you to teach your quarterbacks to read the defenders and check the depth of the safeties. Life will be a lot easier on you. Thank you very much.

6

Training Quarterbacks to Run and Pass

Ralph Friedgen
University of Maryland
2003

Thank you very much. It is a pleasure to be in Cincinnati. I am going to talk today about *training the quarterback*. Some of the things I'm going to talk about are technical. I hope you can use some of the ideas from what I give you today.

I'm going to take you from day one when we start working with the quarterback until the end of the season. It has been my privilege to work with some pretty good quarterbacks. This year we had a quarterback named Scott McBrien. If any of you saw our first game against Notre Dame, you probably were wondering how we were going to win a game. As the season went along he got better and better and ended up as the seventh most efficient quarterback in the nation.

The system is not an easy system. A lot of people don't think they can teach it. You can be simpler, but you are not going to have all the answers. Part of being a good offense is having the answers for problems. We put a tremendous amount of responsibility on our quarterback. It is my belief that he is the last guy who can change the play before the ball is snapped. We work very hard with the quarterback in understanding defenses.

When recruiting is over we start meeting with our quarterbacks a couple of days a week. We only talk defense. We don't talk about our offense. We want them to understand defenses. Before I get into that let me explain our offensive philosophy.

We have to have *balance* in our offense. When I say balance, some people misunderstand what I mean. Balance is the ability to run the ball as well as you can throw the ball. It doesn't mean you run the ball and throw it an equal amount of times.

When I was making a decision to leave the San Diego Chargers and come back to college ball, I talked to my good friend George O'Leary. He was at Georgia Tech at the time. He told me his philosophy was to run the ball 60 percent of the time and throw it 40 percent of the time. I told him he needed to find someone else because that was not a philosophy. There was a silence on the phone, because he was a defensive coach. I told him I wanted to be able to run and throw the football equally as well. When you can do that you can take what the defense gives you.

Defenses want you to beat them with what you don't do well. They want you to play left handed. If you are a passing team and that's all you can do, they will make you run the ball. If you are a running team and that's all you can do, they'll make you pass the ball. When you can do both, the offense has the upper hand on the defense.

When I was at Georgia Tech we lead the nation in offensive production. We were very close in the yards we rushed the ball and the yards we passed it. I think there was four-yards difference in our rushing and passing. Both categories were in the 230-yard area. Last year, which was my first year at Maryland, we were almost identical. There was one-yard difference in our run/pass totals. This year we threw for 198 yards a game and ran for 215 yards a game.

I like to use *multiple formations, personnel groups, shifting and motion*. I look at formations as weapons. I think every formation stretches the defense differently. You as the coach need to know how the formation stretches the defense. We have to know how the defense is going to adjust to motion and shifting. We want to know how the defense reacts to certain personnel groups. The more you can do with the same personnel group the better you are. When I went to Georgia Tech with George O'Leary, he used to talk about personnel groups being synonymous with formations. He thought like a lot of defensive coaches. He thought if you had two tight ends, one back, and two wide receivers, you were going to be in that formation. I didn't understand that.

The personnel on the field can be in a lot of different formations depending on the ability of the personnel. We had a fullback who could be a tight end and a running back who could play wide receiver. That let us get into a number of formations without changing personnel.

We want the quarterback to be able *to put us in the right play* or get us out of a bad play. We use *audibles* and *check-with-me* calls. The quarterback has to recognize the strengths and weaknesses of each of the coverages. It was a shock to me when I was in San Diego that Stan Humphrey, our quarterback, had never checked out of a play. He did check-with-me calls, but never changed the play at the line of scrimmage. It was hard to coach him to audible, but once he got good, he was very good at changing plays. The quarterback has *to prepare for every situation that may arise.* A game plan allows you to do that.

As I get into the technical talk, if you have a question please ask. I tell our quarterbacks to think of defenses as different animals. Each defense has its own characteristics. The first package I'm going to talk is the seven-man front with four defensive backs. Within that package there is a 3-4 defensive front. That defense consists of three down linemen and four linebackers. If it is a 4-3 scheme, there are four down linemen and three linebackers. The first thing in our game plan is to decide what type of front the defense is playing. We want to know if it is a seven- or eight-man front. In both of these fronts there are four secondary players.

The next defensive package is an eight-man front with three secondary players. You 4-4 or 5-3 are the fronts we see in the eight-man scheme. In the 4-4 there are four down linemen and four linebackers. In the 5-3 there are five down linemen and three linebackers.

The new defensive front that teams are using is the *nickel front.* Five years ago you didn't see many nickel fronts in college football. You see it all the time in present day football schemes. The nickel gives the offense five players in the secondary. The two fronts we see are the 40-nickel and 30-nickel. In the 40-nickel there are four down linemen, two linebackers, and five defensive backs. In the 30-nickel there are three down linemen, three linebackers, and five defensive backs. I tell our staff any time we see a 30-nickel defense sirens should go off because that is a real problem.

The *dime package* is something that we see in college. I'm not sure you see it that much in high school. The dime package has six defensive backs in the scheme. We see the 40-dime and 30-dime in our situation. In the 40-dime there is one linebacker and in the 30-dime there are two linebackers. Both of those defensive schemes have six defensive backs in the secondary.

I name all the defensive packages so my quarterback is on the same page with the coaches. When I talk about four down linemen, I am talking about two tackles and two ends. In the three-down-linemen package, there is a noseguard and two tackles. With five down linemen, I have one noseguard, two tackles, and two ends. That is simple, but you have to start simple to be more complicated.

If there are three linebackers in the scheme they have names. The Mike linebacker is in the middle. The Sam linebacker is aligned to the tight end side and the Will linebacker is to the split end side. If there are four linebackers their names are Sam,

Buck, Mike, and Will. The Buck linebacker is the strong inside linebacker and Mike is the weak inside linebacker. There are two linebackers in the nickel scheme: their names are Mike and Will. The Mike linebacker is normally to the nickel side.

Why do you read defenses? You hear that term all the time in the offense scheme of things. The thing that makes a good quarterback is how fast and accurate he can make a decision. If the quarterback can anticipate what the decision is going to be, it increases his speed in making that decision. When the quarterback pre-reads a defense he is putting information into his brain so he can make a fast and accurate decision.

If a quarterback has a gun for an arm and great physical tools, but has no vision and can't make a decision, he will not win for you. Move him to some other position. He is going to create problems and will throw a lot of interceptions.

You have to teach the quarterback to make decisions. The first thing the quarterback does as he breaks the huddle is to look at the 25-second clock. He wants to know exactly how much time he has to get the play off. I like the quarterback on the line of scrimmage with 17 seconds left on the clock. We have a fast cadence and we only huddle four yards from the line of scrimmage. My coordinator gets the play into the game quickly.

The hardest thing to teach the quarterback is to see the *free safety*. If you only take one thing out of this lecture today this is it. Quarterbacks get all concerned about the formation, motion, his mechanics, and everything else, but he forgets to look for the free safety. The free safety is going to tell the quarterback what the defense is doing. From the free safety, his eyes should go to the strong safety and finally at the front. This is the information the quarterback needs in his computer. The quarterback has to know how the strong safety, free safety, and the front are all coordinated.

We identify fronts in a number of different ways. So many quarterbacks never know what the front is. If the quarterback is going to be involved with putting you in the right play in the running game, he has to be able to identify fronts. I'll go over our system quickly on the way we identify fronts.

We define a *50 defense* as a defense with the linebacker aligned over the guard. If there is no one over the guard or a linebacker over the guard, the quarterback classifies that as a *50 defense*. A *60 defense* has no playside linebacker. There is a down lineman over the guard and tackle and the next linebacker is outside the tackle. A *70 defense* has a three-man defensive side with the linebacker over the tackle. An *80 defense* is defense with a four men on one side of the ball. A *90 defense* has a three-man side with the linebacker stacked over the offensive guard or aligned in the A gap.

We have a *stack defense* in which the linebackers are slid to the tight end side. A *solid defense* means the center and two guards are covered by down linemen. A *bear defense* is a solid defense with a coverage player over the tight end and a rush player outside. The term *plus* means the noseguard is shading the center toward the tight end and *minus* means he is shading the center to the split end side.

A *wide defense* means the offensive tackle is uncovered. A 70-wide defense means the defense has a three-man side with the linebacker over the tackle, but there is no down lineman over the tackle. The *tight defense* is the opposite of the wide. The offensive tackle is being covered by a defensive down man.

We use this system in our computer breakdown too. We always describe the tight end side first. If there is a 50 defense on both side we simply call that a 50. If the defense to the tight end side is in a wide 70 defense, and in a 50 minus to the weakside, we call that a *wide-75 minus defense*. In the number 75, the 7 stands for a 70 front to the tight end side and the 5 means a 50 front to the split end side with the noseguard shaded that way.

Something I think that would be invaluable to a high school program is the *center call*. When our center comes to the line of scrimmage he has five calls he can make. That puts everyone on the same page. This is situation where the offense has to communicate. This also helps the quarterback make the call because he knows what the line sees. If the center has a defender on him he calls *odd*. The call takes all the doubt of where the defender is aligned. The *odd* call means the center has a shade or man head-up on him. If the center can block a man who is aligned in the gap, he can call *odd* and the quarterback will treat the defense as an odd defense.

The next call he can make is *even*. The even call means the center has a linebacker over him. If the linebacker is in a shade or a gap alignment and the center thinks he can block him, he calls *even*. If the center can't block a shade or there is no linebacker the center calls *clear*. If the center calls *solid*, the center and both guards are covered by down linemen. If the center sees a player in the guard-tackle gap, he calls *solid*. That takes away any confusion of where the down linemen are aligned. The last one is *stack*. That means the center is covered with a linebacker behind the noseguard.

The center calls what he sees and the rest of the linemen make a front call. For example, the center may make an odd call, the right side might say 50, and the backside could say 70. That means the entire offensive line is on the same page. The line knows what they are dealing with.

The quarterback has to know how to identify coverages. Let's talk about *zone coverages* first. There are a lot of different coverages, but we put them all into some really simplistic forms. The zone coverages are *three-deep*, *two-deep*, and *quarter coverage*. On all coverages there is a *strong and weak rotation*. The rotation coverage puts one of the secondary players into underneath coverage. We define odd numbered coverages are strong coverage rotations and the even numbered coverages are weakside rotations.

In a three-deep zone, *sky* means the safety has flat responsibility and *cloud* means the corner has flat responsibility. If the defensive call is *cover 3 sky*, the strong safety is in the flat and everyone else plays three-deep zones [Diagram 1]. If the call is *cover 3 cloud*, the strong corner is in the flat and everyone else is in three-deep zones.

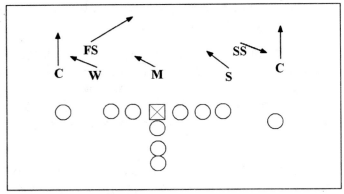

Diagram 1. Cover 3 sky

At Maryland our cover 6 is a weakside rotation. We use the term *fox* or *cloud* to describe the flat player. If we call *cover 6 fox*, the weak safety is in the flat and *cloud* puts the corner in the flat [Diagram 2].

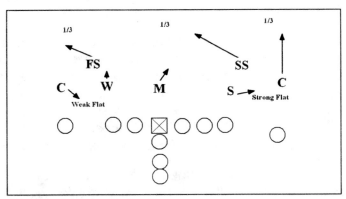

Diagram 2. Cover 6 cloud

I always like to look at things from the hash marks. Defenses try to disguise what they are doing. To disguise the *three-deep coverage*, the weak safety will come off the hash and move into the boundary about two-yards outside the hash mark. Most times it is a yard depending on the split of your wide receiver. If the weak safety is two yards or less from the hash mark, I figure he is going to the middle third. That is what we tell our quarterback. If he is three yards or more, we anticipate him going weak. Since the hash marks in high school are wider, we would use his alignment on the hash marks as the key. The quarterback is anticipating cover 3 sky coverage. On his first step he verifies what he is anticipating. If the weak safety goes to the middle, the quarterback knows the Will linebacker covers the weak flat and the strong flat is covered by the strong safety. He knows he is getting a four-man rush and has three-deep in the secondary. He knows he has strong safety support to the strongside and linebacker support to the weakside on a running play.

The depth of the safeties is very important. If they are going into thirds they are normally going to be 12-yards deep. They have to get that depth if your wide receiver splits are good.

The next category of coverage is the *two-deep coverage* [Diagram 3]. In this ratio you have two people deep, five guys underneath, and four defenders rushing. We never key the corner because there are too many ways for him to play. I know when the safety retreats the corner is rolling at some time in that coverage. If the safety plays flatfooted, the corner is in quarter coverage. If the safety goes to the middle, the corner is in third coverage. The safety will always tell you what the corner is going to do.

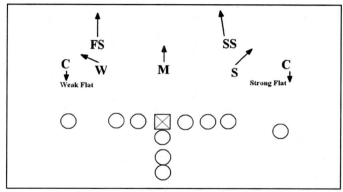

Diagram 3. Cover 2

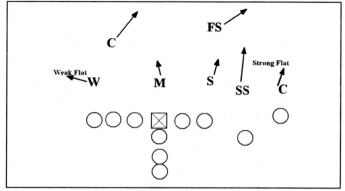

Diagram 4. Strongside cover 2

71

The *strongside cover 2* is usually played against a slot formation. The defense overshifts the front to the tight end and rotates the coverage to the two-receiver side [Diagram 4]. The free safety rotates to the strongside and the weak corner moves to the backside half of the field. The Will linebacker has the weakside flat area. We don't see this coverage much, but that is one way to play this type of coverage.

The last zone coverage we see is called *cover 4*, which is quarter coverage [Diagram 5]. In this coverage, four secondary players are going to about 10- to 11-yards deep. The safeties in this coverage are going to be flatfooted. They are run-support players to either side. In pass coverage, they are keying the number two receiver on their side. If he goes to the flat, they are playing the number one receiver. If the number two receiver goes vertical, they play him. If this defense is true quarter coverage there are three players underneath and four rushers.

In this defense the strong safety is reading the tight end, which is the number two receiver. The corner is reading the flanker back, who is the number one receiver. The weakside reads are the same. The Sam and Will linebacker are dropping to the flat area. The Mike linebacker is probably keying the third receiver to either side.

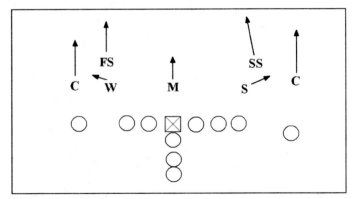

Diagram 5. Cover 4

The *strongside quarter coverage* will probably be played on a slot formation [Diagram 6]. In this coverage the strong safety comes down to play the flat. The free safety and the corner are playing the quarter- coverage reads. The free safety is reading number two, or the slot receiver, and the corner is keying the split end. They are playing quarter coverage off the releases of the slot receiver. The backside corner is playing half the field and the Will linebacker is playing the weakside flat area.

A variation of this coverage is played to the weakside. The corner can roll into the flat with the free safety going over the top to play the backside half [Diagram 7]. The strongside plays the quarter coverage as usual. Everything is the same except the weakside roll or half coverage.

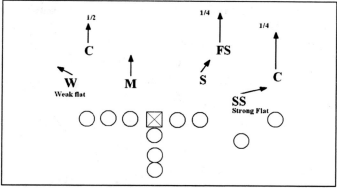

Diagram 6. Strongside quarter coverage

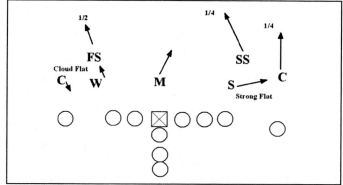

Diagram 7. Quarter-quarter-half coverage

Those are the zone coverages we play against. Now let's talk about man coverage. The first one I want to talk about is called *cover 1*, which I call *man free* [Diagram 8]. When we read man coverage we tell the quarterback to assume he has five-man pressure rushing. The ratio will be five rushers, five underneath, and one deep. We tell the quarterback to expect the linebacker blitz coming from the side that the safety has rolled down.

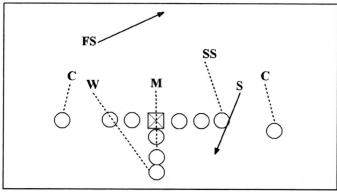

Diagram 8. Cover 1 man free

What we see a lot of is called *one-man hole* [Diagram 9]. This generally is an inside linebacker in a free position playing in the hole in the middle of the field. When the quarterback reads man coverage, but he doesn't get a blitz and there is no pressure, he should be aware of the linebacker playing in the hole.

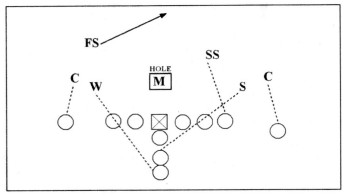

Diagram 9. One-man hole

Another type of the one-man hole player is called *robber coverage*. [Diagram 10] This is the same type of play except the strong safety is free. He is generally playing your favorite pass pattern or receiver. The quarterback knows that when he is expecting five man pressure and doesn't get the pressure, it means the defense has a man free in the underneath secondary.

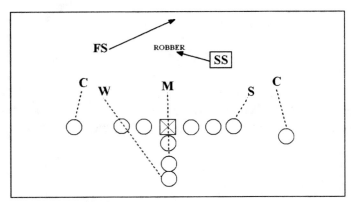

Diagram 10. Robber coverage

We read man coverage when the strong safety is over the number two receiver instead of being outside in his alignment and the free safety is cheated toward the middle or in the middle. We also see the linebacker aligned on the backs in the backfield. The corners are generally in an inside alignment on the wide receivers and are looking at the receiver. When the quarterback sees the secondary rotated strong, he can anticipate the Sam linebacker blitzing. If the Sam linebacker doesn't rush, it is probably a hole-free coverage.

If we read the coverage going the other way, we call that *cover 8* [Diagram 11]. The strong safety is free in the middle. The weak safety is cheating down to cover number two out of the backfield. The Will linebacker is blitzing and the Sam linebacker is matched up on the tight end. The quarterback goes through the same reads as he did to the strongside.

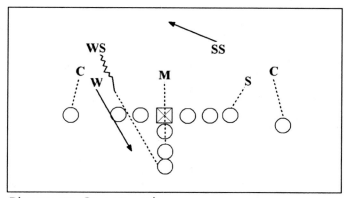

Diagram 11. Cover 8 weak

If the quarterback anticipates the Will linebacker blitzing and he doesn't come, the quarterback knows he has a free defender in the middle of the field playing robber. That is the same read he got to the strongside. The most popular coverage here is the *cover 8 thief* [Diagram 12]. This is like the robber call to the weakside. The free safety is playing the hole in the middle or sitting on a particular pattern or receiver.

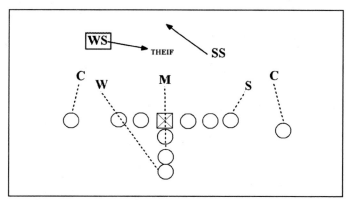

Diagram 12. Cover 8 thief

The next thing we see is called *cover 0* or *pressure-man coverage* [Diagram 13]. That means there is no free safety and both safeties are locked into coverage. A key to the pressure-man defense is the safeties and corners. They will start to creep inside of 10 yards. When the safeties get down to eight yards, there should be an alarm going off in the quarterback's head; he is going to get blitzed. If both safeties are down it is going to be a six-man rush. A change-up the defense could use with that kind of pressure is called *cover 0 hole*. In that case the defense would only bring five-man pressure and play someone in the hole in middle of the field underneath.

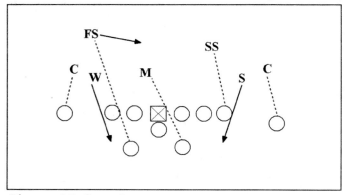

Diagram 13. Cover 0

If we see a *cover 9*, that means we are going to get a blitz by a secondary player [Diagram 14]. It will be six-man pressure with one of the blitzers coming from the corners or safeties. If the corners are coming, the safety to that side will move out to cover the wide receiver. This is a hard blitz to see because the sixth man can come from so many directions.

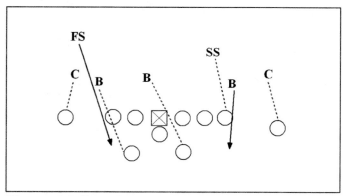

Diagram 14. Cover 9

Some people may bring their safeties down and not blitz anyone. If that happens they are doubling underneath on receivers. If you have a secondary blitz, the free safety will tell you where it is coming from. If he goes over number two strong, the blitz is coming strong. If he goes weak, you are going to get it from the weakside.

The popular thing to do now is *zone blitz*. If the defense knows the offense has a six-man protection, they will try to make the quarterback throw hot. They will blitz a linebacker and drop a defensive lineman. It is tough because they are forcing you to throw the ball to your hot receiver and covering him with someone not in the coverage package.

The quarterback has to know what ratio he is facing. If the middle of the field is closed, that means there is a safety in the middle of the field. We tell our quarterback if the middle of the field is closed, we should be able to throw the ball because the offense outnumbers the defense. The offense is going to throw a triangle route to one side of the defense. That means you should have three receivers over two defenders, and if you can read anything you should be able to complete a pass.

If the middle of the field is open, that means the defense has five defenders underneath and can cover you regardless of the route. The weakness on that defense is behind the underneath coverage where you can get three receivers on two deep defenders.

If the coverage is quarter coverage, you should be able to throw the ball underneath. You are building confidence into a quarterback on how to attack a defense based on how well he pre-reads it. We are trying to help the quarterback learn how to pre-read coverages so he can anticipate and make decisions fast and accurately.

If the quarterback reads man coverage and middle of the field closed, he knows he has 1-on-1 coverage on all his receivers. If the defense blitzes a defender, he has 1-on-1 underneath. If they don't blitz, they have a free defender underneath.

We tell the quarterback a basic rule, if the middle of the field is closed and the Will linebacker is over the tackle, you are always 1-on-1 to the split end side. I watch a lot of high school film and that situation happens all the time. That is the easiest throw in the world. It doesn't matter whether it is man-to-man or zone.

When the quarterback reads pressure-man coverage, he has to watch the free safety. The quarterback asks all the time whether he should look at the hot route or the sight-adjustment route first. In a sight- adjustment pattern, we run patterns into areas where the blitz has vacated. My answer to the question is where is the free safety? If the free safety is down in coverage, the route will be a hot route. If the free safety is cheating weak, it is a sight-adjustment pattern to where the free safety vacated. The free safety will tell you, but you have to read him in pre-snap and post-snap.

Formations have an affect on defenses in both the passing and running games. Knowing where the free safety is tells you as much in the passing game as it does in the running game. If the middle of the field is open, that means there is no free safety. The defense could be in cover 2, 3, or 4 depending on the formation. Our pro formation for us is called right/left. That is two wide receiver, a tight end, and two backs. If the middle of the field is closed, the quarterback is anticipating an eight-man front. That means the strong safety has to be blocked if you are going to run at the strongside.

If there is a weakside rotation with the weak safety down and the strong safety in the middle, you are looking at an eight-man front. If the middle of the field is open, it means the safeties are 12-yards deep outside the hash marks and you are facing a seven-man front. That rule holds for the slot formation with the tight end in the game.

However, if I go to an open-slot formation, which is three wide receivers, two backs, and no tight end, with the middle of the field closed, it is a seven-man front. If the middle of the field is open, it will be a six-man front. That is what the quarterbacks are looking for. It is like a theorem in geometry. Obviously it is easier to run the ball into a seven-man front. Conversely it is easier to throw against an eight-man front.

The *one-back formation* is a very popular formation today. If we have two tight ends, one back, and two wide receivers, it gives the defense an extra gap to cover. The only way they can defend the extra gap is to close the middle of the field. That formation also affects the force of the defense. The Will linebacker will be over a tight end, which makes the linebacker force a little soft. This formation gives the offense an opportunity to throw the football.

I'll give you a case in point. When I was at Georgia Tech we had two tight ends. They were good blockers and looked like tackles playing tight end. We were in the two tight ends and two wideouts formation throwing the football. My good friend Coach O'Leary wanted to know what we were doing throwing the football with those two slugs in the game. Every Monday when we went to the office to do our scouting report, we also did a self-scouting report on our team. Invariably our best passing formation was our deuce formation. Because our tight ends were such good blockers, the defense was closing the middle of the field to get more run support and our two wide receivers were catching a lot of balls. We forced the defense to play the run and it opened up the throw.

A *double formation* for us is three wide receivers, one tight end, and one back. If the middle of the field is open, I'm looking for six men in the box. If the middle of the field is closed, I'm looking for seven men in the box.

In the *spread formation*, I have four wide receivers and one back in the game. Now, we are going to see just the opposite of what we saw before. Before we showed run but passed the ball. In this formation, we show pass but the run is open. If I put my four best wide receivers in the game, the defense is thinking pass. In college, the defense checks to cover 2. They have two deep and five players underneath. Unless the defense goes to nickel or dime coverage, they have some mismatches with their linebackers on our wide receivers. Now, this becomes a heck of a running formation. With the middle of the field open, there are five men in the box. That gives us five offensive blockers on five defensive players. If you run any quarterback option, the odds are more in your favor. If the middle of the field closes on this set, we look to run the ball.

Our quarterbacks understand football. From the knowledge they have gained, they make us look like good coaches. The quarterback is the one making the final decision, not me. If my quarterback can make the final decision, I have a chance to be successful. A lot of coaches won't put their jobs on the line with an 18-year-old kid. I don't mind doing that. I have been pretty successful doing that. I have kids that do well on the next level, because we teach football and they understand it.

We run some *three-back formations*. We run the *wishbone* or *double-slot formation*. That forces the defense to balance up instead of overloading one side. When we can get defenses to lock into a formation or coverage we can attack it. The one thing that allows you to do something like that is to have an option-type quarterback. If you don't have one, it is no good. We had to get out of it this formation this year because we didn't have a quarterback that could execute that kind of offense.

We haven't gone to the *no-back set* at Maryland yet. We are going to start practice in three weeks and that is the first thing on my agenda. That formation lets you displace linebackers and work the ball underneath. It works especially well if you have a running quarterback that can run out of the shotgun.

People want to know how we teach our scheme. I teach the quarterback how formations are defended. I teach those principles and how to recognize fronts and coverages. I teach them how to anticipate what they are going to see.

One of the big things for the quarterbacks to learn is to understand how fronts and coverages are coordinated. The first thing they have to understand is *rotation* and *rush-coverage ratios*. Sixty percent of our quarterback's reads are made off the flat defender. If the quarterback has a 3-4 defense and cover 3 in the secondary, he should anticipate the Sam linebacker rushing.

The quarterback has to be able to identify if the front and coverage are coordinated. If the coverage is a weakside zone with the free safety shifted weak, the quarterback anticipates the front being over shifted to the strongside. He knows that the Sam linebacker is going to be the flat defender. The defense has to slide toward him so he can get outside to defend the flat. If it is strongside coverage, the front should be undershifted. If it is a balanced front, the drop of the linebackers can determine coverage.

If the defense is in a 4-3 defense and playing cover 3 in the secondary, the quarterback is anticipating the Mike and Will linebackers to go to the weakside on their drops. The coverage is rotated strong the linebackers have to go weak to be coordinated.

In an overshifted defense with 3-4 personnel, the noseguard will tell you if the front is overshifted. If the defense is 4-3 personnel, the Mike linebacker will tell you if it is an overshifted defense. If it is a 4-4 defense, the line will shift toward the tight end in the overlook. The same rules apply for the undershifted front. In the 3-4 defense, the noseguard will be shifted to the split end. In the 4-3 defense, the Mike linebacker will shift toward the split end and the line will shift toward the split end in the 4-4 defense.

If you have a 4-3 defense with a cover 3, the Mike linebacker is shifted to the weakside. He knows the defense is coordinated. There is going to be a strongside rotation and the linebackers are going weakside. Conversely, if the Mike linebacker is on the strongside and the free safety is weak, he knows the front is kicked to the strongside and the secondary is going to the weakside. A lot of people think I'm nuts for telling everybody this. I think this is just football.

We number the defense. If the nose is directly over the center, we count him as zero. If he is shading the center, we count him as a half. Here are some of our rules for checking plays. The first group is *two- back running rules*. We teach this concept so as we go into a game plan we can put any two plays together we want. The rule tells us to *never* run the ball to the tight end if there are five defenders on that side. It tells us to *never* run the ball to the split end side if there are four defenders on that side.

The *two-back split end* rule says if there are three or less defenders to the split end side, the ball should be run to that side. If there are three-and-a-half or more defenders to the split end side, run to the tight end side. If you can get your quarterback to count to four, you've got it. If we have called a run toward the three-and-a-half man side, we will go ahead and run it. However, if a check-with-me call has been made in the huddle, we will run to the tight end side.

We have a *reduction rule* that we also use in a 70 or 90 defense to the two-man side. We are going to run the ball to the split end side if the defense has only two defenders that way. If we don't get the two-man look to the split end side, we run the ball to the tight end side.

When we talk about balance on an offense, there needs to be balance between running the ball to the split end and tight end sides. Anybody can run the ball to the tight end. If you don't run the football to the split end side, the defense will stack up to tight end side and you won't be able to run it over there either. If you can run the ball effectively to the split end side, you can run it anywhere.

In the three wide receivers, one tight end, and one back formation we have a *base rule*. Remember what I said before: if the middle of the field is open, we are anticipating six men in the box; if the middle of the field is closed, we think there will be seven defenders in the box. The rule for the tight end side is never run to a four-man side. The rule to the split end side is simple. We count the defenders in the box. If the middle of the field is open, we run the football. If the middle of the field is closed, we throw the football. The problem with that is you get predictable as an offense.

Let me tell you a funny story. When I first went to the San Diego Chargers I was the running game coordinator. We had a running game coordinator and a passing game coordinator. The passing game coordinator told the quarterback if he read a two deep, run the football. In the pro football league, the hash marks are about as wide as this stage. Our quarterback called an audible to a weakside run and almost got the running back killed. They looked at me like I had called the play. I asked our quarterback what he was reading. He told me the safeties were on the hash marks and he read two deep. I told him that two safeties on the hash marks were like the middle of the field being closed. The test for a half-field player is whether he can make a play on the fade route. In pro football, for a player to be a half-field player he had to be aligned half the distance between the hash marks to the numbers.

The importance of that story is to make sure your wide receivers take their maximum splits to spread the defense. It is much easier to read the secondary when they have to move wider in their coverage. If a safety is spread between his alignment and his responsibility, he has to give up his disguise early sometimes to get to his responsibility. That makes it easier for the quarterback to read open or closed in the middle.

We had a *one-back split end rule* that allowed us to run the correct side with seven defenders in the box. If the center is covered, run the ball to the two-man side. If the center is uncovered, run the ball to the three-man side.

If we aligned in a four wide receiver package, we count the box. If the middle is open there will be five men in the box and we are going to run the football. If the middle of the field is closed, we throw the football.

Men, I'm running out of time, but I want to cover our progression on throwing the football. The first thing we teach is the *pre-snap look*. That is the initial thing we do to start to read the coverage. The quarterback must know the position of the weak safety in relationship to the hash mark and his depth. The quarterback has to identify the flat defender. He has to read defenders not receivers. When I coached college football before I went to the pro leagues, I was a progression-read guy. If the pattern was a curl, flat, and a pivot inside, we read curl first, flat second, and the pivot third. We went from receiver to receiver to receiver.

I don't teach that anymore. The only thing I read is the *flat defender*. If he takes the hook away, I throw the ball to the flat. If the flat defender takes the flat away, I'm reading the inside linebacker and throwing the ball to the hook or pivot route. By reading, the quarterback gets a better idea and clearer picture of what is happening. He can see body language of the defender. For my quarterback this year, it took him some time to develop that skill. Progression passers sit in the pocket and wait for a pattern to come open. When you read defenders, if he jumps one pattern you take the other one. When the quarterback gets good at reading, he can make the flat defender cover the pattern he wants him to by using eye contact and fakes.

If the quarterback doesn't read defenders, he is going to end up throwing interceptions. Our quarterback threw ten interceptions this year. He threw six in the first three games. Interceptions get you beat. I have a formula called the *percentage-of-*

error that I use on our offense. It includes the number of penalties, sacks, dropped balls, and number of turnovers. I take those things and divide them by the number of plays we ran. When we come out under 12 percent, I've never lost a game. I've won some when we were over that percentage, but I've never lost one under 12 percent. In the Peach Bowl we were at a four-percent error rate. That's how you play good and win games. When you don't beat yourself, you beat somebody you are not supposed to, because they beat themselves. As long as you don't beat yourself, you have a chance to win the game.

Two years ago we were second in the nation in turnover ratio. That is the first thing I cover with our offense every Monday. We lost three games this year. In each of those games we were at a 22-percent error rate or more. When I interviewed for the Maryland job I had a kid ask me how I was going to make them win. I told him the first thing I was going to do was teach them how *not* to lose. We are not going to beat ourselves. Then I told him he was going to be bigger, faster, and stronger than he had ever been in his life, because he was going to work. Those that didn't want to work are not on the Maryland team any more. It is not hard. Don't beat yourself, work hard, put yourself in a position to win, and let your quarterback make the right play.

To throw the football effectively, the quarterback has to *recognize man coverage*. He has to see the depth of secondary players, key defenders looking at receivers instead at him, the alignment of safeties and corners, and the body language of the linebackers. He has to identify the easiest throw, anticipate the hot receivers, and choose where to go with the ball. If the quarterback reads pressure-man coverage, he knows he has a hot route, but if there is a pressed man-to-man coverage on his flanker, that is where I want him going with the ball. He doesn't have to throw hot just because there is a blitz coming. If the middle of the field is closed, that means there is no defender over the top of the corner. I like that match up. The linebacker may be frothing at the bit to take the quarterback's head off, but the quarterback is not going to throw hot, he is throwing for the touchdown.

The next thing in our list is to *take the first open receiver*. Before I talk about that, I have to tell you this story. I was doing one of these clinics last year and I told this story. This is a story within a story. Whenever I talk to the quarterback I try to give him a visual picture. Throwing the ball and never passing up a receiver is a lot like dating. If you have a girl, and she's all right, don't sit around waiting for the prom queen. If you pass up that girl and the prom queen never comes, you've lost out again. Some of you guys have to take the first receiver that comes open. I told that story. At the end of the lecture I looked up and my wife is in the back of the room. The first thing she said to me was, "Was I the first receiver or the prom queen?" Of course I said she was the prom queen.

I identify *field zones* for the quarterbacks. The first zone is the *no-cover zone*. I expect 100-percent completion in that zone. The types of passes thrown are screens, delays, and swings. The second zone is the *short-game zone*. I expect 60-percent completion in that zone. In that zone we have the quick game that are the three-step patterns. We have the 8- to 10-yard five-step passing game. The third type of pass includes the *check-down routes*. These are patterns that the quarterback comes off to if his primary route is covered. One thing that drives me wild about quarterbacks is they always want to throw the ball deep. I have no problem with going deep with the ball, but when that route is covered, I want a completion. I want them to get me to second-and-two for the first down instead of a second-and-ten. The more of those types of situations I have, the less I'm throwing the ball down the field. We want to come out of the play with some positive gain. Also included are the *seven-step drops* and *play-action passes*.

Zone three is the *intermediate passing zone*. I expect 50-percent completion is this area. In this area the quarterback has to be conscious of linebacker drops. He has to be able to throw the ball over the linebacker or through passing lanes with touch and good velocity. Play-action passes control linebackers. Zone four is the *deep zone*. In this area I expect 30- percent completion. These passes are vital to stretch the defense. The quarterback wants to look for mismatches so he can throw the homerun ball. We want one big play per half. The quarterback has to control and move the safety by his body language and eye contact. Every game we play, we are looking for someone on the defense we can beat deep. When we identify him as the defender we are going after, we try to get the match ups we want.

I want to emphasize again that in zone number two we should complete 60 percent of our passes. The reason we feel this way is because most of our patterns are going to give us a three over two receivers-to-defenders ratio. When we get three over two we need to win. That is a simple pitch and catch.

I give my quarterbacks a test that comes from the quarterback manual. We send the manuals out in the summer and when the quarterbacks report in the fall they this test. The test questions come from the material I have talked about today.

I am going to end with my slide show. When I was at Georgia Tech every player there had a computer. I would do a slide show for the quarterbacks, put it in PowerPoint, and send it to their rooms. What I loved about it was it was in e-mail so they had to send it back to me. That way I knew if they read it or not. What I was trying to do was teach our kids how to see things fast. I gave them a play to be run. I flashed a front and coverage of the defense for one second at the most. From that they had to type in the front and coverage they saw. The frame continued to flash with more time between each flash. You can slow the time frame down because it is just a PowerPoint presentation.

When I first starting doing using this technique I used laminated cards. I would have the quarterback come in and I used the cards as flash cards. Later on my eye doctor told me I could put them on slides and I could do the same thing.

That is a way to teach coverages and reaction. I don't want them to be a robot. I've got a guy coming in next week to talk to me about virtual reality that would possibly let the quarterback use a simulator to prepare for reading the defense. The more the quarterback can see, the more he can read.

To do the slide show at Maryland I give our quarterbacks a floppy disc. They go home watch the slide show and then come back with the answers. There are all kinds of ways to teach football, but this is something that I have been doing.

Men, I am out of time. I have enjoyed the opportunity to visit with you. This is what we do at Maryland. I know everyone can't use it, but if you got something out of it I'll be glad to send you anything you might want. Thanks a lot.

7

Quarterback Passing-Game Development

Mike Gims
Cincinnati Hills Christian Academy (OH)
2006

A lot of things have to come together to have a season like we did this past year. We obviously had some good players, we had great team speed, we had great senior leadership, and our player's work ethic matched their goals. It is okay for your team to say they want to win a state championship if your work ethic matches that. If your work ethic does not match your goals, you have some things to talk about with your players. I am also surrounded by a very good coaching staff. Two of our coaches are with me today. John Robinson is our special teams' coordinator, defensive line coach, and technology guru. He put this PowerPoint presentation together for me. Reed Chacksfield is our defensive coordinator. Every year we have an excellent defense and it is because Reed knows how to get the best out of his personnel. We run a complex defense and every game we are very well prepared for the contest.

There are many coaches who have influenced me as a quarterback coach. I am always looking for camps for my quarterbacks and want to find places where I think they are teaching similar ideas that we are teaching our players. Mike Kapiche has a quarterback camp and certainly teaches outstanding techniques. I have spent some time with Hal Mumme, Mike Leach, and Chris Hatcher when they were at Kentucky. I learned a lot from them. I also have been able to sit down and talk to Jon Kitna. I was able to talk to him about the things that I teach. He was gracious enough to spend some time with me and give me some ideas on how to teach our quarterbacks.

In our offense, we are not just a passing offense, but we do like to throw the ball. I am going to talk about quarterback development in the passing game. I will go over the techniques and drills we use at Cincinnati Hills Christian Academy. I will also go over our audibles and automatics that have been very successful for us. Because we like to throw the ball, our quarterbacks only play offense. So when we are practicing defense, the quarterbacks will stay with me. We will work on individual quarterback drills. We will work on reading drills. We will work on their weaknesses. Sometimes we will watch our defense and I will ask our quarterbacks coverage questions. I will ask them who their read is if we are throwing a smash route. I like our quarterbacks to watch our defense because we use many different coverage schemes. It helps them understand defensive concepts.

I am going to begin by talking about quarterback characteristics. Our quarterback needs to be smart and decisive. He must be able to make quick reads and decisions. He has to take all of the information you have given him during the week and come out and understand who his read is on a particular play. He must be able to narrow things down and know who his read is so he can be decisive. The most important thing for the quarterback is to know what the defense is trying to do.

Next, I believe the quarterback has to be accurate. I do not care how strong a quarterback is, he must be able to put touch on the ball and put the ball where it needs to be. I think a quarterback must be physically and mentally tough. Our quarterback this season was a junior and we put a lot of pressure on him. He does a good job with processing all of this. The quarterback also needs to be able to forget his bad plays. He needs to understand why it happened, but he cannot be looking back. I think it is important that the quarterback be a competitor. If you watched Vince Young at Texas, you may not have thought he was that great of a technique quarterback, but there is no question about how he competes. If you watched the championship game, you saw him win that game because he is such a competitor. The demeanor of his team fed off of his leadership.

The quarterback also needs to be disciplined and team-oriented. He needs to be in the weight room. He needs to be encouraging other players. He needs to be disciplined in all the things that he does. Our quarterbacks also need to be technique conscious. He needs to be thinking about his technique all the time. We would like to not worry about technique during games. We can do that if our quarterbacks have understood the importance of proper technique. That allows us to concentrate on execution and reading the defense in game situations.

The last characteristic we expect of our quarterbacks is good arm strength. He has to have good enough arm strength to get the ball down the field and stretch the defense.

We also have some ideas on receiver characteristics. Obviously, they have to have great hands. I have never thought that if I had a freshman receiver that could not catch the ball that he would be able to develop that skill to become a productive receiver. Therefore, I tend to move those guys to other places quickly. We recently had a young man that proved me wrong in this area as he had 20 touchdowns and over 50 catches as a senior. I guess my attitude toward developing the hands of a receiver has changed because of this one player.

Our receivers have to be able to run good routes. He has to understand when to break down and when to run through. He has to understand the difference in defenses and what they are trying to do. Obviously, it is a position that requires decent speed. I think good receivers also have physical and mental toughness. Our receivers need to be good blockers, and without physical toughness they cannot do that job. He also has to be tough enough to knock balls down if the quarterback has thrown bad balls. I really think our receivers did a great job of exhibiting toughness this season.

Let me move into quarterback techniques. Let me start with how to grip the ball. I want to make sure the quarterbacks understand a couple of things about gripping the ball. I want the quarterback to grip the ball with one or two fingers on the laces. I would like to have two fingers on the laces. There should be air between the palm and the ball. If you palm the football, it will produce a throw that turns the nose down. There should be daylight between the palm and the ball as he grips the ball.

I want the quarterback to grip the ball with just enough tightness so that the ball does not fall out of his hands. Many quarterbacks get sore arms because they are gripping the ball too tightly. Even though we do a lot of throwing, our juniors and seniors rarely get sore arms because they understand how tight to grip the ball. If they are using proper techniques, they are not going to develop sore arms. One of the things that I picked up from Hal Mumme was that the thumb and the ring finger should make a perfect circle around the football. Coach Mumme believes that this helps create a more perfect spiral on the throw.

Next, I want to talk about our quarterback stance. In his stance, I am going to have his toes in slightly. This allows them to be in good balance and to keep from taking a false step. It also allows the quarterback to be able to go in either direction and to use the opposite foot to push off. The heels of the quarterback should be slightly off the ground. Our feet are parallel and we are bending slightly at the knees. Your hands should be set with the throwing hand over the non-throwing hand, with the left thumb under the right thumb. As the quarterback gets under the center, his middle fingers should be right in the crotch of the center. Elbows should be bent slightly, and the quarterback should give pressure with the bottom hand. Pressure with the bottom hand does not allow separation of the hands on the snap.

I would like to talk about the five points of release. I talk often about starting with the ball in the trigger position. This is something I got from Coach Curry. As soon as you get the ball from the center, you are going to get it into trigger position. I want the ball relaxed in the quarterback's hands. The landmark of the trigger position is in between the armpit and the earlobe. If the quarterback takes off running, we want the ball to stay in trigger position until he is ready to release the ball. In trigger position, the nose of the ball is turning down and the left hand is a bit under the ball. Next, we will push the ball back from elbow to shoulder height. We will push the ball back and get our elbow up to shoulder height. We do not want a sidearm thrower and we do not want a passer who is going to bring the ball behind his head. We feel that if the elbow is held low, then sore arms will develop. So we work hard on pushing the elbow back to shoulder height. As the elbow is brought to that height, the nose of the ball should point back.

Next, is our weight exchange. When we step, I would like a six-inch step. I think quarterbacks overstride a great deal, especially if they are throwing deep. If they take a six-inch step, the hips will be able to help in the throw. The quarterback also wants to point their lead toe at the receiver. If the aiming point of a throw is in front of the receiver, the toe needs to be pointed just in front of the receiver. You want to take your step on the whole foot. If you just step on your toe, your knee will lock out and produce a poor throw. We desire that we step with our knee bent. If a quarterback steps with a straight knee, two things could happen. If he releases the ball late with a straight knee, the ball will go into the ground. If he releases the ball early with a straight knee, the ball will sail.

The next point is our index-finger follow-through. As the ball is thrown, the pinky fingers are the first finger to come off the ball. If the ball is thrown correctly, the index finger is the last finger to come off the ball. That should lift the nose of the ball up a little bit. The follow through should be to the side pocket or to the groin area. I do not want the quarterback to end up across his body. I think that is hard on his arm. After the release of the ball, the palm is going to face down and out, the thumb is down, and the index finger is extended.

Finally, we want to finish with the opposite elbow breaking the plane of the back with our chin over the front foot. Our back heel should come off the ground and it may move forward just a bit. Jon Kitna said a great drill to emphasize this is to throw and step through so the hip helps the throw. If you get your hips into the throw, your heel may come off the ground and you will drag your toe to the opposite heel. We want all of these release thoughts to work together to get the shoulders and the hips into the throw.

I want to talk about our drops and then I will go over some of the drills that we work. The three-step drop will be worked on as the quarterbacks are on a line facing me. I will check their stance before we begin. I will say, "Big," and the quarterbacks will take a big step. The key on the first step is to gain separation from center. On the first step, the ball should be moved to a trigger position. As we step, I want to make sure we are heel to heel. I do not want to understride or overstride so that the quarterback ends up over a guard. I will then say, "Little." At that point, the quarterback takes his second step, which is a little step. We repeat that for our third step, and then I want each of them up on his front foot to simulate a throw. I want them to stop on the third step so I can see their finish position. I want to see that no one is overstriding and I want to see that their belly button is over their knee. After we have taken our steps, we repeat the drill at quarter speed. Before we begin, I am looking at their eyes to make certain they are looking up and checking their stances. We then will run the drill at half speed. We will finish our drop drill at full speed. I do not want to see the quarterbacks rush with a bigger second and third step. This will cause the ball to sail. If our footwork is not proper, I do not want the quarterbacks to rush. We will move back to slower speeds and work on our steps.

When we work on the three-step drop and throwing to the left, we work with his big, little, and cheat step, as well as his plant step. His foot is going to come around and turn so that the quarterback's hips can open and turn to the throw. This will get our front toe pointed at the receiver. We will go through the same processes of this drill as we did with our three-step drop to the right. If the quarterback follows proper technique, he will not have a problem throwing to the left.

The five-step drop goes through the same drill work that I have explained with the three-step drop. On our five-step drop, we want the first three steps all to be big steps as we work our way away from the center. The final two steps can be two short, shuffle steps with an emphasis on getting our hips down with a slight forward lean as we prepare to throw the ball. As we begin to work on throwing to the left, we will work on the same cheat step on the final step as we did with the three-step drop.

In our shotgun, our five-step drop is a three step and our three-step drop is a one step. With our three-step-drop routes in the shotgun, we work on just setting our feet with a small step and throwing.

On our spot and bubble passes, if I am throwing to the right side from under the center, I am going to step with my right leg to get my leg open. I am then going to take a gather step with my second step so that I can step into the throw. If I am throwing to the left, the technique is the same, but we really emphasize getting turned so the shoulder gets pointed at the receiver. The step needs to be in the direction of the target and will want to put the ball on the downhill shoulder of the receiver for the bubble. If the quarterback is struggling with throwing the bubble, there is a very good chance he is rushing his mechanics or not getting his shoulder turned. Out of the shotgun, our footwork is very similar, although we do not have to step back as far. We just catch the ball and take a small crow hop to get into proper position.

I will now cover some of the drills that we use. Every day we do our throwing drills. Our quarterbacks will face each other, 10 yards apart, standing with toes pointing toward each other. They will make their throws to each other with a shoulder turn. They do not step or use any lower-body technique in this drill. From time to time, I will walk in between the quarterbacks with my hands up so the quarterback has to learn to put the ball up and over me.

We turn the quarterbacks to the side with their toes straight and throw with a hip turn. We do this to both sides. Next, the quarterbacks will take a knee. This allows us to isolate the mechanics of the upper body. We want to get the ball to the trigger position and work their elbow up into proper height. I also look closely at their finish in this drill to make certain that the position of the arm is correct on the finish. I will also make the quarterbacks freeze their arms after they get it into a throwing position. This allows us to examine if the elbow is at shoulder height.

The last drill we use is to stand on one leg (left leg for right-hander). To throw, we must get a good shoulder and hip turn. The right hip should lead as you throw. This teaches the power you must use in your upper body to throw the ball.

We also work a great deal with our footwork drills. When I have our quarterbacks while the defense is practicing, these are some of the drills we will use. Obviously, we work on the drops that I have previously described. We also work on line jumps. We will be on a line working one-leg perpendicular jumps, parallel jumps, split jumps, and jumping to swivel our hips. We do all of these jumps with the ball in trigger position.

We work a great deal on line drops. We will put our quarterbacks on the sideline and drop to the hash mark. On my command, the quarterback will turn and drop, working on the ball and getting to trigger position in a relaxed fashion. We emphasize strides and speed in this drill. We want to get big strides and good speed in our drop. When the quarterback approaches the hash mark, I will put my hands up and he will set and throw me the ball. When you do these drills, you see what kind of feet each player has, and the mechanics of them setting up to throw the ball.

We also do a scramble drill. I will command to go, and the quarterback drops. I will point in a direction for the quarterback to scramble. If I point back, he will move back. I will also have indicators for the quarterback to throw the ball, or to run towards me. I may put my hands down for him to run toward me and when I put my hands up, he has to move to throw the ball. I will tell them that they can throw on the run or they can stop and throw. I want make sure they understand that they cannot be running away from a receiver and throw the ball to him. They have to stop their feet and step into the throw.

We also use the typical ladder drill with our quarterbacks. The only difference is that we will use the drills with a football being kept in the trigger position. We will do all of the ladder workouts: one foot in each hole, two feet in each hole, sideways, and the typewriter drill. We will then go to our dummy drops. I will align two dummies in seven lines. We will have the quarterback drop. When he gets to the top, he will slide forward, step with his back foot, come to the bottom of the dummies, then drop-step slide, and drop-step slide back around the top of the dummies. The quarterback will go through all seven sets of dummies in this fashion. We work this drill much like our scramble drill in that I will give the quarterback a sign to throw the ball as he is working through the pocket. He may not be able to take a large step to throw because of the dummies. I want the quarterbacks to keep their eyes up and not look down at the dummies.

I want to look at our automatics. If our Y-receiver in the slot is left uncovered, the quarterback will give him a signal and either throw him a spot or bubble route. The quarterback will tap the center before putting his hands underneath. This is a sign to the center that there will be no cadence. When his hands go underneath the center, the ball will be snapped without a call from the quarterback. The quarterback will turn and throw the spot pass without anyone else really knowing what is going on.

The next automatic is to our A-receiver, who would be the middle receiver in a trips set. If the outside receiver is the one left uncovered, we will audible to him and run a quick or fade route. These checks to uncovered receivers are something that has been very successful for us.

If the corner is playing up or well inside our wide receiver, we will signal for a one-step fade route. To practice all of these, we will come out at the end of our morning practice of two-a-days and run nothing but automatics and audibles. This is five minutes, very fast paced, working the quick and fade routes outside. The inside receivers will be working the spot and bubble routes. This allows everyone to get used to our signals. As we get into our scripts in practice, out of 15 plays, two of those will be designed for an audible. Out of the shotgun, we will use hand signals for an audible. We can call plays in our two-minute situation, but often we have situations that allow the quarterback to automatic to something else. This does not take a great deal of practice time, but does allow your players to take advantage of situations that are given to them. The players always have fun with it because they are doing a little of their own thing.

We check our weakside outside receiver often. We will audible his route and change the huddle call route based on the coverage shown. If the defense is giving us a slant, we can change to that. We can also change to several other routes as well. If we audible to the spot pass, we like for the corner to be at least six yards off the line. That would be seven yards if we were in shotgun.

I am out of time. I appreciate you having me at this clinic. I hope you got something out of this and if you have questions, give us a call.

8

Wishbone-Quarterback Techniques

Paul Hamilton
Georgia Southern University
1990

I want to talk in terms of the triple and double options. I want to talk in terms of alignment, technique, and what we look for on the option.

Let me talk about stance for the quarterback. I tell the quarterback to get comfortable under the center. He must be able to get out from under the center in a hurry and make things happen. We want our quarterbacks to have their weight on the balls of their feet. If our quarterback is going out to the right, we want a balanced stance, but we want the pressure on the left toes. If he is going to the left, the pressure is on the right toes. The reason for this is to eliminate any false steps. We cannot have any false steps from our quarterback when we step to mesh with the fullback on the triple option. Our fullback has an aiming point, and we must be consistent. The pressure on the toes will force the quarterback to step in the opposite direction.

Our fullback aligns his hand down six feet from the quarterback's heels. At the Air Force Academy, we had our fullback a little tighter than most wishbone teams. We feel this gives our fullback a chance to be a quicker threat on the triple option. We are a quarterback-fullback offense. They are the two most important people in our offense. We start with these two players. They must make things happen for us. We let our fullback get in a three- or four-point stance. It doesn't matter to us. We want him in a stance that allows him to come out low and quick.

We got this point from the Air Force staff a few years ago. They took a broomstick out on the field. They would lay the broomstick down to give the fullback a landmark to line up on. They could see if the fullback had the right relationship with the quarterback.

Our halfbacks are in a three-point stance with their eyes up. Some teams will put the halfbacks in a two-point stance. We did that one year at Wofford College, but we came back to the three-point stance because we did not feel we could get the momentum from the two-point stance that we needed to block the big ends. Also, by being down we felt we added to the deception on the plays to keep the linebacker from seeing the football clearly. So, we went back to the three-point stance. They are in a three-point stance at the Air Force Academy. The halfbacks put their hands on the fullback's heels. They are three-yards wide from the fullback. This gives us a base landmark as far as our splits are concerned. If our linemen want to adjust their splits, it does not affect our backs. We are going to have a base alignment for our halfbacks.

I will cover the alignments for our X and Y receivers. Coach Sammy Steinmark will cover their pass routes. When the ball is on the hash mark, the majority of the time we want our X end to be in a normal split. He would be two yards outside the opposite hash mark. We teach splits in terms of normal, outside normal, and inside normal. There are a lot of times when our wide receivers will crack block. We may come two yards inside the hash mark. If the ball is on the short hash mark, we are going to line the X end up five yards from the boundary. We tell our wide receivers not to line up with the same split twice if possible. We want the tight end to split three to five yards from our tackle. He aligns on the tackle. We do not want them to have a lot of weight on the hands when they get down into their stance. We do not want a lot of pressure on the hands, because they have to be able to get out.

In our offense, we start with the quarterback and the fullback. We like to load people. We like to get our quarterback out on the force on the perimeter player. What are we looking for in the triple option? The first thing that we want to get is a number advantage if possible. When I say number advantage, this is what I mean: we talk in terms of offensive and defensive structure. We say we are going to have five and a half on one side of the ball and five and a half on the other side of the football. So, what we look for is how the defense is going to align on our offense. We want to see if the defense is going to be five and a half and five and a half against us. This is what we see a lot. This is how we count the defense.

The best way I have found to teach the quarterback to count the defense is with the *box*. We say the box runs from our tackle to the other tackle. We tell our

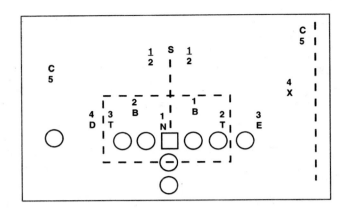

quarterback to look down the middle of the defense and count the number of men on each side of the football. If the defense has a man in the middle of the formation, he is counted as one half on each side. Here, the free safety is in the middle, so he is counted as one half to each side. Here, we have a balanced defense. We have five and a half men to each side of the ball. In this situation we want to work to the wide side of the field. We want to stretch the defense to the wide side of the field. The three people we want to key on in the box are the nose guard, the strong safety, and the free safety. They are the key people. This will tell us the balance of the defense. If we are hurting the defense by going to the wide side of the field, they may move the free safety over on us on a pre-snap move. When they do that, they think they can press the corner. Now, the free safety is moved out of the box and we have six to the wide side of the field and five to the hash mark. When our quarterback sees this, he may change the play and come back into the boundary. Our quarterback is going to look for the advantage. That is the number system for us. A middle linebacker is treated just like a nose guard as far as being counted. The most important thing we want to know is this: how is the defense trying to cover the field?

In this offense, you must have a quarterback who can make things happen. He must be able to beat the free safety in the alley. If the quarterback is not a great athlete, he must be a great technician and he must be able to execute the offense in order to move the ball.

The next thing we look at on the defense is the personnel. We attack the personnel that is to our advantage. Our quarterback is going to put us into the scheme that we are going to run, depending on the call of the offensive line. Most of the time against the seven-man front, we zone block with the line, and load and arc block with the backs. Against the eight-man fronts, we are going to veer block with the line and block the pursuit with the onside halfback. I will cover this later.

What do we tell our quarterback on his steps for the triple option? We use a *clock system* to teach the quarterback his steps. We draw a clock for the quarterback with the ball at 12 o'clock.

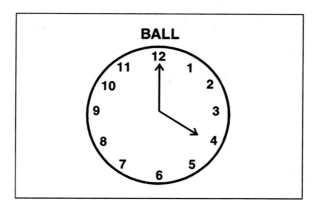

BALL

We give the quarterback a directional step on each play on the triple option. If we are going to the right, I tell the quarterback to step at four o'clock. If we are going to the left, we tell him to step out at eight o'clock. I have found that every quarterback is different. None of them is going to step the same. They may not step right at four o'clock or right at eight o'clock. But the thing you must do is to give them a reference point to start out with. This is where we start.

We teach the quarterback to take the football and to lock the backside elbow on the backside hip. We want him to get the ball to the fullback's pocket as deep as possible. We talk to the quarterback in terms of taking his chin and putting it on his frontside shoulder where he can see through the read key. I want the quarterback flexible in the knees as he comes off the mesh. The key is how they come off in the mesh. We want acceleration off the mesh. We want the quarterback to have his backside elbow on the backside hip, and we want his chin on his frontside shoulder so he can see through the read key. The quarterback's read key is the first man on the line outside the B gap to the outside. If there is a man outside the B gap, we are going to read him.

What happens if the defense puts a man in the B gap that is too tough for us to handle? We can either read the next man outside, or we can go to the double option and take the read off that man. We will not let a team put a man in the B gap and cause us problems in the mesh area. We can block the gap different ways to take care of him.

Our fullback is going to aim for the outside pad of the offensive guard. He is going to run a track. He is not going to come off that track until he is off the mesh with the quarterback. We tell our quarterback not to ride beyond the front hip. On the triple option, we are going to ride to the front hip and we are going to make a decision right there. We do not want to go past the front hip because we feel that is where turnovers occur. If the quarterback has the ball past the hip, he may be making a decision and jerk the ball away from the fullback. The fullback may still be on his track, and the ball could hit the ground. We want the quarterback to make his decision at the front hip.

We want the quarterback to take the ball as deep as possible. We want a tight, soft squeeze on the ball with the fullback. It is the quarterback's decision to decide if he is going to give the ball to the fullback or not. The fullback is not involved in the decision. The thing that I have learned about the mesh is this: it all deals with the *feel* and *repetition*. No two guys are going to be the same. You must repeat this over and over so the players to get used to the play. The starting quarterback must get some repetitions with the second fullback. The backup quarterback must get some work with both fullbacks. The mesh is all based on repetition.

We tell our fullback to take a six-inch step to the side we are going. The aim point is on the outside hip of the guard. We do not want the fullback to take a crossover step, and we do not want him to take a long step on the first step. It is a six-inch lead step to get in that track.

What do we tell our quarterback to do on the read key? When should the quarterback pull the ball on the read key? We read the first man on the line outside the B gap. Let me show you how quickly that can change. If we have a tackle in the *4i technique*, he is our read key. If the defense moves the tackle inside to a 3 technique and the end down in a 5 technique, the end is our read key. We never read a man that shades our guard. If a team plays a tackle in a *3 technique* and plays the end in a 7 technique, then the end would be our read key. We do not see that defense very often, but that is our read key.

4i

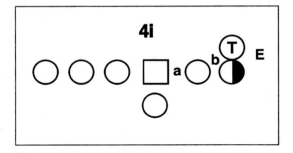

3i TECHNIQUE

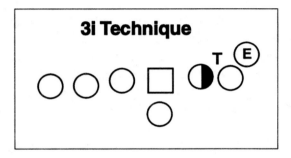

7 TECHNIQUE

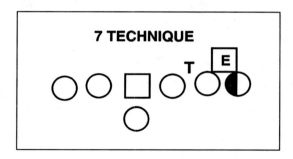

I tell the quarterback when in doubt about the read to give it to the fullback. I try to make it as simple as possible. If the inside part of the read key can get into the fullback's track where he can stop the fullback for less than 4 yards, we want the quarterback to pull the ball. If the read does not show in the track the quarterback should give the ball off to the fullback. We start inside out first. If the defense gives us the inside, we will take it.

There are a lot of different things the quarterback may see at the *mesh point*. I talked about the *mesh charge*. The defense tries to collision the fullback at the mesh point. We have seen a *squat technique* where the defense sits there and squats in the hole and tries to read the mesh. As quick as we hit the hole with our fullback, we should be able to run up and down the field against the squat technique. Also, we see upfield movement by the read key. We hand the ball to the fullback on the upfield movement.

The toughest thing to teach the quarterback is against the *queue stunt*. The read key comes down on the fullback, and then turns up on the quarterback just before the mesh point. You must work against the queue stunt over and over. If you run the triple option and read it, you will see the queue stunt. There are a lot of good football coaches around who know how to attack the triple option. The queue stunt is something we work against every day. I tell the quarterback if he knows he is going to get a queue stunt from the read key, he must stay in the mesh longer. We tell the quarterback he must be fast and accelerate off the mesh, but don't run through the mesh. This is the tough thing to teach the young quarterback initially. He wants to run through the mesh and get outside and make things happen. You must emphasize to the quarterback that he cannot run through the mesh.

We give the quarterback a pre-snap read key. If the defense puts a man in the B gap, he is there for one reason. You can look for a strike from that man in the gap. It is just like the baseball situation with a batter with a 3-0 count on him. He knows the pitcher is going to try to throw a strike on the next pitch. It is the same with a man in the B gap. The quarterback should know the man is going to go for the strike. He is going to rip through the neck of the fullback. Our quarterback can expect that to happen. If we get a 5-technique tackle, it is like a 3-2 count in baseball. We are looking for a strike, but we may get a ball. Because of the down block by our tackle, we are thinking of a strike. We are going to pull the ball on the 5 technique that comes inside.

On the tight-end side against a 7 technique, we look for the 3-0 count. We expect the 7 technique to come to the quarterback, so we are going to give the ball to the fullback. We think it is important to give the quarterback a pre-snap read. You do not want to give the quarterback two trends of thought. He can't be thinking, *Should I give it off or pull it?* He has to have a pre-snap thought and then react off that move.

We try to simplify the reads as much as possible. We have a *read key*, a *pitch key*, and a *support key*. On the 50 defense, our read key is the first man from the B gap outside.

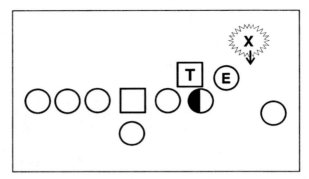

That is the tackle. Our pitch key is the first man outside the read key. It would be the end. The next man outside the pitch key is the support key. That is the rover or strong safety.

On the *Eagle* defense it changes. Now the end is our read key. The man outside the end is the pitch key. The support comes from the free safety as the alley player. They can pressure you with the corner and take the free safety to the top. If they do that, they need a superman at the free safety position, or he has to move before the ball is snapped. This is where the numbers game comes into play. We count them off on each side of the ball.

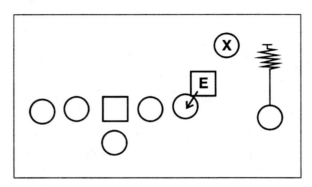

Against the *Shade* defense we go through the same reads. The tackle is the read key. The drop end is the pitch key. The linebacker will try to scrape to the outside. The corner or free safety will be the support.

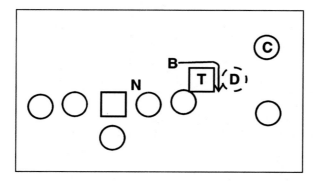

On the pitch key we are going to attack the inside pad downhill. If we get a slow player on the end, our quarterback will attack and try to eliminate him. The quarterback's job is not over when he pitches the football against a slow-playing end. He takes his inside arm and tries to get past the end's pad to cut him off. Our quarterbacks will occasionally get a knockdown block on the end. If the pitch key is outside or downfield, then we must stretch to his inside pad. We know the man the quarterback will have to beat is the free safety. If the quarterback feels the safety underneath him, he stretches it and tries to beat him to the boundary. If the safety goes to the top, the quarterback takes a step inside and tries to get inside his momentum.

Let me get to the *triple option*. The key is getting the frontside linebacker blocked. If you can't get the onside linebacker blocked, you are going to have problems on the option. We zone block against seven-man fronts, and we veer block inside against eight-man fronts. We can put our tight end inside on the linebacker.

When we zone block, the halfback arc blocks outside on the force player. On the arc block, we tell him to pivot and to take a crossover step, and then one, two, three lateral steps before he goes downhill. We want those three steps before they go downhill. We locate support and adjust to the rover. We would like to get to the rover's outside pad where we can use the field. We want to stretch the defense and run away from the free safety if we do pitch the ball. We may have to kick out the corner and run up inside. We tell our halfbacks not to throw the block too early. We tell them not to throw the block until they can step on the toes of the rover.

We will come inside and load block on the man who is the pitch key. When we load block, we step with the inside foot first. The reason we do that is so we can make the block if we get a hot end. If we step with the outside foot first on the load block and the end is coming on an angle stunt, we can't get back inside to pick him up.

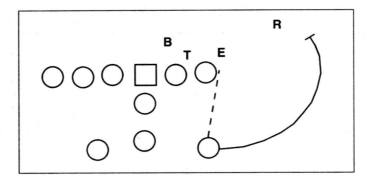

We do have a safety block. We run it against a 50 defense. The end arcs and zone blocks. We read the tackle, and the end is the pitch key. We send the halfback inside on the free safety. But we do not see this defense much.

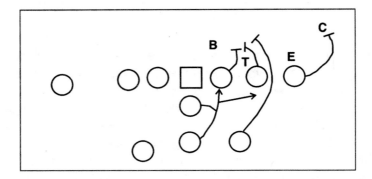

When we face eight-man fronts we veer block. We put our play-side halfback on the pursuit, which means the linebacker. Against the Shade defense we get a lot of stunts with the linebacker and tackle. Again, we have two blockers on the linebacker. If the tackle comes inside and the linebacker outside, the halfback is going to pick him up. Our tackle goes inside. If the linebacker goes inside, our tackle takes him. The free man, our tackle or halfback, flattens out and looks downfield. We tell our halfback to go off the tail of our tackle. He must adjust on the move. He must be aware of a tight scrape and a wide scrape. He looks for the tight scrape first. Furman does a good job on this.

On our wide receivers blocks we teach him to *stalk block*. His aiming point is tight outside eye. He is going to protect the sideline. Again, we want to stretch the field. If the defense wants to widen on us, we may block him into the sideline. We spend a lot of time on the stalk block outside. A lot of the stalk block is desire. You have to find players who are willing to make those blocks.

On the crack block we are going to push three to five yards upfield. Then we aim for the upfield pad. When we crack with our wideouts, we want to invite him up underneath. We do not want to get beat up on top. We are stretching with the quarterback and we can run away from the man if he comes underneath.

Into a short field we have the crack read. Into a short field you are going to get *cloud* or where the defense rolls up or fills with the safety. We come off three to five yards and read the corner and free safety. If the corner backs up, the end comes inside looking for the free safety. If the corner comes, the end blocks him.

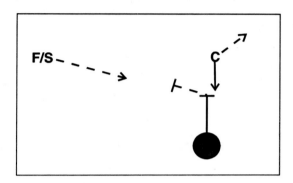

On our tight-end blocks we mix it up with the play-side halfback. We can send the tight end inside on the linebacker and let the halfback load on the end. We can have the end arc and let the halfback go on the linebacker. The thing we tell our end is this: he has to come off low and hard. The defense will try to hold up the end. We can split our tight end on our 10-yard rule and arc him. Now we let the tight end read the support. If the corner presses, we block him. If the corner backs out, we look for the free safety inside. When we arc the tight end, we take our play-side halfback and put him on the linebacker to free safety. We are changing up the responsibilities for the tight end and onside halfback.

On short yardage and on the goal line, we take our tight end and block the defensive end. We block inside on our veer block. The play-side halfback goes inside on the linebacker to free safety. It is a great goal-line play. This is what happens: if the defense is on an angle stunt, the tight end washes the end down as he comes inside. That leaves the corner on an island. He has to take the quarterback or the pitch, and the quarterback can get in the end zone. If the end is taught not to get hooked and widens, then the quarterback cuts up in the seam, and the halfback blocks the linebacker. It is a good play.

If the defense puts a stud in the B gap, we can call off the read. On the double option, we can take the read off and under-block the play. We put the guard on the tackle. We put the tackle on the linebacker. The fullback blocks levels. We can option the end. We can arc with the end, and we can load with the halfback on the end. We can go outside and read the next man outside and run the outside veer. If you run a lot of double option against a B-gap player, you need to keep the fullback in the game, too. We can block the defender in a 4 eye and hand the ball to the fullback. That linebacker is running outside anyway. You can scoop the backside and make it a big play.

We teach the quarterback to read numbers on the read, key, and mesh. They call out the number I hold up when they mesh with the fullback. We run a bag drill on the read key. It is not good, but it builds confidence. Then we run the gap drill with a defender on the fullback. We run a ride-and-decide drill, which is a true look for the quarterback.

9

Developing the Young Quarterback

Walt Harris
University of Pittsburgh
2003

I want to start by talking about Coach John Majors. Early in my career he gave me a chance to become an offensive coordinator for the first time. He was very good to me. Before I joined Coach Majors at Tennessee, I had worked for Coach Mike White at the University of Illinois. We had produced two first round draft choices at quarterback. Then Coach Majors offered me the job of offensive coordinator. I went to Coach White and talked to him about moving. He told me, "I do not think you are ready to be coordinator." That was the wrong thing to say to me because I wanted to prove to him that I was ready. That was a great experience at the University of Tennessee.

I went back to the University of the Pacific in California, which is my alma mater. The school has produced some outstanding coaches. I left there and went to the New York Jets. I coaches there for three years. Everyone knows how tough it is to stay very long in the NFL. After three years in the NFL, I lucked out and ended up going to Ohio State. We were able to recruit a few good players. We were able to win 11 games in a row at Ohio State. We defeated Arizona State in the Rose Bowl. That was a great time for us in that 1996 season and 1997 Rose Bowl. We took a drive down the field in the last 40 seconds and beat Arizona State. Bruce Snyder was the coach at Arizona State and they were only one drive away from being the National Champs. Two years later he gets fired. It makes you wonder a little about this profession. I think it is a great game. Most of the time administrators get very involved and that is the sad part of it. We owe a lot to the game of football. As I go into high schools recruiting today, just talking to the principals, I can tell they know how important the football team is to the morale of the school.

I appreciate you being here today. Hopefully you will get something out of this lecture. I think we are in a great game. It is an unselfish game and it is a challenging game. Every year it is different. We had a real good football team last year. We were only one score away from winning in our four losses. We did resurrect the program at Pitt that had won only 15 games in the five previous years. Coach Majors was a great coach but they did not give him the things you need to be successful. But our A.D. did some great things to help us. He gave us a chance to be somebody.

We have led the Big East in passing for the last six years. I can't wait until we are referred to as *tailback*-U instead of *wide receiver*-U. That would mean we would be getting the job done the way you need to get it done. I say this even though the Oakland Raiders may think differently. By the way, Jon Gruden was my G.A. for three years at Tennessee. He was the first coach that I hired as an assistant when I went to the University of the Pacific. He earns everything he can get. He sees a lot of things that you and I do not see. He never blinks at situations. It was a great victory for Jon Gruden and his staff.

My topic is *developing the young high school quarterbacks*. There are a lot of ways to do this. When I was coaching in high school football, I coached defense. I may not be able to help you a lot in that respect, but I do not believe it is any different in high school as it is in college. I think it a great position. I coach the position and call the plays. I coach a position because I do not want to be a head coach who just walks around and blows the whistle. I like to coach. I call the plays on offense. That way the offensive coordinator does not have to answer the media. The newspaper people come to me on any questions about our offense. All in all it makes my job harder because I still have head coaching responsibilities.

I like to coach. Coaching the quarterback is the most challenging position of them all. Why? Because every time the quarterback touches the football something good or bad happens. They touch it every down. You cannot win without a real good quarterback.

The first phase of developing the quarterback is to *have a plan*. The mental approach is very important to developing consistent quarterback play. You must be able to help the quarterback handle the mental aspects of the game. It is a hard position to play quarterback.

The quarterback must master the proper passing techniques and develop the fundamentals of quarterback. As the coach of the quarterback, you must make sure he creates the proper habits.

First, to execute the game plan we must start from the beginning. Here are the considerations you must consider in working with the quarterback. What is the role of the quarterback? The best thing I ever did when I worked for coach John Majors at Tennessee was to ask him what he expected out of the quarterback position. I think it is important for you to find out from the head coach what he wants from the position. Make the head coach declare himself. Then the quarterback coach must declare himself to the quarterback. He must understand if he is not doing what you want him to do as quarterback; no one has to get upset. If he is not doing what you expect, he is not going to be playing quarterback.

The big factor in the game today is *turnovers*. We play in the Big East and it is one of the best conferences in the country today. The Big E does not stand for the *Big Easy* anymore. Two years ago we had 18 turnovers in our first six games. We were getting our butts beat. We decided to change the situation. We had too many players who were thinking about their stats and their careers in the NFL. I quit being the good guy and decided to make a change in our approach to the game. In the last six games that year we only had seven turnovers. We won all six of those games.

Turnovers are the name of the game. If you do not win the turnover battle you are not going to win many games. You must commit the football team to protecting the football. We work hard to prevent the turnovers. Our quarterbacks, receivers, and backs do not switch the football. Once we put the ball away we do not switch the ball. It is too risky. So we do not switch the ball once we have in our possession. It may not be the best in all situations, but our running back coach really did an outstanding job in that area.

The player I coached fumbled seven times. It is also exciting for the assistant coaches for the head coach to be a position coach. A lot of the times the head coach will walk around and tell the assistant coaches they need to do this and they need to do that, it makes a difference if he is also coaching a position. So the player I coached had seven turnovers. Unfortunately I could not take him out of the game. If you can make the player better by sitting him on the bench when he turns the ball over, then you need to do that if you have someone capable of replacing him. I could not do that because our quarterback was so good in other areas. I cannot tell you enough about turnovers.

You must talk with the quarterback about *field position*. Also, you must talk about *momentum* with the quarterback. You must include those situations in the game plan. It does not matter the level of the game you are playing at, momentum is a big part of the game. I believe every game has highs and lows. One of the great ways to prevent the lows is to prevent the turnovers. If you can do that you will have a lot less highs and lows.

It is important to understand the impact of the quarterback position in winning. I grew up on the West Coast and I was always a San Francisco 49'ers fan. I am a big Bill Walsh disciple. Why? I love to run the football, but the hardest part of coaching is to get good linemen. Linemen win championships and they are hard to get. We try to control the ball with the forward pass. We have gotten better at running the football. Anytime we can run the ball we are going to be hard to beat.

My point on all of this is the fact the quarterback must be able to dump the football. He has to understand what it is like to be a *high-percentage passer*. I talk to him all of the time about making high-percentage throws. Their job is to get the ball into the end zone. They must move the stakes and they must move the clock. We want to keep our defense off the field. That was the best thing we did this past year. We got beat out by five seconds on leading in the total time of possession in our conference this year. We were second in that stat behind West Virginia University. We were second in time of possession in that aspect. We were not close in rushing offense, but we really held the ball in the time of possession area. That helped our defense. Our defense was ranked number 10 nationally in total defense. To do this you must be able to control the football.

We work on the center-quarterback exchange every day. Once a week we run the *wet ball drill*. When you have to take the ball from the center, you never know how the weather is going to be like. We will be using the Nike football this coming year. I feel certain it will be just as good as the other balls we have used in the past. I know it will be good because Nike is outstanding and that is the reason I am here speaking. (Ha, Ha!)

Each day we work between 5 and 10 minutes on what we call *T and A*. This is *timing and assignment* with the running backs and quarterback on the exchange. We go full speed on this. You cannot practice half speed on drill. Those two exchanges, between the quarterback and center, and between the quarterback and running backs, will get you beat if you do not work on them full speed in practice.

We talk to the quarterback about getting on the ground after he gets the first down. We want our quarterback to be able to get on the ground on the dive or to slide after the first down.

Let me move to the interception phase of the game. There has never been an interception that was okay. The only possible exception would be at the end of the half or end of the game. Quarterbacks hate it if they have to throw an interception then. That is part of the game. There is no reason for fumbles or interceptions.

I think it is very important for the quarterback to have discipline. He must take care of the football. I have coached the quarterback position for a long time and it does not change. You try to be nice, and try to be positive, and you try to build them up, but the bottom is that they must take care of the ball. I hope you have enough competition at quarterback so if they are undisciplined they do not play.

We feel simplicity of the offense is important in helping the quarterback. We seem to be fairly complex in our system, but we're not really. It just means a quarterback cannot play early and do a good job. We are simple in staying within our concepts. Our basic concept on the pass is this: *If it is tight getting the ball to a receiver, dump the ball off.*

If the back is not open in the flat, we tell the quarterback to run the ball. To me, you must get the ball down the field. If the pass is open, then fine, but running is part of the game.

The quarterback must understand the pass offense. You can have a lot of routes, but if the quarterback does not understand what he is trying to do it is not going to work. Running routes against man-to-man coverage is not that difficult, but still the quarterback should know where he is going with the football. Against zone coverage he must understand how you are trying to attack the zones.

We have our concepts for attacking *zone-coverage defenses*. We have four concepts we work on against the zones. Basically, they are very simple. Most all teams use these concepts.

If we have a hook route, we will have someone come outside. It will be run with an inside receiver and an outside receiver. We run a simple *curl-flat route* [Diagram 1].

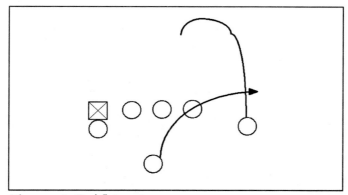

Diagram 1. Curl-flat route

The next route we use is a *high-low route* [Diagram 2]. Against the cover 2 look, we will have the outside receiver run an out release and the back will swing out in the flat area. The quarterback reads the corner on the play. That route is a high-low route. We love throwing the ball to the backs.

Another concept that we use is called a *triangle-read route* [Diagram 3]. When we run a crossing route we have three receivers involved. We use two receivers and a back on the routes. We run a lot of the post-cross routes. The reason we run the post is because we are looking at the angles of the drop of the linebacker. We are looking for the hole. On our crossing routes we will hook. If the ball is not there we will continue to sit. We do not like to run the play against the zone defense. We sit against the zone and run away from defenders in the man-to-man. That is our triangle read or *3-on-2 concept*.

The last concept is what we call the *three-level pass* [Diagram 4]. Sometimes this play is hard to run. The play can be good for the fast tight end. He is going to run an out route at 10 to 12 yards deep to the outside. The wide receiver is going to take off deep. He must be a legitimate threat deep. The back is going to swing to the outside. You must get the corner defender out of the area.

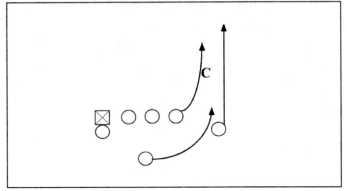

Diagram 2. High-low route

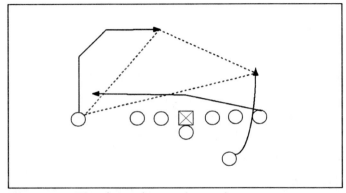

Diagram 3. Triangle-read route (3-on-2)

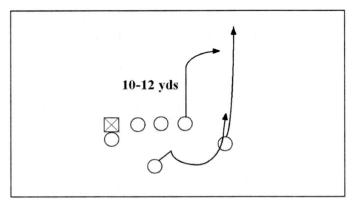

Diagram 4. Three-level pass

Those are the concepts we use to attach zone defenses. They are simple plays but you must work on them a great deal so everyone is on the same page.

The quarterback needs to understand how the pass patterns work and what his *progressions* are versus various coverages. A lot of the time our progression will change based on the coverage. They will change and the players must understand this. It all goes back to the mental approach.

We tell our quarterback he must be able to recognize the various pass defensive coverages. We expect him to know the coverage after he takes one step on his drop. We teach him to read through the goalpost. He will also understand the keys on the linebackers. The linebackers are going to drop back, move outside, or they are going to blitz and come after the quarterback. They will tell the quarterback a lot of what the defense is going to do on a play.

The quarterback is going to look at middle of the field to see how many safeties are there. If there is no one in the middle of the field, it is what we call *cover 0*. If the defense has two safeties in the middle of the field, it is *cover 2*, or it may be a defense with a middle safety and they may rotate. We are going to go away from rotation, so the quarterback has to be able to read the coverage. He has to be able to recognize *man-to-man coverage*.

If the quarterback reads a two-deep coverage, he has one man to throw to. If the man is not open, then the quarterback is going to do something different. We are not going to throw the ball to the back if there is a linebacker running with him.

The quarterback must be able to understand under coverage. He must understand the strengths and weaknesses of the defenses. We have plays that we call *cover-beater plays*. We have a cover 2 beater. If we do not see the cover 2 look, it is the job of the quarterback to get us some type of completion. It is the *save-the-day* pass so to speak. Otherwise, I would be afraid to call the cover 2 beater play. If we do not get a completion, I will not be able to trust the quarterback on the play.

We grade the quarterbacks on every play. We have an end zone view and a side view of every play in practice. I coach the quarterbacks so I grade the practices for the quarterbacks. It is a written grade. I may be tough on them, but I am going to do everything I can to get them ready to play. I want to give them all the help I can so they will know what to do in a game.

We talk about *practice field approach*. When the quarterbacks come to the practice field we want them ready to go. That does not mean they cannot be relaxed and be able to have fun, but they must be focused. When they come to practice they must come with a purpose. They must learn that we cannot let one quarterback take every snap. This is especially true for the second-team quarterback. He is not going to get every rep. If the starting quarterback needs reps, then the second-team quarterback is going to get less and less reps. If the first-string quarterback is a quick learner, the second quarterback may get more snaps. We do not try to get more than two quarterbacks ready for a game. We will run the first quarterback four plays and the second quarterback two plays. It is very important to stress they will play like they practice. The players should be tired after practice. Why? Because they must concentrate mentally while on the field. As I said before, I believe strongly in mental reps.

Now I want to talk about the basic techniques and fundamentals of *throwing the football*. The first approach to this area is to determine why we have techniques, which are covered in the following reasons.

The first fundamental reason for throwing techniques the quarterback must focus on is *accuracy*. A quarterback can improve his passing accuracy. Steve Young of the 49'ers was a good example of a quarterback improving his accuracy. When he was with Tampa Bay he was not very good. But when he went to San Francisco he improved a great deal. Why? Obviously the system had a great deal to this. He went to a much better system. He was older and he had been cut so his eyes were open more. His focus was a lot better. He became very good at putting the ball in a spot. He learned to hit the receiver where he wanted the ball to go. He was not just getting the ball to the receiver, but he was getting it to a spot where the receiver could catch the ball. I like to say we want to *hit the receiver in the eyeball with the ball*. If we throw the ball at his eye, the receiver should have great hand-eye coordination and he can see the ball. He should be able to catch the ball in that area.

Quickness of decision is another fundamental to consider when working with quarterbacks. When I was working with Jeff Blake with the Jets, he used a phrase that I liked: *Process it quickly*. The faster you can go through the progression and get the ball out, the better you are going to be at throwing the ball.

The way I like to help the quarterback with this process is to have him drop back to pass. It is amazing how much the whole process speeds up when he is dropping back.

Quickness of the release is another fundamental to consider when discussing techniques for the quarterback. *Arm strength* is another part of it. *Movement in the pocket* is another factor to consider. *Being able to scramble* is very important in the techniques for a quarterback. When we have to scramble on a play, I tell the quarterback I want those plays to be the highest percentage of plays for the whole day. Why? Because most of the time we can give the quarterback the looks he is going to see or what we expect to see in a game. But when the quarterback is outside scrambling right or left he will see his teammates and the defenders in all different areas. He must make sure what he does with the ball in those situations is correct. We want a very high-percentage rate of success when we are scrambling on a play. He must understand why he is scrambling in the first place. He is scrambling because someone else made a mistake. It may be a missed block or a missed route. But the quarterback must write a check for the entire football program and make the play right. We want him to be very sure of what he does when he scrambles. I tell him to make something positive happen. To us a positive play is a throw away.

We have 11 coaching points or proper techniques and fundamentals in working with the quarterback. I would *never* coach all 11 of these with a player. We call it *paralysis by analysis*. Hopefully when you pick your quarterback he will have some ability to throw the football. It is best if you do not have too much to change as far as his habits. You must analyze what your player must do in order to improve his skill. That is your challenge as a coach. Even though we can recruit, we still have to talk to our quarterbacks about their throwing technique.

The first technique relates to the feet. It all starts with the quarterback's *feet*. This means he must get into the proper angles to throw the football to be consistent. He must get his body aligned to make the best throw and it all starts with his feet. You cannot just have a tall player at quarterback, especially if he's slow. He will have problems against a quick defensive team because he will not be able to get his body aligned to throw the ball with defenders around him. Do not fall into the trap of playing a guy that looks like he can throw the ball but he can't move. If you do have a kid that can throw the ball it is your job to get him to be a lot better. Things we do to help the quarterbacks improve their speed are to jump rope and do the wave drill.

We use this *tennis ball drill* to help the quarterbacks [Diagram 5]. You have them start by facing the coach. Take a shoebox and place it near a line. The quarterback starts out and shuffles 10 yards to a second line and comes back to the shoebox. He picks up a tennis ball out of the shoebox and shuffles 10 yards gain. He picks up a total of three tennis balls out of the shoebox on at a time. A time of 12.2 seconds is really good. This teaches the quarterback to accelerate and get going.

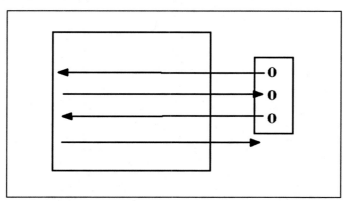

Diagram 5. Tennis ball drill

As I mentioned, the *wave drill* is another good drill to help quarterbacks improve their speed [Diagram 6]. The drill is set up with two receivers and the quarterback. The coach is in front of the quarterback. The quarterback takes his drop and the coach yells, "Now!" Then one of the receivers will hold his hands up with both hands open. The other receiver will hold up his hands but they will be crossed. The quarterback must pick out the receiver with the open hands.

When the quarterback drops back to set up, I will direct him on the wave drill. We call a play and he must execute the play. When I call out, "Now!" the quarterback must hit the receiver with the open hands. I will tell the receivers what I want them to do before the quarterback makes his drop.

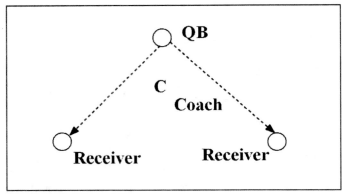

Diagram 6. Wave drill

Again, the wave drill is based on accuracy. We want him to throw the ball quick but we want him to make the throw accurate. However, the focus of this drill is to improve the mobility of the quarterback in the pocket.

The next drill helps the young quarterback find the safe spot in the pocket. We call this drill the *avoid drill* [Diagram 7]. This drill is used in the spring practice or early in the year. We take four receivers and line them up and down the field at a set distance. We have the quarterback take his drop for the play called. We have four defenders that are going to rush him, one at a time. The fist defender will go to the area where the quarterback will be setting up. We want the quarterback to climb in the pocket and not just flush out of the pocket. As soon as the first defense gets halfway to the top of the pocket the second defender is going to be on his way toward the quarterback. When the second defender is halfway to the quarterback the third defender is going to come. Now the quarterback must move over in the pocket. As soon as the third man gets halfway to the quarterback the fourth rusher goes toward the quarterback. Again, the quarterback has to move over in the pocket. Any time during the drill I can call the word, "Now!" and the quarterback must come up to see if he can find the open receiver with his hands up. He must try to throw the ball with the defender's hands in his face. He must try to get rid of the ball and throw it accurately to the receiver with his hands open. It is a good drill for the quarterbacks to get the *feel of the pocket*.

We can change the avoid drill and have the defenders run straight at the quarterback. We can change the order of the pass rushers so he has to flush to one side of the pocket or the other, or he must scramble to one side or the other. You can teach a lot of escape techniques in this drill.

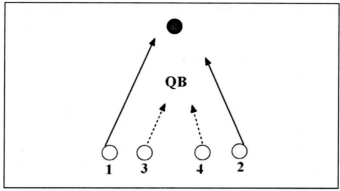

Diagram 7. Avoid drill

You can have the inside defenders rush first and force the quarterback to go sideways to avoid the rush. So, any four of the defenders can flush the quarterback. You control the drill and you can mix it up from day to day. If you point at one defender he can run straight at the quarterback. Now he must work on his escape against that man. We run the avoid drill about three-quarter speed.

Our next coaching point is *alignment*. First we talked about the feet. Now we must talk about the shoulders. I am talking about right-handed quarterbacks for this lecture. We always talk to the quarterbacks about having their shoulder pointed toward the target. We refer to their shoulder as a *radar gun*. It becomes a problem when you are throwing the ball outside. We try to get our quarterbacks to align to the target.

We do a simple *shift drill* to help the quarterbacks work on their alignment [Diagram 8]. We have the quarterback set up at 10 yards from two receivers on the line. We will move the two receivers from one side to the other as much as 20 yards from the original spot they line up in. The quarterback must move or shift to the side the receiver has moved to and make the throw.

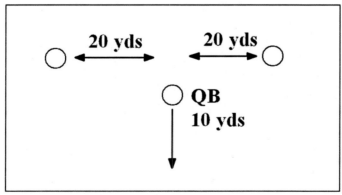

Diagram 8. Shift drill

We stress two hands on the ball on the quarterback's dropback. I do not want him to set up and sit in the pocket patting the ball with his off hand. This is just a bad habit. They see this on TV and think it is a good technique. I tell them, "When you make it to the NFL, you can pat the ball all you want." Until they make it to the NFL, I do not want to see the pat-pat on the ball.

To add to the drill we will put four receivers in. Then the quarterback has to shift to find the receiver we want him to throw the ball to. Keep in mind that you should not emphasize too many things at the same time on a drill. To be fair to the players you should work on one fundamental at a time and coach that fundamental. If the player learns the fundamental but does something else that is not perfect, do not criticize him for that aspect of the play. If he did what you wanted him to, compliment him on that aspect of the drill. Again, it is very difficult to change bad habits, but you must always work on them.

The shoulders come into play on throws like the out route and on comeback routes. If the quarterback is a right-handed passer, the out route and the comeback route to his left side becomes a problem. There are a couple of different ways to run the play. One way is for the quarterback to come back four steps and to kick on the fifth step. The quarterback gets a little wider to make the throw when he does that, but I also think he gets so much momentum that he ends up falling off the throw. Most of those throws are then low and away.

What I like to teach them is this: If we are going to throw to the left side, I want the quarterback to *step to the right when* he is throwing to his left. He takes the four steps and on the fifth step he swings himself outside and is aligned to the target. Another coaching point is the quarterback should be a little deeper from the defensive end who has his hands up in the air. If the quarterback is not going to throw to the number one receiver, he will be more in an area where the offensive line expects him to be.

When the right-handed quarterback is throwing the out route to the right side, it is a hard throw to make. If the defender intercepts the ball there is nothing out there except a lot of green grass. It is a dangerous throw but a lot of teams on defense will give you that throw. How do you take the out route if they are giving it to you?

We try to get the quarterback aligned to the target. We have thrown the ball off the plant step and now we are throwing it off the hitch step. This has helped us on the play. We think we can be more accurate on the out route although we do not throw a lot of out routes.

The next area to consider for the quarterback is his *legs*. Whenever possible he wants to get his legs into the throw. The reason for this is because most guys are not strong enough to throw the ball with their arm. As quarterbacks get older and stronger they can throw the ball with their arm. Dan Marino and Brett Favre are upper-body throwers. With young quarterbacks, they need to get their legs into the throw. Most of the throws should come off the hitch. If we are taking a five-step drop, we come back and plant the foot, hitch it up, and let the ball go to the primary receiver. Most of our plays are timed out at 10 to 12 yards in depth on a five-step drop. This times it up pretty good for us.

We will run the plant step when we run the straight vertical routes and when we are coming right back down the pass-route stem. It is a form of the out route, but we do not have the receiver break to the outside. That throw we will throw off the plant step. The quarterback is moving backwards and he must stop, change his momentum, and get his legs into the throw. This is very difficult. To help our quarterback on the play we tell him to chop and try to stop on the fourth step. He will probably stop on the fifth step and plant his foot. His body will be in a position where he can straighten his leg and make the throw. If his weight is on his back foot as he gets to the fourth step, he will have to wait until he can get his balance before he can make the throw. Or, he will throw the ball out of the hole and he will not get much on the ball. That is a dangerous throw because it is out in the flat. He needs to plant his foot and then make the throw. We throw the plant route off the plant step.

We do the same things off the seven-step drop and call it the turn route, which is at 16 yards. On most of our drops we try to throw the ball off the first hitch and try to get the quarterback to get his legs into the throw.

The plant drill has the quarterback dropping back and throwing the ball off his plant step [Diagram 9]. We do not want him to exaggerate the throw, but we do want to know if he exaggerates getting his body into the throw. We want to know if he gets his legs into the throw. We are not concerned about the kind of throw it was. If he is not getting his legs and body into the throw this is what we must work on.

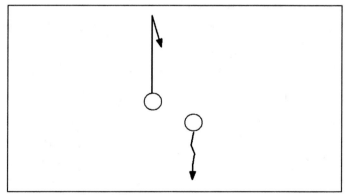

Diagram 9. Plant drill

As I told you earlier, there are 11 fundamentals that we work on with quarterbacks. You are only going to get him to work on one, two, or three of these techniques at any given time, and he may only need one or two of these to improve his game.

The next fundamental to work on is *weight shift*. The goal for the quarterback is to shift his weight so he can throw the ball from a bent front knee. He should not lock his knee out. He can get a lot of power if he can get his weight over the front knee. A lot of kids will straighten their knee to get more torque on the ball. They will straighten their left knee to get more whip or snap into the throw and it will lock the knee out. That used to be a five-hour surgery. It does not take that long now, but when the quarterback gets hit with his legs locked he is in big-time trouble. Do not let them throw the ball with a straight front knee. They need to have a bent front knee.

We will go back over these fundamentals with the quarterbacks in the spring. I will tell the quarterbacks they must be able to coach themselves. They must get a video and watch the film. They must learn what it feels like on these drills. I do not worry a lot about the fundamentals during practice. I am working on the reads. He must work on the individual techniques in the early spring and on his own time. The fundamentals do not get as much attention as the decisions do once the season gets underway.

We always make the quarterback take the steps he will take in a game in working on the fundamentals. Always have them drop back on the drills. Make it realistic for them.

We stress accuracy in our drills. When we are working on the passing drills, we want the receiver to give the quarterback a target just before he lets the ball go. We are going to be good at what we emphasize.

The next coaching point is the *draw back*. We are talking about drawing the football back in the passing motion. We have two hands on the football and we want the ball up under the chin on the chest. We do not want it down low or up high. We talk to the quarterbacks about drawing the ball back. We tell them to get it back, cock it, and throw it.

Pro football is not good for younger quarterbacks. The young kids see the NFL quarterbacks and the bad habits they have. One of the reasons for the bad habits of the pros is that the offensive coordinator is coaching the quarterbacks. He is not coaching techniques very much. The coordinator is coaching the system and expecting the individual player to work on his techniques. He cannot do that. That is why we coach the techniques. Now most pro teams are getting quarterback coaches.

The next fundamental is the *quick release*. The quickest release in football was that of Dan Marino. Dan did drop the ball down on his dropback, but his muscles were so developed that he could do that. You can explain to you quarterbacks that they are not in pro football so they need to adhere to the basic fundamentals you are teaching them.

The next point is that we want a *slight tilt of the shoulders*. It is important to get the ball over the tips of the defenders' shoulders on the pass rush. I do not want the quarterback with the ball up high and his shoulders flat. If this happens it slows down the release of the ball. Do not let him get the ball up over his head.

If the quarterback has his shoulders squared up with the turf before he throws the ball, and then tilts his shoulders forward just as he is ready to release the ball, it forces the tip of the ball to come up. What happens then is the quarterback gets the ball up but he does not have the ball behind his head. The slight tilt of his shoulders gets the ball out higher. The ball is alongside his body and not behind his head. He must not overtilt to the point where he is off balance.

There is a theory that goes something like this: If the quarterback can get the ball up with the tilt of his shoulders, he will get in a groove where he can throw the ball with consistency. It is a lot like the golf swing. If you can get the swing down where you are in a groove, it makes the swing a lot more consistent. Golfers want the same swing and we want the same throw. We want the same motion all of the time.

The next fundamental we stress is to *lead with the elbow*. We want the quarterback to lead with his elbow so he is in the groove and every throw is the same, unless he is under stress and he throws the ball sidearm like Rich Gannon does. We want every throw the same with the elbow leading.

Next we want to *pronate the wrist at the top of the release*. This helps with the spiral on the ball. With a tight spiral the quarterback really pronates the wrist at the top of his throw.

This is the last of the techniques for the quarterback. As the ball comes off his hand, the quarterback wants to put his *right thumb in his left pocket*. Some quarterbacks will stop their thumb at their midsection. We like to see the quarterback turn his hand to get his thumb down inside and turned toward his left pocket. This is the way to get a nice tight spiral on the ball.

I want to wind this down with a few general comments. There are a couple of important points I want to talk about. We stress *key habits*. We want two hands on the ball in the pocket. We stress *rhythm* and being on time with the ball. The difference between a college passer and an NFL passer is when the quarterback lets the ball go on the release. In the NFL they let the ball go early. That is because the corners in the NFL are so good and they never play zone defense. They will play a combination of man and zone coverage.

A drill I like to use that develops confidence in the quarterback's accuracy is called the *confidence drill* [Diagram 10]. The best way for him to gain confidence is to develop accuracy. We place a coach, another player, or another quarterback five-yards apart. We want the quarterback to throw the ball to another man and throw at his numbers. We have him to throw five passes in a row to where we designate.

Next the quarterback takes a step back and throws the ball five more times to where we designate. We want him to develop some confidence in his accuracy. The off-season is the time to work on the techniques and fundamentals. We want our quarterbacks to work on these before they get into 7-on-7 drills and team drills.

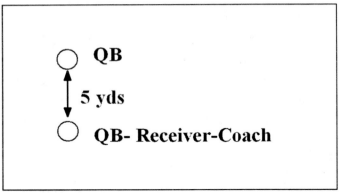

Diagram 10. Confidence drill

We ask him to step back each time after he hits five passes in a row accurately. We work until he gets 15 yards from the receiver. We want him to start thinking he is more accurate. If he does not throw five accurate passes in a row, then we move him back five yards and do it again. It is all about developing the quarterback's confidence.

We can use different targets on the body. We can have him throw at the receiver's hands. We do not want him to aim his toe toward the target. We want him to aim his foot toward the target and the toe will aim slightly to the right of his target.

I want to end with a film clip so you can see the quarterback fundamentals and techniques I have talked about. I have a second tape on quarterbacks that I will share with you. I will stress the coaching points we have discussed here today.

Men, I am going to be here a while longer. Hopefully you did get something from this lecture.

Finally, we are going to be expanding our recruiting territory. If you have a quarterback that is interested in playing for us let me know. I have coached 13 players that have had a chance to go to NFL camps. We have had seven first-round draft choices in the NFL. If you have any other players you think we may be interested in give us a call. You will not be disappointed with the facilities we have and the program we run. Thank you very much.

10

Developing Quarterback Fundamentals

David Huffine
Chaparral High School (AZ)
2007

If you know much about Arizona high school football, you know about Chaparral High School. Over the last decade, Chaparral has had a very successful run under the guidance of Ron Esterbrook. Chaparral has had three state championships and seven state semi-final appearances in the last 10 years. Ron Esterbrook recently retired, but he hired me a couple of years ago. I owe a debt of gratitude to Ron.

Prior to my arrival at Chaparral, they were a wing-T team. The wing-T has its fundamentals and principles, and he was an expert at the wing-T. He was great at teaching the offense, and he knew how to get the timing down which you must do in that offense.

Before I went to Chaparral, I was the offensive coordinator at Moon Valley High School for six years. We ran a different style of offense. We ran what we referred to as the multiple offensive system. It was not necessarily multiple as much as it was personnel driven. What I mean by that is the fact that we tried every way we could to get our playmakers the ball. In the beginning, we did not have very many playmakers. We had a running back who was talented, and we devised as many ways as we could to get him the football. We made an effort to get him between 40 and 50 touches per game. We did not have anything else that we could be that successful with.

As the system started to develop, we started to become a little more creative. One of the reasons for this was the development of our quarterbacks and the quarterback system we were using.

It does not really matter the type of offense you run, it boils down to this: It is the fundamentals and how you teach those fundamentals. It could be any type of offense, but how you teach it and how you get the players to understand what you are doing is more important than what you run. That is the direction we have gone. We focus a lot on fundamentals and techniques.

What I am going to dwell on now will focus on what I consider to be the most important single position on the field, and that is the quarterback. I am not talking about the linemen, or the other defense. I am talking about the person who handles the ball every single snap, and that is the quarterback.

By being the offensive coordinator and quarterbacks coach, I get to work with the quarterbacks every day. Over the last four years, we have had quite a bit of success at the quarterback position. I do not know how many of you know how the NFL calculates the quarterback efficiency ratings, and I have never talked with anyone who can tell me exactly how it is done. You can go to the website, input the data, and it will figure it for you. Over the last four years, according to the NFL quarterback efficiency ratings, we have had the following marks: 101, 122, 126, and 126. Over those four years, we have averaged over 34, 45, 48, and 50 points a game. We won a state championship and had three semi-state appearances.

A lot of people say that since we are located in Scottsdale, we have access to a lot of good players. If you are familiar with the area, you may know there is a little bit of money in the area. People can afford to send their kids to camps to get the best instructions possible for their kids. They do send them to camps. There are high expectations of the kids.

This past year after our spring practice, and after we finished the seven-on-seven tournaments in June, we met as a staff and we talked about one subject constantly, which was the fact we had two players who were competing for one position. We had a senior and a junior who were battling for the quarterback position. We were trying to decide which one of them would do the best job as quarterback. Both athletes were gifted, and both had experience at the position. But what we did not get was the things we felt we were going to need for the upcoming season.

Our receivers coach said it best. We were talking about the fact that both of the quarterbacks were struggling at that position. He came to me at the end of June and said, "When the game is on the line, and when we are playing in the playoffs in a close tight game, who do you want to be the quarterback?" My answer was simple. "Everything being equal, I would want our starting cornerback to be the starting quarterback. He is the one guy that I think can get the job done." He looked at me and said, "Exactly!"

We met as a staff and made the decision to take our cornerback and make him our starting quarterback. Our pre-season camp was only four weeks away. Everyone agreed to make the switch.

I went to the cornerback and told him he was going to be our starting quarterback. He looked at me and said, "What?" I told him he was the guy. Then I went to talk to his father. I told him the same story. I told him his son was going to be the starting quarterback. He said, "You know, I do not think I can remember him ever throwing a football." I knew this task was not going to be easy, but what this player had was all of the attributes you look for in a quarterback.

I am going to talk about the quarterback development within our multiple offensive system. Most of this is window dressing. Quarterback development is fundamentals and techniques that can be used in any system. I am going to walk you through the things we did to get the cornerback ready to play quarterback in our system. By the end of the year, he had thrown over 2,000 yards, had 31 touchdown passes, and ran for nine touchdowns. He only threw six interceptions. He was the offensive player of the year for our region. In the quarterfinal game, because he had been a defensive back, we decided to play him on defense. In the quarterfinal game in the third quarter, he broke his arm. That was the beginning of the end for our team. We got beat in the state semi-finals 24 to 14.

I am going to talk about the traits we think are necessary for the quarterback in any offense you want to run.

Attributes of a Firebird Quarterback

- Student of the game
- Leadership
- Poise
- Intelligence

The first point we must decide is if he is a student of the game of football. Does he have a deep love for the game and does he know what to expect on and off the field as a quarterback? He must be aware of the number of hours it will take for him to become a quarterback. Is he going to be willing to sit in film sessions? Is he going to be willing to speak up when he has questions? These are the intangibles.

This past year, we got a new video-editing system. This allowed me to do a lot more with our quarterback. We live in a video society. I walked in the exhibit and saw Coach Comm and they were advertising the fact you could put all of your offense in their system and then you can play it like a Madden video game.

The system we have allows me to do cut-ups and make DVDs. It is voice-activated. I can talk on the computer and I can talk to the quarterback while the game is going on. After the game, I made him a DVD and he takes it home where he can put it in his computer and watch the film. With this he can hear what I said during the game on each play. He can hear me telling him to "Watch the corner on the right. He is going to squat on the play." We worked on this throughout the month of July and August. He got very good at picking up the concepts that we wanted from him.

When you give the players a copy of the offensive playbook, or video, or whatever you use to teach them the plays, they are going to put what you give them into their John Madden video. They will come back and tell you what happens when they put in our plays into the video systems. They may come back the next day and tell you the play we put into our offense the day before was not a very good play for them in their video games. "The Indianapolis Colts could not run the play, so why should we think we can run the play?" The players have a point in this regard.

I can't stress enough to you the importance of the leadership attribute. Is he going to be a leader? This may be the most important point here. Is he going to be consistent in everything he does, both on and off the field? Many of you are teachers. Many of your best leaders are the students that you never hear about. They are never in trouble. They are not sitting in the office for some discipline problem. Is he a leader in drills? Is he the first to finish? Is he going to be the person who makes sure everyone is on time for practice and class? Is he the player who is going to finish the last rep when no one is watching? That is what we are looking for. In the end, he must be a leader on and off the field.

I do not know how many of you call the plays, but I am the offensive coordinator and I call the plays. Four years ago, I made a decision. I had been down on the sideline. I called the game from the sideline. I had another coach up in the press box assisting me. I was not satisfied with the way things were passed on to me. I switched around and went to the press box and had the assistant coach come down on the sideline. Since I have been in the press box calling the plays, we have gone 47–7. That isn't bad, although that is not necessarily the answer. It got me out of the intensiveness of the battle and allowed me to focus on play calling. We spend all week looking at film. That view in the film comes from the top or from the press box. Then when you get on the sideline it is a different view. You can see so much better from the press box. We have established a system for the bench to get the play signaled in to the quarterback, and we have been very successful.

The quarterback must be an extension of the coach. You spend so much time with the quarterback he should finish telling you the play before you do. That is when you know you are on the same page.

The next point is poise. I am not just talking about the quarterback staying in the pocket against a pass rush. I am talking about the way he handles situations on and off the field. Does he get rattled when he plays away from home and the fans get on him? They can rip the quarterback. Can he handle that situation? Does he get into a verbal spat with players from the opponent's team? Is he going to keep his poise and focus in on the task at hand? That is very important. It is a high-anxiety situation playing quarterback. They get way too much credit if we win, and too much blame if you lose. They must know how to handle this. They must maintain control of the situation.

The quarterback must be intelligent. Can he master the system you want to put in place? Can he learn the concept you are trying to create? I am not just talking about our offense. Can he understand defenses? Can he understand strengths and weaknesses? One advantage we had this year by playing a former defensive player at quarterback was the fact he understood the defense. This was very helpful for the offensive coordinator.

This year on the first day of fall camp, the "new quarterback" came in and he was wearing a green t-shirt. On the t-shirt, it had this across the front. "2005 Calculus Camp." I just said, "Oh my goodness." I did not think we needed a Harvard scholar playing quarterback, but we accepted him as he was. He understood, and he was able to grasp everything we were trying to get across to him.

The last point was his mechanics. This kid had absolutely no mechanics as a quarterback. He had no technique in throwing a football. He did have the ability to throw a baseball. He was a centerfielder on the baseball team. Our school has won the state championship four years in a row in baseball. He had been in situations in games that put a lot of pressure on him to make plays. One of the things we had to do was to develop his mechanics.

There are three areas of quarterback mechanics. We break these downs and talk about them over and over.

Three Areas of Quarterback Mechanics

- Throwing
- Drops
- Play-action

First is the throwing mechanics. In drops, we are talking about the footwork. The third area is play-action passes. Let me spend some time on these three areas.

The Art of Throwing a Football

- Ball on the shelf of throwing shoulder
- Ball away from body

- Wrist straight
- Front shoulder stays closed
- Six-inch step

When I talk about the ball on the shelf of the throwing shoulder, it is a term I heard Jeff Tedford of the University of California talk about in working with his quarterbacks. He talked on putting the ball just inside the throwing shoulder. The arm is at a 45-degree angle. This is what we teach our quarterbacks. Some quarterbacks want the ball up higher, and some want the ball lower. We want the ball in a comfortable position for him where he can throw the football.

One of the things you do not want is for the quarterback to squeeze the ball. The young quarterback gets a little tense and tends to get the arm up too high. We tell them to relax and get their elbows at a 45-degree angle.

When you start the loaded motion and the ball is cocked, we work on this action two or three minutes per day. We start out without a football. We want the hands in position so he can get the ball back in a throwing position.

Next, we want them to get the ball away from the body. We stress the following points.

- Elbow above the shoulder
- Release at highest point away from body

The more you can get the ball away from the body, the higher velocity you will have on the ball. Some of the quarterbacks can throw the ball sidearm and still make the throws with a lot of velocity. When you are throwing the ball to the far sideline, you need to get the ball up and away from the body. You need to get rid of the ball. To do this, we do a couple of things.

Let me put this another way. If you have seen the movies about the gladiators and the battles they have been engaged in, you see the same principle. If they want to hurl a large object toward a given target that is a long way, they get the long caterpillar out. It is the same concept here. That long arm or the long caterpillar can generate more force and get more velocity on the object they are shooting at the target. It is the same thing with throwing the football. You must get your shoulder up and away from your body. I say this about 30 times per practice. "Get that arm above the shoulder." For young quarterbacks, this is one of the hardest things they go through. They want to throw with the arm down next to their shoulder. When they do that the ball sails high on them. It is like they are throwing a pie. It will go up and away. I work with them getting the arm above the shoulder and getting on top of the football. They need to release the ball at its highest point.

When all of the pro magazines come out, they have action pictures of the quarterbacks. Look at the point where they release the ball. You will see the ball above the shoulder and the arm will be practically straight. It does not matter what level we are talking about. They do the same thing.

Prior to coming to Moon Valley High School, I was in Oregon. I was able to go to a small college where I played football and baseball. You can do that at small colleges. Also, I had the opportunity to coach football and baseball in college. The same concept came into the picture. You have to get the elbow above the shoulder and the ball away from the body.

As a quarterback, you need to keep the wrist straight. We do not want a bend in the wrist. When you throw a football, it is different than when you throw a baseball. In baseball, you are behind the ball and you are coming from different angles. In football, you must keep the wrist straight. If you throw the football like you are throwing a pie, it is not going to work. It is going to sail on you. You will not have control over the ball if you do that. You need to keep the wrist straight.

The drill we have done over the past few years is to work on the goalpost. We go down to the end of the field or on the practice field. We line the quarterbacks up six yards behind the goalpost. They have a receiver 18 to 20 yards down the field. The quarterback has to throw the ball over the goalpost on a line. That teaches the quarterbacks to get that elbow up and to keep the wrist straight. We have two rules on the drill: The ball does not go under the goalpost, and we do not want a balloon throw or the high arcing throw. Quarterbacks want to drop the elbow on the drills and throw the ball up high. I want them to throw the ball, not lob the ball. It is an exaggerated move for the quarterbacks, but it teaches them to keep the ball up high. It takes a while for them to master this technique. We work on it for five minutes a day for two or three weeks. Eventually, they will start throwing the football where the ball has a nice spiral and the ball will come nose down.

This is the drill to get that point to come nose down. They have to drop the shoulder, and keep the ball away from their body.

The next concept is to keep the front shoulder closed. I mentioned I coached baseball before. I had an opportunity to talk with Tom House, one of the leading pitching coaches in the game today. He has been the pitching coach for several major league baseball teams. Now he is just a paid consultant to many teams and players. We talked about throwing a baseball and throwing a football. He said that young players are taught to take the front shoulder and to get maximum velocity on the ball they need to throw that left shoulder back and replace the front shoulder with the back shoulder. He said the front shoulder needs to stay closed. What he was talking about was this. When you make the throw the elbow and front shoulder never go past the point of being perpendicular to your target. When you finish the throw, your numbers are pointed at the target. You do not finish with the front shoulder pointing down at the target. The shoulder stays up. The back shoulder does not come around.

It does not matter the type of throw the quarterback makes, every throw should be with the shoulder in front of the body. If it is a sprint-out pass or a dropback pass, the action is the same. Everything in the mechanics should be pointing in the direction of the target. On the sprint-out pass, everything should follow a straight line to the target.

We touched on the six-inch step over a bent knee. Some quarterbacks may be from six-to-eight inches on the step over the bent knee. We put our quarterbacks on a line and have them take that six-inch step. We can do it on the sideline. We put them on the line and have them take that six-inch step and make the throw. We do that five minutes each day. If they overstride, the ball is not going to be accurate. It must be a short, six-inch step. You are not trying to see how far the quarterbacks can throw the ball. It is a six-inch step over a slightly bent knee action.

When the ball is released, he wants the body in a position where it is balanced. When the right foot comes across, you are perfectly balanced. That is in a perfect world. If you are being chased in a game, it may look a little different.

Next, I want to talk about our straight dropback components. I am not going to get into the sprint-outs and the rollout action. But when we talk about the straight dropback action, we talk about three components.

Dropback Pass Components

- Drive step
- Speed steps
- Settle steps

The first step is the drive step. It is the step that goes at 6 o'clock. He is taking a long stride and he is trying to get back to setup. We call that the drive step. We want depth, and we want speed. We want the quarterback in a good football position with his legs and to drive back on the long step. We work on this action for five minutes a day.

Then we have our speed steps. This is our crossover step. I can call them crossover steps, but I like to refer to them as speed steps because that is what we are stressing. Quarterbacks tend to slow up after they take that first step. They need to get back and get setup. We tell them they are running for their life. That is the nature of the game. We ask the quarterback to throw the football. In order to do that, he must be good on the speed steps.

To teach the speed steps, we talk about taking the drive step and then keeping the front hip open. One of the things that young quarterbacks at our level are seeing is the backside blitz. We work on the hips and shoulders being open slightly. That allows the quarterback to turn his helmet so he can see the backside as he retreats. If he closes that front shoulder and hip, he cannot turn the helmet and see that backside. The shoulder pad must be open so he can see this.

To teach this we work the down-the-line drill. We have the quarterbacks drop to a spot and we throw out numbers from sideline to sideline. They will get to a point where they can go down the line on the drop. It does take work.

The last step is the settle step. This is the last step to put the quarterback in position to throw the ball. This puts the quarterback in position to throw or to hitch and throw, depending on the drop.

The eyes and the feet must match up. We do progression drills to teach this. When the quarterback drops back to the right, he must turn his hips and shoulder in that direction. The hips, shoulders, and eyes must all rotate together. They must all be on the same wavelength.

We have four or five receivers at different lengths on the football field. We take those first steps and work on the types of drops we use.

Types of Dropback Passes

- Three step: Drive step, two settle steps

- Five step: Drive step, two speed steps, two settle steps

- Seven step: Drive step, four speed steps, two settle steps

I will get behind the quarterback on this drill and I will point to the player on the field to throw his hands up. The quarterback has to pick that receiver up and throw him the ball. The quarterback must open the shoulder or he will be late with the pass. It is a great drill to teach the components of the dropback pass.

Our three-step drop is our five- to six-yard route. They include the hitch, outs, and slants. Our five-step drop is our intermediate route, 10 to 12 yards on the route. The seven-step drop is our dig, comeback, delay, and screen pass.

Play-Action

The last aspect of the mechanics is play-action passing. These are the points we stress on play-action:

- Create big plays.

- Most effective off base runs

- Sell it.

- Be aggressive up front.

- Pull whenever possible.

- Make it quarterback-friendly. Have a checkdown.

To be a good play-action team, you must be able to execute your running-game offense effectively. If you can do that, the defense will have to honor the run. I have heard coaches say, "When it comes down to it, the team that can run off-tackle wins the football game." We are a run-first team. We have gone to the I one-back offense.

A few years ago, I researched all the teams in our division. I found that teams, generally speaking, run the ball 75 percent of the time. Every coach that sits down and talks offense with you will tell you they want a 50-50 balanced offense. No one in our conference was balanced or even close to a 50-50 balance. This was in Arizona at the 4A level. I know a lot of other states have teams that may throw the ball a lot more than we do in Arizona. I was shocked when I saw the numbers. Most of the teams in our division were between 60 and 75 percent run-oriented. The team that won the state that year was Cactus High School, and they threw the ball 40 percent of the time. They were good at throwing the football.

We want to know what our best running plays are. We have looked at all of our running plays. We looked at the base runs and we are going to create play-action passes from those plays. Teams know what your base plays are. They are going to game plan to stop those plays. If you run play-action, you can take advantage of this.

When you run play-action, you are trying to do a couple of things. You want to take advantage of linebackers and safeties, and help your perimeter blocking. When you can do that, the defense starts to become tentative. The ends do not rush so hard up the field. Now you can give your quarterback time to throw the ball.

Play-action passing is good for teams that do not have good offensive lines. You have to sell the play-action pass. The last couple of years we have filmed our play-action passes from the linebacker position. We would get a cameraman and put him in the middle of the defense. He filmed our base run, and then he filmed what our play-action passes looked like off those base run plays. It was remarkable. If you are a linebacker, you must have the ability to recognize play-action. We started to see things that hurt us on the play-action passes. The quarterback may not have carried out the fake as well as he should have. We want the quarterback to sell the play. I think filming the play from the linebacker position was very helpful. After that, we became more effective with the play-action pass.

We need to be aggressive up front on play-action passes. I have heard this before. The play-action pass must "sound" like a running play. When you run the play and when you pass, it is two distinctive sounds. When you run, you hear the "thud." When you pass, you do not hear the pads pop because the line is sitting back to take on the rushing linemen. We are looking to make the linebackers step up on the play-action passes.

You need to pull the guards on play-action as much as possible. If you pull on the running plays, you need to pull on the play-action passes.

When we run the counter, we pull the guard and tackle. When we do that, the linebackers flow. We want to pull them when we run the counter pass. Things will open up for you if you can make the plays look the same.

We need to have a checkdown play. We want to make the plays quarterback-friendly. We may have a back sneak out of the backfield, or we will have a checkdown coming over the middle when we run the dig route.

We run a multiple offense. We put the quarterback through these steps in developing him in our offense. I think this can be done at any level and at any system. We will start working with our quarterbacks in a few months, and, hopefully, they will become just as effective as our other quarterbacks.

If you have questions on our offense or any other phase of our program, I will be here for the rest of the clinic. If you want me to talk football with you, let me know. Thank you.

11

Quarterback Drills and the Passing Game

Bobby Lamb
Furman University
1997

First, I want to talk about seven traits of a great quarterback:

- He must demonstrate leadership and responsibility. The quarterback must be able to communicate in tough situations. He must be willing to take the blame and the glory. He must be a leader on and off the field.

- He must be a competitor. He must hate to lose. He must be competitive in practice. He must be ready to compete in all phases of the game.

- He must be confident. He must have confidence to the borderline of being cocky. He must inspire confidence in his teammates.

- He must have credibility. We hear the expression, "You're the man." In football, the quarterback must be *The Man*. His teammates must believe in him. When it is third-and-six on the last drive and you must stick the ball in the end zone, *the team must believe in him.*

- He must have an instinctive mental process. He must be able to react on the move. He must know all of the assignments for the entire team.

- He must have a quick delivery. I know it is great to have a quarterback who is big and can run, but if you are going to throw the ball today, you must have a quarterback who has a quick delivery. He must not wind up to throw the ball. He must be able to get the ball out of his hand.

- *He must be a playmaker*. This is the most important of these seven traits. He must make the difference in winning and losing.

A quarterback must believe in himself, and his work must convince his teammates that he can be trusted when all else fails. I think this about sums everything up about the quarterback's position. The quarterback is the man who must step up and make the play. He must get the ball in the hands of the best receiver or the best running back. He must be trusted by his teammates.

Passing Efficiency Ratings				
Year	Quarterback	Rating	C. Rank	N. Rank
1989	DeBusk	156.00	1st	4th
1990	DeBusk	134.17	1st	18th
1991	Swilling	157.22	2nd	3rd
1992	Jones	123.38	3rd	Min
1993	Jones	131.48	2nd	26th
1994	Bonaventure	132.94	2nd	28th
1995	Bonaventure	137.60	1st	12th
1996	Bonaventure	154.70	1st	4th

The big thing we look at in the passing efficiency rating is this: how many interceptions did the quarterback throw? The next thing we look at is percentage of completions. I will talk about accuracy percentage later.

Next, I want to talk about drills we do in practice. First, we run *air routes*. We start with wide receivers. Later we bring in the tailback, fullback, and tight ends. We want a lot of air routes thrown during the early practice.

The next route we work on is one of the best for the wide receivers. It is a *1-on-1 versus the defensive backs*. We also use the tight end in the drill. We split the receiver, and the defensive man lines up and plays him man-to-man.

We have a stopwatch on the quarterback because we do not want him to hold the ball too long. We want the ball gone in less than 2.8 seconds.

Next we work on a *combo route*. We have two receivers going against two defenders—a safety and a corner. The defense will play what we call a two-read coverage, or they will be playing quarters. It gives our receivers a chance to see what the defense is doing with their coverage. I like to get the linebackers involved in the defense. We add them to the drill later on.

The next drill is with our tight end, tailback, and fullback against three linebackers. We call this the *Dallas drill*. The defense can play different coverages as we run our different routes against them.

Then we go to our *skeleton drill*. This is where we bring our skilled people on offense to go against the entire defensive secondary. This is our team passing drill. This is our best drill. We never want our quarterback to get hit in this drill. He must stand in the pocket and throw the football. Then we go to an 11-on-11 drill. This is where we let it all out, and the quarterback must make the play.

We keep an accuracy percentage on our quarterbacks. Also, we keep a completion percentage on them. If the pass is dropped by a receiver, it is counted as a completion for us in this chart.

If the ball is batted—and we see this in the film—I give them the benefit of the doubt and count it as a completion. If the quarterback throws the ball away to prevent a sack, we do not count it as anything. It is not counted as a catch or an attempt. Every day in practice we have a goal for the type of passes we throw:

Air routes	**100%**
One-on-one	**95%**
Dallas	**95%**
Skeleton	**85%**
11-on-11	**70%**

Last year, our quarterback had a passing accuracy of 77 percent. He did a good job of getting rid of the ball, although we had several passes dropped.

Next, I want to get into the drills for our quarterbacks. We are going to do four drills every day before practice. A lot of you have been to our camp and know these four drills. I do not want my quarterbacks to warm up unless I am out there with them. I do not want them to get into any bad habits.

- *Toes-on drill*—We want the quarterback to put his toes on the line about shoulder-width apart. The quarterbacks are going to be 10-yards apart. We want the quarterback to rotate his shoulders and use his upper body. His feet should never leave the ground. We want him to set the ball, turn the hips, and work on the shoulder rotation. He must come over the top with the ball. He rotates his shoulders from one sideline to the other sideline. This drill helps him to get loose. We really stress setting the ball. We want the ball up high on the drill.

- *Weight-shift drill*—The quarterbacks are still 10-yards apart. They take their back foot and put it on the line. We do not want to rock all the way back, but we do want them to shift their weight. We talk to them about finishing the throw just as they would if they were a baseball pitcher. We want them to transfer the weight, take a six- to eight-inch stride, and set the foot. Again, we stress the follow-through.

- *Step-n-stride*—Again, the quarterbacks are going to put their foot on the back line, take a short stride toward the target, and throw. They are working on a short stride, and they are standing tall. Again, we concentrate on the follow-through. They are just like a baseball pitcher. We want them to come over the top.

- *Crossover plant*—We simulate being at the top of our drop. Now we are going to cross over, plant the foot, and throw the football. We stress balance and the weight transfer with the shoulders level. The most important step in the drop for the quarterback is the fourth step. He has to break the momentum to cross over and plant. If the fourth step is too long, he will never be able to throw the ball without gathering his feet. We do these four drills every day. We make sure we are on the field to supervise them. We want reps, reps, and more reps.

Next we go to a series of *quarterback-drop drills*. The quarterback is not throwing the football; he is dropping back. We do all of these drills on the lines. We start on the sideline.

First is the *distance drop*. I blow a whistle, and they start the drill. The quarterbacks drop all the way across the field. It is full speed all the way across the field. We want them to stay on the line and to keep the head up and shoulders level and work the football. This is sideline to sideline. The drop is second nature, and it helps lengthen the drop. This is how we warm up. You can vary the distance if you want. At times in practice, we may have them drop 100 yards. We put them on the goal line and have them drop all the way down the field. This is usually after they have made several mistakes.

Next is the *swivel-hips drill*. Again, they start out on the sideline. I blow the whistle, and they are going to drop. I blow the whistle again, and they swivel or rotate the hips. We want them to stay on the midline. We do this all the way across the field. I blow the whistle and they rotate. On every whistle they must rotate the hips. We want them to try to stay on the midline. We want them to keep their feet working.

The third drill is the *carioca drop*. This drill is used to improve footwork. The upper body remains the same. This drill goes well with our big-five drop, which I will discuss later. Again, we are sideline to sideline. We start out and carioca all the way across the field. We want to stay on the midline. The upper body remains the same. The lower body must do the work in a carioca-type style. It is very good for developing footwork. We like to stress this point with our quarterbacks. Playing quarterback starts from the ground up. Feet, feet! If they have good feet, they have a chance.

Next is the *tapioca drop*. It is the same as the carioca drop except the quarterback is giving a quick washing-machine action. We want real short, choppy steps. We go from the sideline to the hash mark on this drill. We start out by straddling the sideline. Everything is the same as the carioca drill, except we are speeding things up. Again, this drill goes well with our quick-five action. We do not take many seven-step drops anymore. The defensive ends in college are too good. We are a quick-five-action team and a big-five team.

The fifth drill is what we call our *alternate drops*. Now, the mind and body must work together. It is the same thing. They start on the sideline. We may be working on the big five, quick five that day, or we may be working on three quick steps. We may be going three quick and big in the drill. I will blow the whistle, and the quarterbacks go 1, 2, 3, and throw to the right. When I say, "throw to the right," they get the ball and bring it to the other hand. Then they reset and go again down the line. They throw and reset all the way across the field.

The sixth drill is one that we have been doing a great deal of lately. It is what we call our *mental drops*. I line the quarterbacks up in front of me, and they get on the hash mark. I will call the formation, the play, and the defensive coverage to them. Then I will say, "Sam runs to the flat." Then I blow the whistle. They take their drop, a quick five or a big five. Then they must throw the ball to the receiver they think will be open. The quarterback drops and goes through his reads mentally. I know who they are throwing to. If they screw up, I help them. This is the way they are going to learn to throw the ball in a game. This is something you must do over and over.

Next, I want to go over our *throwing drills*. The first is what we call the release drill. We have two quarterbacks standing side by side. We have a wide receiver in front of the quarterback, but it could be a manager, another quarterback, or another player. The coach stands in front of the receivers. If we have an injured wide receiver who can take part in the drill, we will use him. The quarterback is in a set position. When the coach throws his hand up, the quarterback must release the ball to the receiver.

RELEASE DRILL

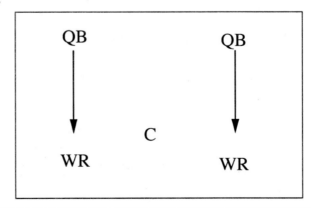

The quarterback is in a set position. The coach will throw his hands up in the air. The quarterback releases the ball as quickly as possible. Start at 15-yards apart, and vary the depth and angle of throws. Get the ball out of your hands!

Next is our *carioca drop-n-throw* and our *tapioca drop-n-throw*. We have a quarterback and a wide receiver. First the coach blows the whistle. The quarterback must carioca and set his feet. The whistle blows again and he throws the football to the receiver.

CARIOCA DROP-N-THROW AND TAPIOCA DROP-N-THROW

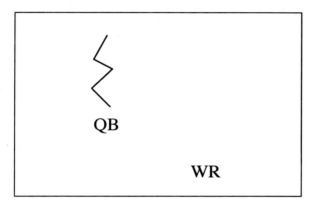

The coach blows the whistle. The quarterback takes the snap and carioca- or tapioca-drops. The coach blows the whistle again. The quarterback sets his feet and delivers the ball. You can vary the spots for the receiver. The whistle may blow while the quarterback is in the middle of the carioca. If that happens, the quarterback must get set and throw the football as soon as possible. We do not want to run the drills where we are throwing the ball straight ahead all of the time. We like to practice throwing at angles. Throw at a spot. If you run a curl that week, work on the curl route. We like to let the quarterback throw to spots that he will be throwing to in a game.

In the tapioca drill we take quicker and choppier steps. Now we want to get the ball away much quicker. That is what our quick-five pass drop is. We take the short, choppy steps.

The fourth throwing drill is what we call our *avoid drill*. You may not want to work on this, but we feel we have to.

The quarterback takes the snap and drops on a quick-five or a big-five drop. He sets on the fifth step. He must avoid the rush to the right or left. Then he must sidestep and throw the ball to the wide receiver. He must reset his feet before throwing the ball. If he gets pressure from one side, he must slide, reset his feet, and then throw. We have the dummies set up deep enough to simulate the depth that we want the

AVOID DRILL

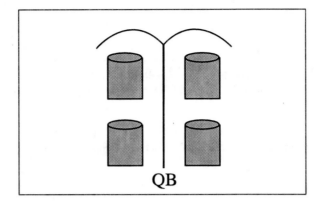

quarterback to drop. Most quarterbacks want to get out of the pocket when they get pressure. If is a feel-type thing that the quarterback must experience. The way to work on that is running this drill over and over. You work on throwing from both sides.

Next is our *step-up drill*. Now the quarterback must step up in the pocket to make the pass.

STEP-UP DRILL

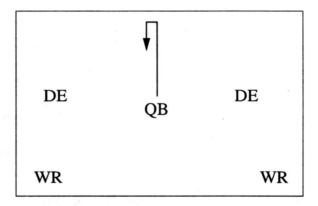

We take two defenders, who can be other players, quarterbacks, or managers, to rush the quarterback. The quarterback takes his drop and checks the rush. We rush at the angle that the defensive ends will be rushing in the game. The quarterback must step up in the pocket and make the throw.

Next is our *pressure drill*. Do not let anyone do this but the coach. As soon as the quarterback releases the ball, the coach throws a hand dummy at the quarterback. Do not hit the quarterback anywhere near his throwing hand. Again, do not let anyone throw the dummy except the coach.

PRESSURE DRILL

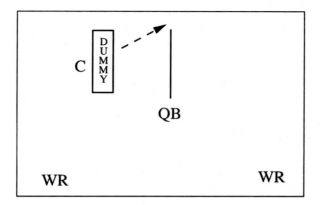

I like to use this drill on individual routes. I have a hand shield, and I throw it at the quarterback as soon as he releases the football. I do not sling the dummy; I throw it at the quarterback. Again, we do not want to hit the quarterback on his throwing arm. We want to simulate the type of pressure he will see in the game.

The last drill we use in our throwing drills is our *clock drill*. The coach will point to the wide receiver. The wide receiver flashes his hands. The quarterback must work from his right to his left and from his left to his right. The quarterback must step and turn on each target. You can have as many receivers as you want. We want the quarterback to move his feet and shoulders together.

CLOCK DRILL

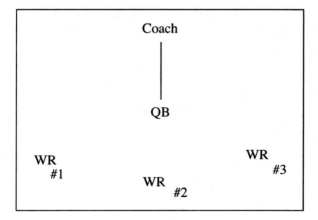

If I flash my hands to the number 1 receiver, the quarterback must throw the ball as soon as possible. If I flash the number 2 receiver, the quarterback can look at number 1 and then come off to the number 2 receiver. You can build this in with the different pass routes you are running. We mix it up on the patterns.

We feel it is very important to take the first 15 minutes in practice and work on these drills. It is very important for us to do them, especially this year. What we like to do is to get out to the practice field and warm up, then do our flexes, and then get into our drills. After we get through with the drills, we go to individual routes.

Next we go to our *quarterback throwing techniques*. These are the things we work on:

- *Lower body*—Step toward the target, and shift the weight. We want a flex in the left knee. We want the quarterback to allow the hips to come through. We want to take a short stride. We want to follow through toward the target. That is the number one thing that we stress. When the quarterback throws the football, he wants the hips and everything else to follow through straight forward.

- *Upper body*—We want to set the ball high. We want to get it up in the air. We want the quarterback to turn the ball away. We like to say that we take the football off the shelf. This is what we teach in our camp in the summer. The elbow must be at 90 degrees. The elbow must be higher than the shoulder. The lead arm must assist with rotation of the shoulders. We want to snap the throw off.

I am not a big grip person. We want the quarterback to snap off the throw with his finger rotation. If the quarterback is throwing with a normal rotation, I will leave him alone. If the ball is wobbly, we work on the rotation with that quarterback. We want the quarterback to use as little motion as possible in throwing the ball. We want to get the ball out of the hand of the quarterback.

The next area is the *passing sequence*. This is after the drop. First, we want to stand tall and be balanced. We want to set the ball high. Next, we must step toward the target. We want to throw the ball with finger rotation. We want RPMs on the ball. And last, but not least, we want to follow through to the target.

Let me go back to our summer camps again. I want to talk about the problems that high school quarterbacks have. The first problem is *overstriding*. This causes the ball to sail as the hips sink. We can make a videotape and look at the quarterbacks throwing the ball. When the quarterbacks' hips sink, the ball sails.

The second problem is that they are *unbalanced* after the drop. The front shoulder should be up.

The third problem is that the lead *arm folds*. This does not do them any good. We want to make sure that the lead arm pulls them through.

Next I want to talk about the *two-man game*. This is where we break the routes down. The first thing we do that is different from what most people do is that we put the tailback in the halfback position behind the tight end. Most teams put their fullback in that position. We move our tailback to that position. We have our tailback and tight end working together. Our fullback goes to the split-end side. This is a standard set for us, especially in a passing situation. I want to break it down, take about three individual routes, and go over them.

First is the *flat route*. The depth of a flat route is three yards from the line of scrimmage. If the tailback is deeper than three yards, he is wrong. We stress width. We say width is more important than depth. He wants to reach the line of scrimmage three yards outside the tight end. After he gets to the three-yard area, he should bend it outside. As soon as he reaches the line of scrimmage, he must snap the head around and look for the ball. More important than depth is for the tailback to get leverage on the Sam linebacker.

FLAT ROUTE

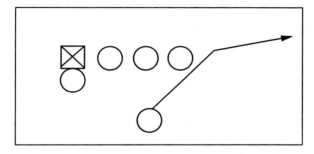

The fullback runs the *choice route*. He goes to a depth of four yards versus a zone and six yards against man coverage. When he reaches the line of scrimmage, he wants to be four yards outside the tackle's alignment. Against the zone, he wants to snap his head to the outside and anchor his feet to the ground. Against man coverage, he wants to get vertical and give the Will linebacker a jab step to the inside. The key to the route is to get vertical. If he does not get vertical, he does not have a chance out there.

CHOICE ROUTE

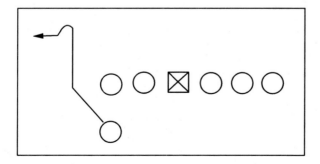

Next is our *option route* by our tight end. All of these routes can be run out of all three wideouts. This route is for the inside receiver. The depth is six to eight yards. All it is is a backyard route. The receiver does just the opposite of what the linebacker does. The receiver has three options:

- If the linebacker walls the receiver off, he must plant and break to the outside. He wants to lean back to the quarterback.
- If the linebacker drops over the top of the receiver, he hooks to the inside.
- If the receiver passes the linebacker, he turns back to the inside.

OPTION ROUTE

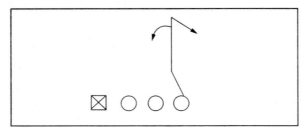

If we make a quick-five call, our quarterback is going to take five quick steps and shift his weight to his back foot and throw the football right now. This is our two-man game. His first option is to read the Sam linebacker. If we have Sam outflanked, we want to throw the ball to that receiver. We throw that route until they change the defense. A quick five to us is usually a five- to six-yard drop of our quarterback, but we are getting the ball away very quickly.

If Sam has our first receiver covered, the quarterback will reset and throw the option route. If the option route is covered, the quarterback resets and throws to the choice receiver. It is a quick 1-2-3. It is just like the clock drill we did.

This is what the routes look like against what we call *cover 2 float*. The Mike linebacker cannot cover the tight end if he is going deep enough. If the safety gets uptight, we send the wideout deep inside behind him.

R-L VS. COVER 2 FLOAT

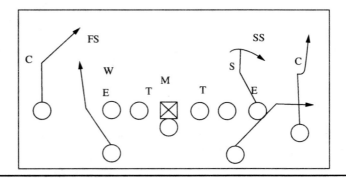

What happens if we see *cover 3?* If we get cover 3, we can work on either side. We work against both sides. We like to work the backside post. We want the wide receiver to break inside at eight yards and catch the football on the hash mark.

ROW–LEE VS. COVER 3

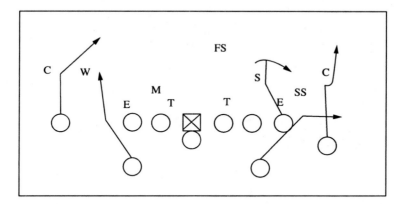

Let me show you the same route from different sets. These are what we call our *Row* and *Lee* sets.

ROW–LEE VS. TWO FLOAT

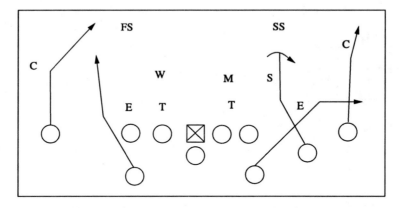

If we call *move*, we can set the tailback to the split-end side, bring him back in motion, and run the same play. It is simply 830 flat choice.

ROB–LIZ–MOVE VS. TWO FLOAT

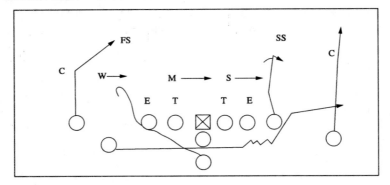

We went with a one-back set and ran the same plays.

DOUBLES—ONE-BACK SET

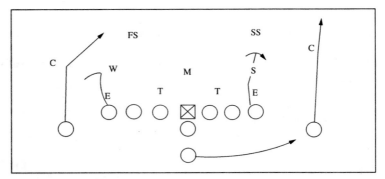

Everything we teach on routes develops off this route. This is where we start out teaching. In the no-backs set, notice where the B receiver is lined up. We ran the 839 flat-choice route.

839 FLAT CHOICE—EMPTY

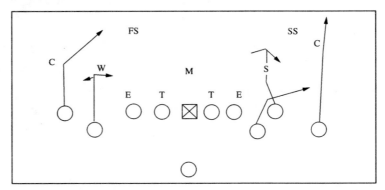

This gives the defense a different look, but it is the same route. We want to give the quarterback as much of an edge as we can. That is our two-man game. There are a lot of ways you can do it.

12

Coaching Quarterbacks
From Head to Toe

Tom McDaniels
Canton McKinley High School (OH)
1998

Every person here knows something about coaching quarterbacks. Some coaches know more than just a little, and some of you know a lot. What I want to do is to share some theories I have about coaching quarterbacks. I am sure some of these points that I share we will have in common. But I am just as certain some of my thoughts will clash with your own ideas.

I've been the head coach at McKinley for 16 years, and I have coached quarterbacks for 26 years. What I know about quarterbacks can be traced back to Don James when he was the head coach at Kent State. It was before he went on to Washington where he had great success. I learned a lot from Don and his quarterback coach at Kent State. What I learned back then I have used for all 26 years.

We give our kids a manual at our meeting at the end of school before we dismiss them for the summer vacation. In that manual we list position skills that we feel a kid must master and learn to be the best at his position. We do this for all 22 positions, offensively and defensively. It is important to let them know what they are competing against in order to be the starter. It lets the position coach know the things you have to cover in order to get that kid ready to play the best he can play. I am going to concentrate on two specific areas—*quarterback decision making and passing accuracy*.

I want to begin with the head of the quarterback and work my way down to his feet. I have five or six points I need to make about the use of the head and hands as far as playing the game. I want to finish up by making several coaching points about the feet and how that impacts the way a kid plays.

I ask the position coaches to come up with the skills for the position they coach. We think this has helped us a great deal.

POSITION SKILLS—QUARTERBACK

- Stance
- Faking
- Footwork—Run and Pass
- Decision Making—Option, Pass, Calling Package, and Checking Plays
- Reading Pre-Snap Keys
- Reading Post-Snap Keys
- Ball Security
- Quarterback/Center Exchange/Shotgun
- Ballhandling—Handing Off and Making the Pitch
- Passing Mechanics
- Passing Accuracy—Executing the Short Pass, Executing the Intermediate Pass, Executing the Long Pass, and Executing the Running Throw
- Game Awareness

Down/Distance to gain/Time remaining/Timeouts

- Defensive Recognition
- Coverage Recognition
- Reading Play Signals from the Sideline
- Huddle Discipline
- Cadence
- Running Ability—Scrambling, Avoiding a Rush, and Open-Field Running
- Pass Drops—Three-Step Drop, Five-Step Drop, 34-35 Pass, and Boot
- Executing the No-Huddle

Of all the traits the quarterback must possess, I think confidence, decision-making, and passing accuracy are head-and-shoulders above anything else. He must master all of these to be a good player. Accuracy and decision-making are number one and number two. We would all like to have a rifle-arm quarterback. In 26 years of coaching,

I have had a couple of those type quarterbacks. We have had a couple of quarterbacks sign with Division I schools, but all in all we have not had that many go to Division I. In most cases our quarterbacks are just good athletes.

I think you can coach accuracy. Accuracy is the most important trait a quarterback can have in throwing the ball. If the quarterback can throw the ball 100 miles per hour but can't hit his receivers, he is not any good to anyone. If we can put the ball where our receivers can catch it and their defenders can't, we feel we have a good quarterback. We feel accuracy is more important than having a strong arm.

Decision making goes hand in hand with accuracy. In our passing game, we believe in flooding zones and putting two receivers where you have two defenders or two receivers where you have one defender. We ask our quarterback to make decisions as to which receiver he is going to throw the ball to.

I also require the quarterback to make a lot of decisions on our running game. We package a lot of our running plays. He makes the decision if the play is going to be 38 scoop or 39 scoop. We will also package a pass play with a run play. In order to run the play he must know what to call. He must make that decision on the line based on what he knows.

I think you can coach accuracy and decision making. You can make the quarterback more accurate and you can make the quarterback a better decision maker. I do not think you can coach confidence. But, I think confidence is a by-product of being accurate and good decision making. When a quarterback throws a pass and it ends up where it is supposed to be, and we get a catch and we make a gain, and he does that again, again, and again, his confidence grows by leaps and bounds. When a quarterback makes good decisions that result in plus plays for us, he feels good about it. That builds his confidence. I am not going to tell you that you can coach confidence, but I think you can coach decision making and that creates confidence. When you have a confident quarterback I feel that you have an edge.

The term *coaching the quarterback from head to toe* is a nice, catchy phrase for a clinic talk, but that is exactly what I want to do. I want to start with the head and work my way down to the feet.

I am just like everyone else. I do not always get 100 percent of these points but it does not mean that I am not coaching them.

Some of these concepts are very basic and fundamental. I think that is where coaching begins. If you cannot coach the basic fundamentals and the kids cannot understand them, I am not sure they will be able to understand the more complex things.

I want to start with mechanics to mental awareness. I will start with the head, and then hands, and then down to the feet.

HEAD

Look left to right as you set the defense. Locate your key. If a quarterback is going to make a decision, he must gather information. He gathers information using his eyes. We want him gathering that information the same way on every snap. If we are going to throw the ball in the flat, we want him to find the cornerbacks and decide on the side that is the short throw. If one corner is at eight yards and one at six yards, we are going to throw the ball to the side where the corner is at eight yards because that is the soft corner. That is part of his routine. He scans the defense and looks left to right.

When we run the fullback-wedge play, I would prefer to run it at the 1 technique rather than at the 3 technique. The quarterback looks left then right and finds the 1 technique, checks the play, and runs it to that hole. We cannot have him do that only when he is throwing to the flat or running the ball, or only when we are checking the plays. It must be a habit and he must do it every single time. It is just like crossing the street. He looks left, right, and then makes the play call. It is critical in how he gathers information in order to make the right decision. It is a little thing but it is important at the same time.

Pre-read coverage every snap. Anticipate who your open receiver will be. We ask our quarterback to pre-read the coverage. We coach him in reading coverages and we expect him to know it. Fortunately, we play two or three different coverages and our kids get comfortable with it, at least against those two or three. Certain coverages work against certain plays better than others. We want them to know that certain coverages make it difficult to complete certain passes. Based on what the quarterback sees, he wants to anticipate who our open receiver may be. If he can anticipate the open man he will not have to wait until he gets back to set up to make the decision.

We tell our kids that coverages never defend anyone. People playing coverages real well defend things. Just because a team is playing a cover 2, it does not mean they are taking the flat away. But we do want our quarterbacks to anticipate what they are seeing at the line before the ball is snapped.

Read coverage after the snap on your drop. Recognize disguised coverage. This is something we are seeing more of in our area. We want our kids to understand this point. Just because a defense is lined up a certain way before the snap it does not mean they will stay in that defense once the ball is snapped. Teams we play are showing cover 2 but playing cover 3. They are showing cover 3 and playing cover 4. They are showing one thing and moving after the snap to another defense.

We feel it is important to get the quarterback to read the coverage after the snap. This is very important against teams that disguise their coverage.

We got a good drill from Coach George Curry of Berwick High School in Pennsylvania. We set up a secondary and tell them to line up in cover 2 and move to cover 3 after the ball is snapped. We stand behind the defense and check all of the quarterbacks. As soon as our quarterbacks get back on the drop they must raise three fingers to indicate it is cover 3. Again, we are teaching them to read the coverage before the snap and then to read it after the drop. That affects the decision the quarterback will make once he gets ready to throw the ball. He makes decisions before the snap, but the decisions he makes after the snap are more important.

Listen for the silent alarm. Know when the timing for that play has expired. Run the ball or throw it safely away. On each pass play there is a normal period of time from the snap to the release of the ball. In the three-step drop, that period of time is shorter than it would be on a five-step drop or on a bootleg. But even on the bootleg, there is a normal period of time that expires and a quarterback must know when that time has expired. At that time it is like an alarm going off in his head to warn him. He has to listen for the silent alarm. He must know the time period for each play from the snap to the release of the ball. Anything that happens after that may not be good. If he does not get the ball away when that alarm goes off he attracts defenders to the area he is going to throw. If something happens to disrupt the normal timing on that play the quarterback must know what to expect. It is a decision the quarterback must make. After that alarm goes off we want him to tuck the ball and get back to the line of scrimmage, or throw the ball safely away.

Never focus too long on a receiver before delivering the ball. Your eyes will attract defenders and invite interceptions. In the zone coverages, the defenders are looking at the eyes of the quarterback as they are dropping into their zones. If our quarterback drops back and looks to the right side and does not deliver the ball, he is going to attract defenders there. We do not want our quarterbacks to focus in too long before they throw the ball. The defensive backs are taught to break on the football. If we look too long the secondary can get a break on the ball and has a chance for the interception. It is important for the quarterback to know that he cannot stare at a receiver. He cannot focus in on a receiver too long because his eyes are like magnets. If we can get him to understand that, we can cut down on interceptions.

Use your eyes to move or hold defenders during your drop. The best example I have of this is this: if my fifth point is true, then this one is true. If my eyes will invite defenders to go for the interceptions, then I should use that to my advantage.

HANDS

Set the defense with your hands. We think the quarterback sets the defense with his hands. We play teams that like to stem on defense. We play teams that like to use two different fronts. They will show one front and then move into another front. When the quarterback comes to the line of scrimmage and looks left and then right, he must get his hands under the center immediately. The defense does not have to stem their front until the quarterback is ready to take the snap. Once the quarterback is under center the defense had better be where they want to be. If we go on a quick count we can catch them before they move or in the move. It is the same with the secondary that will disguise their coverages. They do not have to get into the coverage they really want to play until the quarterback is under center and ready to take the ball. They can delay their movement and stall if we are not under center. We will go on the quick snap enough to keep them honest.

It is important to use the hands. We want them to get into the front they are going to play after the snap as soon as possible. Something as simple as putting your hands under the center forces the defense to declare, and that helps the quarterback make a decision. This is a decision-making process. We want to make them play the defense they want to play when the ball is snapped. Then I have a better chance of making a better decision and we have a better chance of being successful.

Carry the ball high. This is a mechanics thing. The quarterbacks watch a lot of pro football but they do not learn this because some of the NFL quarterbacks do not carry it high. They don't have to because they are great athletes and they have great arms. They can do things our kids cannot get away with. If the ball is going to be thrown from the shoulder area, we want to carry it there. We want the quarterback to carry the ball high on his drop. We want him to carry the ball in the breastplate area. If we do that we feel it improves accuracy because we have the ball in a position where it can be thrown. We do not have to do something with the ball to get it ready to throw.

We do not want any loss of time between the recognition of seeing if the receiver is open and the release of the ball. If we carry the ball from the position that I am going to throw the ball from then there is no loss of time.

Ready the ball for the throw. This is very important when the quarterback throws on the run. My experience in working with kids who throw on the run are thinking more about running the ball and not on the pass. Most of the time they have to move the ball to get ready to throw it. We do not want that to happen. If we are throwing the ball on the run we want it up and ready to be thrown. When we are running to the left, we bring the ball over to our right shoulder and carry it up by the ear so the ball is ready for the pass. All we have to do is to let the play develop and get an open receiver. We do not want to have to do something to get the ball ready for the throw.

A term I use all the time is to *ready the ball for the throw.* If the quarterback has to bring the ball from his waist to his throwing position, that could be a wasted second. That can impact his accuracy. If it is ready to be thrown there is nothing to happen to affect his throw in terms of having the ball ready to throw. If the quarterback is to throw on the run, he does not need to do anything to run it. We do not want them to have to do anything to throw the ball.

Lead with your elbow. Everyone knows this is important on the throwing hand. We want to get the elbow out ahead so you can get good snap on the ball. It increases velocity and distance. But the off-elbow is the one I am talking about here. We feel it is important to get both elbows up. That is the trigger that gets everything started.

If you coach quarterbacks, you know that off arm helps the quarterback to maintain balance through the throw and at the finish of the throw. But we also think it is important that the elbow comes off and stays cupped tight to the side. If the elbow comes off at the outside I think he loses some velocity. If we keep the elbow straight down to his body we increase velocity and accuracy.

We coach this during warm-up. During the 7-on-7 drill is not a time to coach accuracy. You coach that in the quarterbacks-only drill. When they are warming up we talk to them about leading with the elbow. It improves accuracy.

Hide the hands with or without the ball. This has nothing to do with decision-making and accuracy. It does have something to do with winning football games. We tell them to hide their hands with or without the ball. A couple of years ago we were a big bootleg passing team; recently we have been a big isolation passing team. We want to show the ball to the defense and then pull it away. We hide the ball with our hands if we keep the ball. If we give the ball to the tailback then we want to hide our hands after we have given the ball off. We want to hide our hands as much as we can when we have the ball or when we do not have the ball. From the sideline it all looks the same. This has nothing to do with accuracy and decision making but it has a lot to do with the success of the play.

FEET

Step and throw on the same line. Your momentum should be in the direction of the throw. This is where we get into the accuracy part more than anything else.

Run and throw on the same line. The momentum should always be in the direction of the throw. Most young quarterbacks have a problem when they throw left. If they do not step in the direction they are throwing they lose velocity and accuracy. *Step and throw on the same line*. When I say that, I do not have to give the complete lecture after they have heard it one or two times. Step and throw means something to them. It means they will have more velocity and accuracy because they have all of their bodies going in the same direction.

Step and pitch on the same line. We are not a big option team, but we do want the quarterback to step and pitch on the same line. I do not want them to pitch without stepping to where I am pitching. We are a toss-sweep team and we want to step and pitch on the same line. If the ball is low or high or in front of the back, I would bet the quarterback is not stepping and pitching on the same line. Our pitch is truer if we step and pitch on the same line.

Start on balance and end on balance. This has to do with the feet. It impacts accuracy. It is important to start on balance. This is not hard for kids to learn. If a kid is not on balance to start with then perhaps he is not a quarterback. A lot of kids do not end up on balance. If he can end on balance he will have more accuracy and more velocity.

Redirect your feet as you redirect your eyes when checking to an alternate receiver. If the quarterback checks off to another receiver and redirects to another receiver, he can't just redirect his upper body. He must redirect his feet as he redirects his eyes and upper body. If he only redirects part of his body he is going to lose something. He gives up accuracy and velocity.

I want to finish up by talking about *mental awareness.* These are things we are coaching our quarterbacks.

MENTAL AWARENESS

- Throw timed routes on time.
- Never throw late to the flat.
- Never throw late down the middle.
- Make a profit every snap. That may be a throwaway. Do something to profit the team.
- Favor moving targets vs. man coverage.
- Favor tight ends and running backs vs. man coverage.
- Favor crossing routes vs. man coverage.
- Know what your man beater is in every pass pattern.
- Let the defense dictate decisions. Never predetermine choices.
- Incompletions are better than interceptions. Practice throwing the ball away.
- A safe throwaway is better than a sack.
- Know who your dump or outlet receiver is on every snap.
- Hit the window on the fade vs. cover 2 and 20 yards or less.
- Throw to the receiver and away from the defender. True vs. zone, but especially true vs. man coverage.
- Don't be greedy. Take what the defense gives you.
- Don't pass up something you have for something you might have.
- Put the ball on the receiver's facemask. That is your concentration point.
- Carry out all fakes. Cheat the fake and you cheat the play.

- Expect man coverage in the red zone.
- Know the down the opponent likes to blitz on. Look for defenders to tip off the blitz.
- Key the safeties to read coverage. The corners are liars.
- The huddle belongs to you. Take charge.
- Know your checks and audibles—script into practice.
- Don't get your receivers killed.

We coach our kids with these special phrases. Over a period of time they learn to understand them. I am not going to tell you that all of our young kids understand all of these things. If they are with you and are in the program very long, or if they happened to be your son, they have heard these terms a lot over the years. These are things we feel are really important.

13

Quarterback Drills and Techniques

Jay Paterno
Penn State University
2003

My dad is a tough act to follow. Today is the first time I have ever gotten the last word at my house. As far as my mother's concerned, she thinks I am a good coach. At least she thinks someone in the family can coach. If any of you have an opening on your staff let me know. I may not have a job at Penn State after that last comment. I really do appreciate the Pittsburgh Clinic giving me the opportunity to speak with you. I am going to keep it very basic. I want to cover some of the things we do to develop our quarterbacks. I will cover the entire package. I will cover the mental and physical aspects of the game and the things we do to get them ready to play.

It is neat for me to speak to the coaches of southwestern Pennsylvania. Coach Joe Paterno mentioned Bob Phillips earlier. Bob was the quarterback coach at Penn State when I was in the ninth grade. I went to the football camp at Penn State when I was in the ninth grade. Art Bernardi was my individual group coach. Twenty years later I am coaching on the Penn State staff and Art Bernardi is working at our camp. I am sure it freaked him out to see me coaching at Penn State. But it has been neat coaching at Penn State. It is just a nice place to coach. I have really been impacted by a lot of coaches over my career. I feel I owe something back to the game of football.

I want to start out by giving you a scenario of what we ask our quarterbacks to do at Penn State. Playing quarterback at Penn State obviously has great rewards. However, there is a lot of responsibility that comes with the position. On game day we dress in our practice facility. Our dressing room is about one-half mile from the stadium. We get our pants, shoes, and t-shirt on and put the jersey on over the shoulder pads and helmet. Then we take the bus ride to the stadium. It is a neat experience going to the game on that bus. When you are a player, you do not really appreciate it. We take the bus up to the stadium and the people tailgating honk their horns.

It is a tradition at Penn State to have the head coach in the front seat on the right. The front left seat is for the starting quarterback. It is an unspoken tradition, but it is symbolic of how we feel about the quarterback at Penn State. The quarterback is our *coach on the field*. When we get to the stadium, the first person off the bus is not the head coach. It is the starting quarterback. When he gets off the bus there are 2,000 people cheering for him. When he walks into the stadium there are 110,000 people cheering him. When we played Nebraska there were close to 111,000 in the stadium. The first player the fans are going to cheer or bitch about is the quarterback.

When we evaluate the quarterbacks, we find there are things that we want them to have in their passing package. There are a lot of great passes out there. Some players can throw the ball through the wall. They can throw the ball 70 yards. They can do all kinds of things with the football.

The first thing we look for in a quarterback is *mental and physical toughness*. We talk about toughness and that is number one. The second thing we look for in the quarterback is his *footwork*. The third thing is his *vision*. If the quarterback has those three things, you have some talent.

As a coach, we feel we can develop two-and-a-half of those three things. By the time they get to our level, they either have the physical toughness or they do not have it. When our freshman quarterbacks come in that first year, we do not put a red scrimmage vest on them to keep them from getting hit by the defense. Now, after they have had a year under their belt and have played in games, we do put the red shirt on them. We do not feel we need to beat them up after they have had that experience of being hit in a game. Our defense knows if they see a quarterback under the center with a white jersey on, it is tee-off time. The defense waits for that day. That is one way we try to build toughness.

A lot of the mental toughness comes with *classroom work*. Joe talked about teaching your players. The most underestimated phase of coaching is in the meeting room. I am talking about our classroom setting. We have to do a great job as coaches in the classroom.

We used to give the players a scouting report. The players look at the report when you hand it to them and they comment on the fact they have played against some of the players on the other team. They will tell you they know all about the opponents.

Then they lay the scouting report down and it never leaves the room. So what I have done in the last three years is to make them write down everything we have on the scouting report. I have a lot of board space in my meeting room. On those boards is the game plan laid out. We go over the personnel, our goal line package, and all of the other facets of the game. We plan it on the board for them.

On Monday we talk about the *personnel of the opponents*. We talk about the personnel groups. We may pick out one cornerback and decide we can beat him easier than we can beat the other cornerback. Sometimes we are right and sometimes we are wrong. We make our quarterbacks write all of this info down. We make them write down our goal line package. "These are our passes we are going to use on the goal line." We have them write down the two-point plays for the week. We have them write down all the new plays we are going to use each week.

Next we go into *situations* with them. We have them write down the different down-and-distance situations we can face in the game. We give them our game plan for *going in* when we get down on the goal line. They are writing all of this information down. We go over all of the first-down plays. Then we cover the second-and-long and second-and-medium plays. I talk with them in terms of the thought process that goes into the game plan.

We sit down and go over what we want to do in the passing game each week. I discuss the passes we pick for the week and go over the situations where we will use each pass. As the week goes on, they get a feel for the game plan. By Monday night we have the game plan for the passing game all set. We go into Tuesday with all of the game plan for the passing game. If we cover it in the meetings we have them write it down, we look at the films, and then we go out and practice the plays selected.

Certain aspects of the game we practice every day. On Wednesday we work on the going-in offense and the red zone offense. We look at the defense we expect to see in those situations. The only thing I write into their game plan is at the bottom of their sheets. I will write down the defenses our opponents have used in their last five games in the goal line situations. I cover the number of times they blitzed, and their top coverage in each situation. I quiz the quarterbacks on this information. When we are watching the tapes of the opponents, I will give them the situation and ask the quarterbacks what they expect in each situation. They must be able to respond immediately. This is the way we build the game plan.

Next we go over our *coming-out offense*. We go over the running plays. We cover plays coming out from our end zone. We cover the deep passes coming out. We go over the formations that give us the best chance to be successful. Again, these are things they write down and they learn as they go through the week. You would be surprised at the number of times the quarterbacks tell me they knew I was going to call a certain play. They may tell the person on the headset to tell me in the press box they knew that was the play to call. They know we have practiced these situations all week. At least I know they are paying attention.

As Joe mentioned, we want to spend time with our players. We do not spend time with them just to get to know them, but we want them to learn how their minds work. Don't be afraid to explain things to them. "This is why we are running this play."

We talk about coverages. I make the quarterbacks draw up the coverages. I do not give them a scouting report. I make them draw up the fronts. They have to know how everything works. When our quarterbacks walk on the field they have almost as much information as the coaches have. They can react accordingly. That is how we build the mental-toughness level. They have learned it in the classroom, they have watched it on the video, and now they go to the practice field and put the game plan in action.

We run our two-minute drill at the end of practice. We want them to practice the two-minute drill when they are tired just like they would be in the fourth quarter. Again, that is another way of building mental toughness. We are in a fortunate situation in that we can recruit the players we want to play with.

The thing I would tell you as you look at quarterbacks for your team is that you always get one player that looks like he has all of the potential in the world. On the other hand, you may get the player who gets in the game and never complains and gets the job done but is not flashy. Do not underestimate that player.

I want to put on a tape of the drills we use for our quarterbacks. These drills are *footwork drills*, *visual drills*, and at the end we will show you some *combination drills*.

(Film)

The first drill is the *board drill* [Diagram 1]. We use this drill to start most of our practices. It is a footwork drill. We are teaching them to move their feet in a tight space. The quarterback takes his pass drop and then sets up using the shuffle. They do not take the big steps. We want them to the point where they are almost hopping. We want their eyes downfield.

I stand down the field and look to see if they are looking downfield. If they are not looking downfield, I will hold up my hand with a certain number of fingers up. I make them call out the number of fingers I have up to make sure they are not looking down at the board.

After we hold up the numbers to make sure they are looking downfield, we make sure they have both hands on the ball. We try to strip the ball from the quarterback as he takes his drop.

Next we go to the *six-yard square drill* [Diagram 2]. It is just a five-step drop square. We want to spend as much time as we can in our individual drills working on our drop run. I spend a lot of time working with them on their running techniques because they spend a lot of time in that run in the six yards. As they run around the cones, their eyes are straight ahead. The players are not down looking at the cones. They eyes should be downfield. When we are in spring practice or preseason practice, we will move the cones out to 15-yards apart. Now it becomes a 60-yard drop for them.

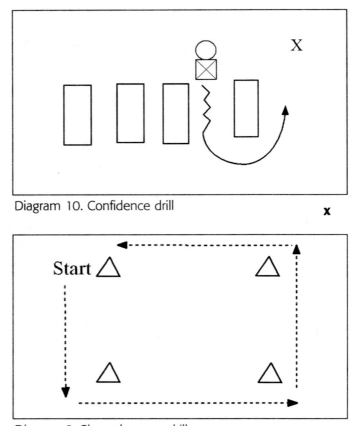

Diagram 10. Confidence drill

Diagram 2. Six-yard square drill

We stress getting back and away from the center as fast as we can. The ball is moving from side to side as the quarterback drops.

Next we go into some vision drills. This is a *peripheral vision drill*. To set up the drill, we tell the quarterbacks to go back and set up where they would normally drop on a pass play [Diagram 3]. We tell them to set up on their drop. We place two receivers in the drill on the outside of the quarterback. They start moving outside almost to the point where the quarterback cannot see them. We want the quarterback to see the entire field or area between the two receivers. He must be able to see both receivers without staring at them. I am going to be in the middle of the field and the quarterback has to look at me. He can still see everything that is going on in this area. I will tell one of the receivers to raise his hand when the quarterback gets to his fifth step on the drop. The quarterback must find the receiver who raises his hand. Then he turns his head, locks on, and makes the throw.

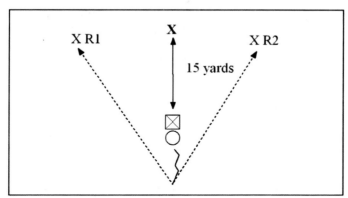

Diagram 3. Peripheral vision drill

I do not know how many of you saw the movie *Top Gun*. In the fight scenes where they were flying those jets, once the pilot got the target in range he locked on the target and shot the missile. It is no different than this drill. He is not staring at either receiver. We want him to be looking straight down the field so he can spot the open receiver. In the game, the defenders who are going to tell you who the open man is will be in the middle of the field.

The next drill is the *anticipation drill* [Diagram 4]. The hardest thing to do is to get the quarterback to throw the ball before the receiver is open. The difference in a good quarterback and a great quarterback is the ability to throw before the receiver is open. When we first started using this drill when I was coaching at James Madison, we used dummies on the drill. Now we use live defenders on the drill. As the quarterback drops back he is looking straight down the field. We put the receiver down the field at 10 yards. We do not want the receivers running 15 to 16 yards on the plays every time. The receivers do not start to run until the quarterback hits on his fifth step. Once the quarterback hits his last step on the drop, the receiver takes off on his route. The linebackers drop to their spots. The outside linebacker takes the curl and the inside linebacker takes the hook area. The receiver comes into the window between the two cones. We want the quarterback to know where that window is going to develop. The ball should be gone before the receiver gets around the cone.

This drill teaches the quarterback to anticipate the receiver's move to the open area. The other thing we want to teach the quarterback is to hit the receiver in the front part of the window. The reason for that is because the near linebacker is opening his shoulders to the outside. It is very difficult for him to turn his shoulders back to the inside. We also want to stay away from the farside linebacker. He has the best chance to tip the ball based on his shoulders tilted toward the receiver and can flow to the area. Our receiver has a chance to make the catch and get upfield and make a big play. Now we want to get the ball to him early in that window so he is away from the linebacker and he can turn and get upfield.

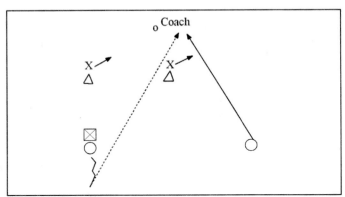

Diagram 4. Anticipation drill

Using films is a great way to show the quarterback how to throw the ball before the receiver is open. He can see where the receiver is when he lets the ball go. The receiver has not made his break when the quarterback releases the ball. When the ball is released, the receiver is not open. But based on where he is going to be when the ball arrives he will be open. The quarterback must anticipate the receiver being open. The quarterback keeps his eyes downfield until he sees the receiver nearing the window. Then he turns his head and throws the ball.

If we have a young quarterback who has a hard time getting this concept down, I will get on the backside of the window and tell him to throw the ball to me. I stand at 16 yards and tell the quarterback to hit on his fifth step and then throw the ball to me. This gives the quarterback a mental image of the receiver already being in the window. Again, we want to throw the ball where the receiver is going to be and not where he is at the time of the release. We do not want the receiver to leave on his route until the quarterback hits on his last step.

Next we go into read drills. Again, these are vision drills. Now we run a *2- on-1 drill* [Diagram 5.] We have one receiver run the curl and the other receiver run the flat. You can run the smash combination. You can run the curl with the outside man and have the inside receiver run the flag behind the curl. However you set up our 2-on-1 passing situations in the game is how you should set this drill up.

The big mistake we all make is to go out and run the 7-on-7 drill. Coaches do not break it down into the basic components. In spring practice we work on these drills in our individual drill periods. When the quarterback drops back he is not staring at the receivers. When he hits on that last step he turns his head and shoulders in one motion. He locks on the receiver and throws the ball to the flat.

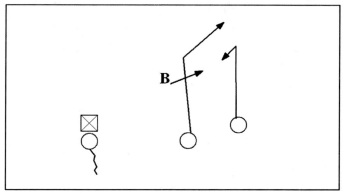
Diagram 5. 2-on-1 drill

Next we go to our 3-on-2 drill [Diagram 6]. Now we have a receiver running the inside route, another receiver running the curl, and the third man running the flat route. You can set it up the way you run the 3-on-2 situations in a game.

Now the quarterback must see five things happen. Again, we are building up on the drill where he can get into the 7-on-7 situations. The more you can break it down for the quarterback, the easier it will be for him when you get to the 7-on-7 drill.

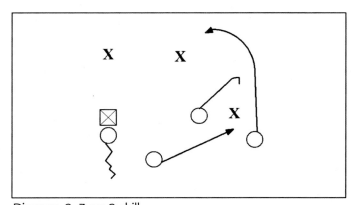
Diagram 6. 3-on-2 drill

The next drill is what we call our *board-scramble drill* [Diagram 7]. We go back to the boards. We have two receivers downfield. We are teaching the quarterback to scramble. He scrambles to his left or his right. You set the drill up the way you want him to scramble. We work on the drill both ways. The quarterback goes back to set up and scrambles to his left. We have a defender that shadows the quarterback. The defensive man can come up any of the lanes he chooses. As the quarterback scrambles we still want his eyes downfield reading the receivers. As he starts to move he must be able to feel the rush defender. If the defender gets in front of him, we want him to come underneath the defender. He may have to step up in the pocket as he would when he is flushed out of the pocket. It is not just a reset-and-throw situation.

The big mistake quarterbacks make when they get flushed out of the pocket is they tuck the ball and run. They do not look downfield for the receiver. As quarterbacks gain experience, they gain the confidence and start looking downfield. That is where the big plays come from. We want our quarterback to find the receiver at 16-yards downfield and then have the receiver turn it into a 60-yard play. Those are back breakers for the defense.

In the drill, we point to one of the two receivers downfield and tell them to scramble with the quarterback. I can wave them off on the drill. I do not want the quarterback to think he has to throw the ball every time he scrambles. The quarterback must read and make a decision and go with it.

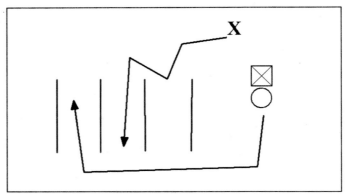

Diagram 7. Board-scramble drill

A key coaching point is for the quarterback to keep his eyes down the middle off the field as he scrambles. Now this drill becomes a peripheral vision drill as he moves. As he scrambles out of the pocket he must be able to read the receivers on the run.

Now we take the drill one step further. Instead of getting flushed up in the pocket, we get flushed outside the pocket [Diagram 8]. Now we are outside on the run. We use live defenders on the drill. You can use live defenders on the board drill as well. The quarterback comes outside looking downfield at the two receivers. If the defender comes up to force the quarterback, he dumps the ball to one of the receivers. If the receivers do not come to the ball, the quarterback has to run the ball if he is gets pressure from the outside.

Here is one coaching point for this drill. We do not want the quarterback looking all the way back to the other side once he has been flushed outside. If he sees someone open deep he can throw the ball deep. Even if the ball is picked off it is just like a punt. That does not bother us. We do not want the quarterback to throw anything underneath on the backside.

Our next drill is our *pass-reset drill* [Diagram 9]. Here we work against the defensive end coming upfield. In this drill we are not getting flushed. It is a situation where the defensive end has gotten a big jump on the offensive tackle. The tackle is still on the defensive end and he is going to run the end beyond the quarterback. It could be the end makes a move inside and the tackle runs him by the quarterback. The quarterback is only taking two shuffle steps in the drill. As he takes the two shuffle steps, he keeps his eyes downfield. He can see what is happening in front of him and he can react to them. We tell the defensive ends what we want on the drill and I tell the receivers what I want on the drill.

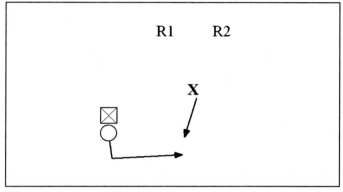

Diagram 8

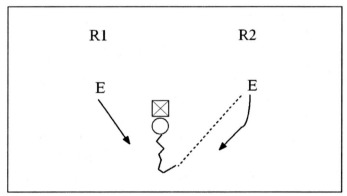

Diagram 9. Pass-reset drill

The quarterback takes two quick shuffle steps and throws the ball. We do not what him running out of the pocket. We want him to reset his feet. That is why we call it the reset drill. The quarterback can see what is happening downfield.

The next drill is our *play-action read drill* [Diagram 10]. It is hard to create a read drill when the quarterback is on the move. It is a play-action pass as we fake to a back. We read the free safety. We have a post receiver and a flat receiver. After the quarterback makes the fake he must get his head around on the play. It is a hard fake and the quarterback is going to stick the ball in the mesh area and pull his hand out.

After he gets his head around he must find his keys in a hurry. He must find the safety very fast. If the safety bites, we will let the quarterback pull up and throw the ball deep. If the safety stays deep, we want the quarterback to come off to the linebacker. He must be able to read these defenders on the run. As he gets his head around he can read the defense.

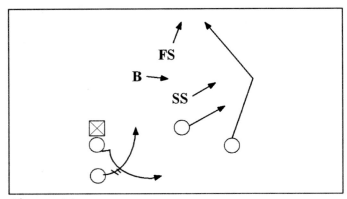

Diagram 10

One thing to help the quarterback on the fake is this. We have the other quarterbacks stand where the defensive end will be and have him tell the quarterback if he can see the ball. If the defense can see the ball, they know it is not a handoff. As the quarterback comes out of his fake, he must get his shoulders turned and he must find his target and get himself headed in the direction he is going to throw the ball.

Any time you can break down the drills so they can see what is happening, it makes it easier to teach. Once the quarterbacks learn the basics they can go to our 7-on-7 drill.

One last point I want to cover. I am a big fan of Dave Letterman. I am sure you have seen the *Top Ten List* that Dave does on his show. I decided to come up with 10 things I have learned about coaching quarterbacks. Here are the 10 things I think you should know about coaching quarterbacks.

Ten Things You Should Know About Coaching Quarterbacks

- You never want to second-guess them or make them look bad in front of their teammates. It is okay to get in their face, but you cannot second-guess them. If you do, it becomes very difficult for them to be the leader in the huddle. It is vital for them to have leadership in the huddle.

- Even in bad situations, find things the quarterback does correctly. For example, the quarterback may be making the correct reads but is missing the throw. If he is making good throws but reading the wrong man, tell him he is making good throws but try to find the open man.

- Encourage the quarterback to take chances and to force throws in practice. We let them force the throws in practice. This lets them test their ability to get the ball into tight spaces. If he does not try it in practice, he will never know if he can do it in a game. It does not matter if he throws 10 interceptions in practice. Now, by the time of the game, he should have a good idea of what he can get away with as far as forcing the ball into tight areas.

- In terms of dealing with the press, take the blame for a bad game as much as you can. You can say things such as, "We did not help him out very much. We could have called a better game for him." This will help alleviate the blame and it will help build his confidence for the future.

- If the quarterback senses a lack of confidence in him, he will play the way he feels. You may not feel good about the quarterback, but you must get it out of your mind. You must show confidence in the quarterback or he will know it.

- Make the quarterbacks write down their five favorite passes. Don't be afraid to use those plays. If you get in key situations and the quarterback is struggling, you can pull out one of those five plays and call it. The guy has all the confidence in the world in those plays.

- You can never do enough footwork and vision drills. We have talked about those situations.

- Always stress speed in setting up on the pass. The longer he holds the ball the more the pass rush will come.

- It is hard to teach the quarterback to throw the ball before the receiver is open. Again, we covered that point.

- The quarterback must think like his coach. If you are calling the passes and the plays, he must think like you. You must spend time in meetings and outside of meetings talking about situations so he can get a feel of how you call the game.

What we do in our meetings and what we do on the field all tie in with these 10 points. Let me give you my email address. I have a drill packet and I will send you the drills. Just send me a note at jvp4@psu.edu. Make sure you include your mailing address. Thank you for your time and attention. I appreciate coming to visit with you.

14

Quarterback Techniques and Reads

Frank Rocco
Shaler Area High School (PA)
1999

The one position that I feel I know and that I feel most comfortable about is the quarterback. I have a couple of things I want to share with you. I will start out by talking about the technique of throwing the football. I want to cover the mechanics of being a quarterback.

We are a run-and-shoot-type team. We have evolved into a one-back offense. We do like to throw the ball around. We try to do this in a very simple way. But in doing that, reading secondary coverages is everything. I will try to get into that area after I talk about quarterback techniques. We try to show our kids what we are doing so they can understand what we want on offense.

Let me get to some things related to the quarterback. These are points that we consider fundamental, but are very important.

QUARTERBACK FUNDAMENTALS

Huddle Discipline

This is very important. The quarterback must be a leader and he must be able to eyeball people. How many kids today give you that firm handshake and look you in the eye? How many of them look away from you or look down? We want our quarterback to be able to eyeball someone. He has to be able to speak clearly.

Mental Zone

This is the area between the huddle and the line of scrimmage. There should be something going on inside the head of the quarterback during those eight yards as he approaches the line of scrimmage. He must have a progression of what he is looking for as he comes to the line. It is the *what if* list, so to speak. Obviously he must make sure his receivers are in the right spot and that his backs are in the right spot. As he comes to the line, what should his eyeballs be on? He must be focused on the defense that will give him some sort of pre-snap read to indicate to him where he is going to throw the ball or run the ball. We will talk about this later. It is a very important step for the quarterback to get the pre-snap read. He must know that something is happening in a certain area of the defense.

Sometimes you have to literally take the quarterback by the hand and take him up the line of scrimmage. We break the huddle, looking from the right to the left down the middle of the field. This is where the reads for the coverages will come. After he reads the coverage then he can put his hands under the center as quickly as he can.

Position Under Center

I just mentioned this aspect. The quarterback must get up to the center *quickly*. Good defensive coaches like to disguise the defense today. They like to stem and run a lot of blitzes. I believe the quicker you get your hands under the center the better. The longer you give the defense time to move around and make adjustments, the tougher it is on your offense.

Cadence

We practice cadence like crazy. We use a *nonrhythmic* cadence. We want him to change the inflection of his voice. We use what we call a *free play*. We use two different manners. We will use it to draw you offside to get the five-yard penalty when it may be a first-and-ten. That will give us a first-and-five situation. Or we will use it on fourth down to draw the defense offside to get a first down. If we do not get the defense to jump offside we will call timeout. The second part of the free play is that we have a play attached to the call. The reason we use this on the first down is because we know we are more likely to draw them off on first down than we are on fourth down. During the game we will use this 8 to 10 times. We just call, "Free play—toss right." The quarterback comes out and goes through a nonrhythmic count. He will do whatever he can do to get the defense to jump offside. If the defense does not jump offside, and we do have a play tagged to the call, the quarterback steps out from center, calls the play to the right and then the left. He gets back under center and we go on the first sound and run the play called. You do not want to use a timeout every time you want to draw them offside. This gives you an alternate. It has been good to us.

Center-Quarterback Exchange

Most of you have your own philosophy on this. The one thing I would add to that is this: I do not like to see a quarterback bent way over the top of the center. I like to see our quarterback in an *upright position* with his chest up where he can have good vision. I like to see a little flexion in the arms so if he is coming back away from the center he can ride the center as he comes out. If the quarterback gets his chest over the center, he does not have room to ride the center as he comes out.

Ballhandling

You want to take a look at your running plays to make sure that the passes that come off the runs look exactly the same. We videotape from the other side of the scrimmage to see what the run looks like. We will show everyone the run. We tell them when they do the play-action fake it has to be the same. Then we take the play-action passes and we critique them. The plays should look the same.

You can correct quarterbacks from throwing errant passes. *Passing mechanics* is something that can improve with coaching. If you understand what the body goes through you can recognize certain problems in passing the ball. You can determine the problem if you see the ball sailing or driving to the ground. If you know the mechanics of passing you can correct these mistakes.

PASSING MECHANICS

Grip

Our middle finger is the longest finger on the hand. The *index finger* should be the last finger to touch the football as it is released. If the pointer finger is too close to the middle finger as I release the football, my pointer finger will not be the last finger to touch the ball. If that happens it will be the middle finger that is the last to touch the football. That index finger should be the last to touch the football. You want it back on the football as far as you can. What that does is this: at the last second, it lifts the nose of the football so it spirals evenly and smooth. Now, it is much easier to be caught. If the middle finger is the last to come off the football it is up near the center of the ball on the laces. Most quarterbacks cannot get friction on the ball and lift it up if the middle finger is the last off the football. As a result, the ball dives all of the time. The ball hits at the feet of the receiver. The problem could be as simple as adjusting the grip and getting the nose of the football up.

I tell our quarterbacks that they want to have at least one finger on the laces. When I played, I used two fingers on the laces. As time went on, I adjusted the nose of the ball so I ended up with only one finger on the lances. I tell our quarterbacks if they will hold their forearms up perpendicular to the ground, they should see the nose of the football slightly pointed upward. If it is not pointed upward you will not throw a good pass.

Pre-Passing Position (Armpit Drill)

Penn State uses what it calls an *armpit drill*. They put the quarterbacks on a line and have them half-speed run, or run the carioca with the football at the sternum. What they are doing is reinforcing the settling of the football at the sternum about two or three inches away from the chest. The elbows are at a nice, relaxed position. They do not want them to drop the elbows. They do not want to jerk the ball up and down from the waist to the shoulders. The natural motion should be for the elbows to be relaxed along the side and rocking from armpit to armpit. We run this drill like crazy.

From that position, what actually starts the throwing motion? We hear coaches talk about quarterbacks having a rocket arm. My grandfather was a great boxer, and he used to tell me that athletics were played with the feet. He would say that the game is played with your lower half of the body. I believe that same thing is true for the quarterback. You need to have a rocket arm and a quick release and a strong arm. But, if you cannot get your feet, your hips, and your body in the proper relationship of where you are throwing the ball, you are not going to be a good passing quarterback. The first thing that initiates the throwing action is the pointing of the toe toward the target. We do everything with our quarterbacks on the line. We have them straddle a line and throw the ball. They have to get the hip around and end up on a landmark. You can see how far off target they are on the drill. They point the toe in a six-inch step and have it come down the line. That initiates the throw. The next point is the off-hand. You want to get the off-arm through on the throw.

Pull (Wipe the Glass)

Now you are starting the arm motion. We want to *wipe the glass* with our hand. When we tell our quarterbacks they are not wiping the glass, they know exactly what I am talking about. They must throw the belly button at the target. They know how to get their hips through on the throw. We tell them they are like a top that is wound real tight. They are almost cocked a quarter away from the target. He is coiled up to a degree. Now, when he starts turning the toe and wiping the glass he is uncoiling his body. That is where the energy comes from.

Release

As the quarterback follows through, here is a key point. He wants to snap the wrist so the pinky finger, the ring finger, the middle finger, and ultimately the index finger touch the ball. That is what gives you the spiral.

Follow-Through

Now comes the *follow-through*. In the old days, they talked about reaching through to the off-pocket and pulling out a dollar bill. There is nothing wrong with that. However, I feel it is a little unnatural, because you are throwing across your body in getting the throwing hand over to the opposite pocket. We just talk about getting the pinky finger to the sky. They follow through and finish up with the throwing shoulder pointing toward the target. If they start with the opposite shoulder pointing toward the target, then they have gone all the way through the cycle. If the pinky points toward the sky then you will get that follow-through.

There are things you can correct with quarterbacks just by eyeballing them. They should be able to start coaching themselves. I know a lot of you feel as I do. You can take a kid that is a good athlete and make him a quarterback.

I want to go into a couple of unique drills for you. This is just to pick up on what we have just talked about.

UNIQUE-TECHNIQUE DRILLS

We do about 20 minutes of special teams per day. When we are working on special teams, we have all of our other coaches around the perimeter of the field leading drill work of some sort. How many times have you seen special teams practice and you see 40 players standing over on the sideline? Some teams may need to use the coaches to run the special practice, and that is unfortunate. We want to make every minute count.

Armpit Drills

We put the quarterbacks on the 45-yard line and run the drills. We run them rapid-fire for 15 minutes. They do *armpit drills* down the line to the hash mark. The first time we

Armpit Drills

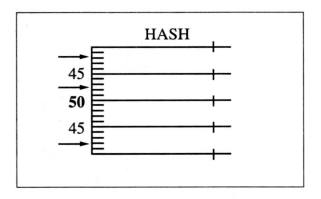

may just have them work on high knees, working the ball from armpit to armpit. Then we turn around and come back doing the carioca down the line working the ball from armpit to armpit. We want them to secure the football. Next, we have them turn to the sideline and execute opening up from the sideline working the ball armpit to armpit down to the hash mark. Coming back he has to open the hips to the other side. We work on securing the football in an adverse body position.

Next we work on the *quick drill* and *air-it-out drill*. We are not in a group drill and we have our receivers with us now. The receivers are one yard outside the hash mark. Some people call this drill the *pat drill* where the quarterback pats the ball and calls hut and the receiver runs a route. The first man in the line runs a go route. The second man runs a three-step out route. We have two quarterbacks in the middle throwing the balls. One is throwing right and one left. We are getting the quarterback loosened up. They just keep alternating. They run a go and an out route. This is where we air the ball out. We line up the quarterbacks in the middle and have them throw the ball.

Quick/Air Out Drill

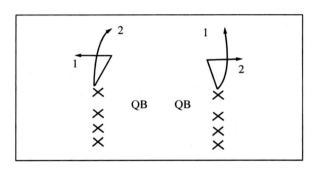

We add to the drill after we work up. It is like the basketball drill where the team lines up around the free-throw line and has to make 10 free throws or they have to run at the end of practice. We do that with the passing drill. We tell them we have to catch 12 passes in a row or we will have to run or do push-ups or something. We have two quarterbacks throwing so we get two catches each time. We have the receivers count the catches out. If we drop a pass before we get to 12 we have to start over. We use this drill early in the season or in preseason camp where we can put them in those pressure situations. Catching the long ball is difficult. You have to practice catching the long ball.

Next, we go to the *special teams period*. This is where we work our quarterbacks on the sidelines. We are in a limited area because the main field is being used. Now we work on cadence during this time. We practice the pre-snap. If you do not practice it, they will not do it on their own. You have to take them by the hand and lead them to water. We can work on different techniques on those lines.

Then we can go to the *knee drills*. Then we stand them out checking their mechanics.

Then we work on throwing on the move. I know you see this drill a lot. This is where we work on our bootleg passes. We work on getting the hips squared and work on running toward the target.

Next, I want to talk about the *net drills*. We have a net at the bottom of our goalpost. We have stitched in various targets on the net for our quarterbacks to throw at. This is to reinforce focusing in on a target. Our quarterback focuses his eyeballs on the belly button of the receiver. He throws the ball and his eyeballs stay focused on the target. He does not need to follow the flight of the ball because it is not going to change its flight in the air.

The other point I want to cover is the art of throwing the football away. This is very important. We actually work on this in our passing drills. When we are calling out the target for the quarterback to throw to, we actually use the *throwaway* as a pass. Instead of calling out hook or curl, we call out throwaway and the quarterback throws the ball out of bounds, or over the goalpost, or into the ground. We want to get the quarterback ready for every situation. You have to practice everything the quarterback will see. If he does not get a chance to work on it, don't expect him to do it in a game.

Now the quarterback has to start putting everything together. We take in all of the receivers and backs. Now we are going to teach the quarterback to read defensive coverages. When the quarterback leaves the huddle and enters the *mental zone*, something has to be going on in his head. It does not matter if it is a run or a pass; he still must know how the receivers and backs are going to line up. He has to know the cadence and all of the other things, but we are talking about passing now.

As we break the huddle, we teach the quarterback and receivers to get lined up first and then to turn their eyes directly to the middle of the field between the hash marks. This will give you the over-the-top coverage. I should say that will give you indicators of what the over-the-top coverage is going to be. If there is one safety in the middle of the field, there is a likelihood that the defense is in man-free coverage. We call that cover 1. It could be cover 3. I will talk about the underneath coverage later. If we see two safeties on the hash marks, the likelihood is that the defense is in cover 2 or zone or 2 man. This makes us feel comfortable about the situation if we know the deep coverage. We do not know the underneath coverage yet, but we know a little more about the deep coverage.

You can look at the defense and see what we call a flat secondary. It could be two things. It could be the corner coverage, or it could be straight-man coverage across the field. If it is straight man, you can look for the blitz because it is coming. You better find out where it is coming from and who is being covered up for. The defense will have to cover up somewhere for the blitz.

When we break the huddle and come up to the line, everyone looks to the middle of the field. We want to know if it is a 1 safety, a 2 safety, or a flat secondary.

The second thing we tell all of our receivers is to use the *D.E.L. theory*. This stands for the *depth, eyes,* and the *leverage* of the defender that is playing in your area. How is he lined up depth wise? Where are his eyes? How is he playing you? Inside or outside, deep or tight? That is the indicator for zone or man coverage.

We break the huddle and come out and look at the *M.O.F. box*. If we see one safety in the middle of the field in the box, we have a good feeling that the defense is in cover free, or it could be cover-man free. Now my eyes start scanning right to left and start picking up DEL of all of the other defenders underneath. If the defender is up tight and turning his butt inside and looking at the belly button of the receiver, there is a high probability that they are playing man coverage. If the man is backed off and his eyes are turned inside looking at the number 2 receiver in the backfield, there is a high probability that they are in a zone. It could be man free or cover 3. Defenses are so good today at disguising the coverages. They can rotate around on the snap and change coverages. We work on that, too, but I am just talking about the pre-snap read now.

Another thing we use a lot is to use *motion* in our offense. This can be a very strong indicator if the defense is playing man or zone. If the defense goes with the motion man, it is likely man coverage. If they rotate, it is likely zone coverage.

Let's jump back to an area and that is the main concept to grasp in reading coverages. Against zone coverage, the receivers must understand when they read the zone that their job is to execute their pass routes. They must find the window in that zone coverage and catch the ball. We school our quarterbacks to throw the ball into the window and let the receivers catch the ball. We want him to throw the ball an equal distance between the two opposite-color jerseys.

We take the defensive secondary and place them in their positions on the field in the zone coverage. We have our quarterback throw the ball into the window. We want to let the ball fall to the ground. We want to impress on him that all he has to do is to throw the ball to the window. We do not want to get the ball intercepted. The receiver is to go catch the ball in the game. That helps him throw the ball against the zone.

Window Drill

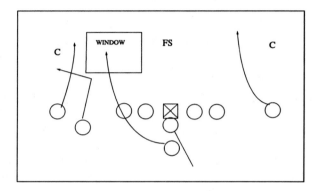

If we read man-to-man on the underneath coverage, our receivers are taught to stick and run away from the defender and to stay on the move. Against the zone we settle and come back to the ball. Against man we stick them and run away from them. If we do not stick them the first time, we run upfield and then run away from them. If we can stick them downfield we will. What starts out as a 10-yard route may now be a 12-yard route because we did not shake the defender the first time. It is a concept to understand for the offense.

We have the quarterback read one key and then we have a throwaway. The throwaway may be as simple as putting the ball up in the press box. However, many of our routes have a safety valve or a receiver in an outlet area where we can throw the ball. It may be a simple dump pass, and it can be as a throwaway as well. We try to make our passing game very simple. We want the quarterback to read one key and one throwaway and then make his decision.

The last concept is *don't throw an interception and don't get sacked*. This year we threw the ball 258 times and only got sacked three or four times all year.

To design an attack against the zone coverage, we want to create a 2-on-1 situation or a 3-on-2 situation. That is the one read. We send out two receivers and read one defender. If the defender covers one receiver he throws to the other receiver. The 3-on-2 situations are the same as the 2-on-1 except the 3 is the man we go to on the throwaway.

Also, we want to stretch the field or zone horizontally or vertically. Create a pattern that will stretch the field each way. This is against zone coverage.

Against the man-to-man coverage, we want to create mismatches. We were blessed this year to have a receiver who was 6'2" and one who was 6'4". They had athletic ability. A lot of the time we could get the mismatch and throw the ball up in the air and they would go and make the catch. So we look for mismatches and take advantage of them. We run a lot of trips where we try to get a fast receiver matched up on a linebacker or someone who is not as quick as he is. We look for mismatches in speed, size, and quickness. You can disguise the routes to take advantage of your talent.

There are several drills you can use to take advantage of reading coverages. We use the *mental-picture drill* in two- or three-receiver situations. Let's say we have a curl/flat pattern. We have the quarterback throw the curl and then throw the flat Routes. Next, we throw the defender into the picture. Now we get them reading that man. There is so much in throwing the football. A lot is just getting the hips into position. Each pass is a progression and we put them through these steps. Now, not only do we have the mechanics involved, we are asking them to read and throw.

I want to show you a couple of pass routes to put together what we are looking at. No matter what formation you are in, you can design a play that will go vertical down the field and read the defense. We teach the quarterback to look the defender off and still throw the ball to the receiver. If you have a quarterback who can put some zip on the ball and throw it downfield 17 yards, you will have success throwing the ball.

We start with the *4-vertical concept*. Then we go to what we call *turns* or *hooks*. We turn up at 10 to 12 yards. Then we go with the *hitch routes*. After the hitches, you can throw the turns, and then we throw the vertical routes.

When we break the huddle and come to the line, we want the defense to think we are going to run 4-vertical every single time. They know our quarterback is good enough to stick the ball in there to one of the four receivers.

When we first went to the run-and-shoot concept, a friend of mine at Phoenixville Area High School in eastern Pennsylvania went to the same offense. He wrote an article in one of our state coaching magazines that was a mock-up of the same things we do. He covered four routes that are the same thing that we do: slide, curl, smash, and switch-and-go. Let me show those to you.

Slide Route Read vs 3 Deep

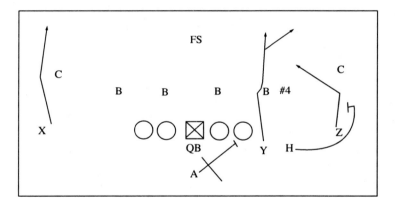

- Quarterback—three-step drop read #4.
- If #4 plays Z hit H.
- If #4 plays H hit Z.
- Coaches read if corner bites on slant call Y Hot.
- Z—4-step slant (find window in zone).
- H—Replace Z upfield five yards.
- Y—Push vertical to seal FS (if corner breaks on slant, push route to flat).
- X—Vertical stretch

Curl Route Read vs. 3 Deep

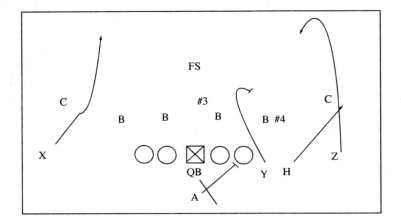

- Quarterback—Step drop heads #4.
- If #4 sinks, hit H.
- If #4 plays H, hit Z.
- Z—15 yards curl (find window in zone).
- H—Run 45 degrees to sideline five to seven yards.
- Y—Hook up at six yards, keeping #3 out of the play.
- X—Vertical stretch.

Smash Route Read vs 2 Deep

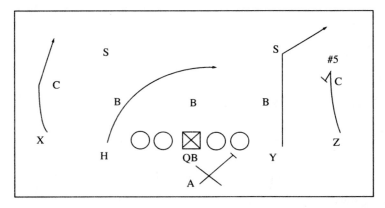

- Quarterback—three-step drop read #5.
- If #5 plays Z, hit Y on flag.
- If #5 sinks, hit Z on flag.

- Coaches read Y drag.

- Z—six-yard stop.

- H—Drag six to eight-yard drag (find window).

- X—Vertical stretch.

Switch Route Read vs 3 Deep

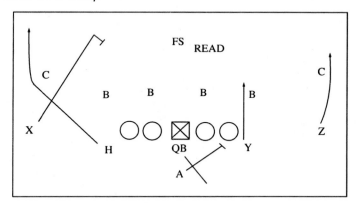

- Quarterback—three-step drop read FS.

- If FS moves to cover Y, hit X on dig.

- If FS stays deep, hit Y after he clears under coverage.

- Coach reads H rail.

- Z—Vertical stretch

- H—Rail (stay close to sideline).

- X—Run on a 45-degree angle to the hash 13 to 15 yards deep and find window based on FS reaction.

This route can be used vs. 3 deep. The quarterback's pre-snap read is still the same because Y is now covered. The quarterback's read goes back to the X receiver running the dig.

15

Quarterback Techniques and Drills

Randy Sanders
University of Kentucky
2007

My topic today is quarterback techniques and drills. Coaching the quarterback is one of the most challenging things a coach will ever have to do. At the quarterback position, there are certain fundamentals that must be taught. Those fundamentals must be accomplished to get the ball snapped and complete a successful play. The quarterback touches the ball on every play, and his ability to execute is directly reflected in the success of that play.

The quarterback under the center must have a balanced stance. We do not want a staggered foot alignment. We want a bend in his hips and knees. We try to keep it all the same. We do not want a foot dropped back because it may tip a pass or the direction he is going. We want his elbows flexed as he goes under the center.

He places his index finger of his dominant hand in the crease of the center's rump. His bottom hand is slightly tilted to the side. I like the bottom hand to the side so it can stay in place and the hands do not separate when receiving the snap. When he receives the ball from the center, he must move his feet as the ball is coming up. He wants to get away from the center as quickly as possible.

If the hands are placed end to end, the center snap has to be perfect for the quarterback to receive the ball. Tilting the hands to the side allows for a margin of error.

As the ball comes up from the ground, it turns slightly putting the laces into the hands of the quarterback.

At Tennessee in 2002, I learned something that was invaluable. We had a junior quarterback and center who had started the year before. We played Florida on national TV and it began to rain. We fumbled six out of eight snaps. When you play Florida on national TV and that happens to you, the quarterback coach is not a very popular guy.

We were clueless as to what the problem could be because they had no snap problems in the past. We found out later, the center thought he had to snap the ball harder because it was raining. It was raining hard and the ball was wet. When he put the extra velocity on the ball, it skidded through the quarterback's hands. If it is raining hard, ease up on the snap.

I cover that with every one of my centers and quarterback now. The quarterback has to know if the ball is not coming from the center as hard he has to stay under the center longer to get the snap.

Every Tuesday after practice, we practice snapping the ball in a wet ball situation. All the centers and quarterbacks take snaps while we hold a water hose on the ball. They do not like it, but it serves the purpose. We sprayed it on their arms, hands, and the ball. Do not neglect working with a wet ball.

One thing I learned from John Majors was to keep a checklist. I played for Coach Majors and coached under him for five years. I have a checklist of quarterback items. Every year I pull out the folder and go through the checklist of things I have to cover with the quarterback. On the checklist are the drops, wet-ball drill, two-minute procedures, four-minute stall offense, scramble drill, and other items. It is about three or four pages of little notes.

I make the checklist to be sure I do not forget something that could be important. I do it every fall and spring. One thing that I personally hate is to hear a coach say it was not the player's fault because he had not gone over that point with him. That is why we coach. We have to cover all the items that will affect the way the player plays. Some of the things on that list are obvious and some not so obvious.

The first thing the quarterback wants to do after he receives the snap is to seat the ball. It does not matter whether it is a run or pass play. The quarterback pulls the ball right to his belt buckle. I do not want a guard to pull and knock the ball out of the quarterback's hands because he has not seated it.

As I go around, I do not hear coaches talking about running game mechanic for the quarterback unless it is an option team. I think the running game is very important. When I was coaching running backs at Tennessee, I had some great running backs. As good and talented as they were, it was amazing how much better they became when they received the ball at four yards deep instead of three-and-a-half yards. The earlier they received the ball, the better they became. That has to do with the quarterback mechanics.

When we talk about quarterback mechanics leaving the center, we refer to the clock face. The direction the quarterback uses as he leaves the center is six o'clock, seven o'clock, or four o'clock. If the quarterback wants to run a draw to the right, his first step is at seven o'clock, His second step is a crossover step and from there on it is a full sprint back to the running back. We want the ball given to the running back as deep as we can.

I want the quarterback to run through the mesh with the running back. I expect the quarterback to be a good enough athlete to run to the mesh and still make a good handoff.

When the quarterback hands the ball off, his target is the base of the numbers of the running back's jersey. I want his eyes on the base of the numbers. We want the quarterback's arm extended as he hands the ball off. It is much easier for the running back to receive the ball from the straight arm instead of a bent one. If the quarterback's arm is bent, he is blocking half of the running back's vision. When the quarterback extends his arm, it allows the running back see what is happening in front of him. We want the running back looking at his reads to see where he has to go. We do not want him looking for the ball. It is the quarterback's job to hand the ball to the running back.

As the quarterback extends the ball, the opposite hand is on his belt buckle. That sets up the fake in the play-action pass. We want the hand off to look exactly like the fake.

Question: On the play-action pass, do you ball fake or hand fake?

Answer: It depends on whether we are in two backs or one back. If we are in a two-back set, I do not like to put the ball out because the fullback might hit it and knock it out of his hands. In the one-back set, I like to show the ball because it is a better fake. When you talk to Peyton Manning, they show the ball. He actually sticks the ball into the running back's stomach, before he pulls it back to throw.

The quarterback has to carry out his fake. He may be setting up to pass or faking the bootleg, but it is important to continue the fake, whatever it is. The quarterback has an opportunity to make a block with his fake. If he can occupy someone, he has done a good job. When you coach quarterbacks in a pass-oriented offense, do not slight the running-game mechanics. The running backs are so much more effective if the quarterback can get them the ball deep and get out of the way.

THREE-STEP DROP

In the passing game, it all starts with the mechanics of the drop. In the three-step drop, I believe in crossing over on the second step. Some coaches teach the quarterback to take a big step and shuffle to get ready to throw on the third step. Personally, I do not like that. We play against defensive backs who read three steps and set down on the pattern. I do not want to show the defensive back a three-step drop any sooner than I have to.

If the quarterback uses a crossover step in his second step, it does not show the defensive back the three-step drop quite as fast. I do not believe it is easier to get on balance and get ready to throw if you do not cross over. Therefore, we try to hide the three-step drop by using the crossover step.

It does not matter whether the quarterback takes a three-step, five-step, or seven-step drop, the last two steps are gather steps. On our three-step drop, the quarterback gets his depth on his first step. On the second step, he crosses over, and on the third step, he puts his foot into the ground. If the quarterback wants to throw the ball on the third step, has to stop his momentum on the second step. That allows him to shift his momentum and drive the ball where he wants it to go.

That mistake occurs in quarterback camps all the time. We tell them to throw the ball off the plant and they have trouble shifting the weight because they do not stop the momentum on the next-to-last step. They have trouble driving forward with the body on the throw.

If the quarterback wants to throw the ball off his plant foot, he has to get the center of gravity to come forward as he stops. He cannot do that if he does not start to stop on the next to last step.

FIVE-STEP DROP

I teach two different kinds of drops off the five-step drop. I teach them as two different drops. We call the first drop a fast five. That drop is like the three-step drop because we prepare to throw the ball off the plant foot. If we throw the out cut using a fast-five drop, on the fourth step we kill our momentum. On the fifth step, I plant and drive the ball to the out cut.

We call our regular five-step drop the big five. I am not worried about throwing the ball off the plant foot. He is driving for more depth in his drop. When he hits his fifth step, he hitches up and gets ready to throw. We do not ask him to throw the ball off the plant foot because it is hard to get into balance.

Typically, if we throw the fast five, we throw something in the 10-yard area. The quarterback has to make a decision on where to throw the ball before he gets to fifth step. On those plays, it does not matter what coverage the defense plays. His progression as he drops is to find out whether the receiver is open. If he is open, the quarterback delivers the ball on the plant step. If he is not, he hitches and goes to the number-two receiver or shifts his body and goes to the number-three receiver.

A coaching point for a right-handed quarterback in his drop deals with his last step. If he has to throw the ball to his left, his plant step moves toward his right side slightly. That naturally lines the body up to throw the ball to the left side. I think body alignment and balance is a big part of throwing the football. Body alignment allows him to drive the ball where he wants it to go.

SEVEN-STEP DROP

Last year we did not use the seven-step drop. The reason we did not use the seven-step drop was the protection scheme. When the quarterback drops to that depth, it makes it difficult on the offensive tackles to block the speed rushers. The only reason for the seven-step drop is to occupy the quarterback while the routes are getting deeper downfield.

The quarterback position is a big rhythm position. To deliver the ball accurately, the quarterbacks want to stay in a rhythm of the drop to the throw. One, two, three, settle, and throw is the rhythm you want to establish with the quarterback. When the quarterback takes five steps and has to wait for the receivers to get deeper, he gets nervous. He begins to get happy feet and starts to creep up in the pocket. They wait for the route to happen and end up sacked because they crept back to a depth of three to four yards.

The extra two steps in the set occupied the quarterback and let the routes get further down the field. When you use this type of drop, you can get the backs to chip on the speed rushers to help the offensive tackles. Sometimes the seven-step drop is good if you can protect it.

When the quarterback drops, I want the ball carried at chest level. I do not want it too low or too high. Chest level seems to be a natural position. When he hits the fifth step, he makes the adjustment with the ball to throw it.

There are many ways to throw the ball. I do not like to change the way players throw the ball when I get them. When they come to me, they have obviously been successful in throwing the ball or they would not be playing quarterback in college. We may fine tune a few things, but I do not mess with the actual arm motion or techniques.

I believe you learn from your players. The quarterback at Kentucky has a different throwing motion. I have never coached a player who throws the ball that way. As he brings the ball up to throw, his elbow is higher than the ball. Usually the less you do with the ball as you bring it up to throw, the more accurate you are. However, the simpler the motion, the less velocity you have on the ball. The more you do with the ball to increase the velocity, the less accuracy you have with the ball. In addition, quarterbacks with simple adjustments in the ball position can throw it when it is wet.

Peyton Manning has a simple throwing motion. When he throws the ball, half the time it does not spiral. When it does, it does not spin very hard. He does not have an extremely strong arm, but is deadly accurate. That is because he has a simple, repeatable motion in his throw. If you remember the weather in the Super Bowl, he had no trouble throwing the ball.

If you coach young players, there are two things you never want them to do. You want the ball higher than the elbow at all points, and the point of the ball parallel to the ground. With the ball pointed toward the sky, it puts pressure on the grip to get it rotated back. It is easier for the ball to slip—especially if it is wet or cold.

If you change something in the arm motion of the quarterback, you must change something with the feet. It is all tied together. Arm strength does not come from just the arm. It comes from the legs, hips, and abdomen. If you change something on top, you have to change something down low. I spend most of my time working on their feet. I am big on getting the body in line. I want the weight on the balls of their feet. I do not want them on their toes or their heels.

If your quarterback is practicing his footwork correctly, you should be able to take the two cleats off the heels of his shoes, and he would not know it. I want him on the balls of his feet.

We describe the mechanics of the quarterback as BEEF. That stands for balance, eyes, elbow, and follow-through. Balance is the body lined up on the balls of the feet, knees slightly bent, and everything under control. The eyes have to be on the target. They cannot look at the rush or the defenders. They have to see the target. The elbow has to be up. Everyone has a different motion, but I have never seen anyone throw the ball well when his elbow was not higher than his shoulder.

People talk about Tiger Woods being able to fix his swing problems in the middle of a round. The follow-through gives the quarterback an opportunity to do that. When he has good follow-through, it is almost like trying to put your thumb in your pants pocket opposite the throwing hand. For a right-handed passer, the hand should end up on the left hip or thigh area. If he finishes too much in front, he is too much over the top. If he finishes on the right side, his elbow is not up. Where he finishes on his follow through tells you about his delivery.

After you throw the ball, you should be able to pose on the finish and hold it. If you cannot hold the pose, you are not in balance. If they throw and rock to the side or fall back, their balance is off. In practice, I have them throw and hold the follow through. If you coach them on those things, it gives the quarterback a way to correct what is going on with his throw.

When we throw the football, we want a bent front knee. I do not want it flexed, but bent somewhat. If the knee locks out, the hip locks also. I want them on the balls of their feet when they throw. I do not want them on their toes, their heels off the ground, or the heel hitting the ground first. It is almost impossible to hit on your heel and stay in balance. The same thing is true when you lock your knee.

When the quarterback's follow-through gets bad, it means they are dropping their elbow. When that happens, I put them on their knees. I have them throw with their right knee on the ground and then the left knee on the ground. Another drill to help this problem is to throw with someone standing about two yards in front of them with their hands up. I tell them to throw the ball as if the player is not there. I do not want them throwing with the purpose of getting the ball over the player. I want them to throw it as if they are throwing it through the man.

I have our video man come out and video our quarterbacks. He isolates on the quarterback throwing the football. We tape it from the side, rear, and front angles. Then we go inside and look at the throwing motion of each quarterback.

The next thing is the progression reads you want him to make. We read high to low in our five-step game. We read from low to high in our three-step game. We can read with a horizontal progression from the outside moving inside or inside going out. If we throw it outside, the delivery has to be on time.

I want the progression happening where the quarterback's eyes are focused. Before the snap of the ball, the quarterback gets a pre-snap read. He reads the safeties and tries to determine which side of the field to work. Once we snap the ball, the quarterback reads half the field. I do not want him trying to read the whole field. I do not want him going through a progression to the right and then turning back to the left and trying to throw the ball there. If he cannot find a receiver after a one-two-three progression, he tucks the ball and runs, or he throws the ball away.

When the focus of the quarterback is to one side, he has an idea of what is happening to that side. If he turns back to the other side, he does not have a clue as to what has happened since he snapped the ball. That is how quarterbacks end up throwing the ball directly to a defender. We have a few plays where the progression may reach to the fourth receiver, but not many. We do not have time to run a progression through four possible receivers. If we hold the ball over 3.2 seconds, a sack will occur. It is hard to take a five-step drop and go one, two, three, and four in three seconds.

The exception to the rule is what we call an alert. That term applies to a receiver. He may not be in the progression, but because of the defense or adjustment in the coverage, he becomes an option.

I like progression reads that are similar for the quarterback. An example of this is a three-wide receiver formation. The split runs a dig route, the slotback runs a curl inside, and the strong split end runs the post. The tailback runs an option route off the linebacker, and the fullback flares into the formation. We want to get a triangle read from the dig, option, and curl [Diagram 1]. The post route could be an alert and the fullback would be a number-four read.

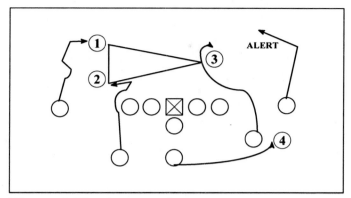

Diagram 1. Triangle progression

The post is the alert. That means if we have a certain coverage, we have the opportunity to go over the top and hit the home run. If the coverage is three deep with a single high safety, the quarterback does not look at the alert pattern.

Here is an example from the same formation [Diagram 2]. We circle both backs into the hook area and option area. The slotback runs the alert. The strong split receiver clears. The backside split end runs a dig. We have the same triangle read progression on different receivers.

We can put in the crossing route and keep the same kind of triangle for the quarterback [Diagram 3]. In this formation, we align in a trips set right with a tight end to the right. The outside receiver in the trips set runs the alert pattern. The inside receiver runs the dig pattern. The tight end runs an option checkdown on the linebacker. The tailback follows the tight end out and crosses the field. The split receiver to the backside runs the clear. The quarterback reads the dig, checkdown, and cross as his triangle read.

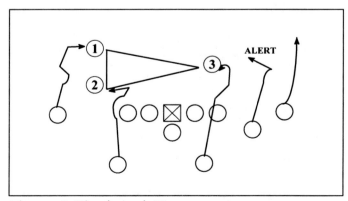

Diagram 2. Triangle read #2

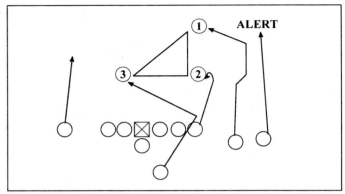
Diagram 3. Triangle read #3

One year I had a true freshman quarterback. We used different reads to keep it simple for him. We used the armband, and he had a bunch of plays on that armband. He may not have known what receiver was running which pattern, but he knew that a Willie call was a triangle read. All the triangle reads are alike. It allows the coach to be flexible as a play caller, but keeps it simple for the quarterback. There are certain things the quarterback has to do with the automatic calls to get you out of bad plays. However, the less they have to think about it, the better they can manage the game.

In the shotgun, the quarterback is five yards deep in a balanced stance. If they drop the right foot into a stagger in the shotgun, I do not have a problem with it. From the shotgun, the five-step depth is the same as three steps in the shotgun. I want the weight on the left foot, and that happens in the stagger. My quarterback drop steps and then takes three steps. He cannot figure out why he takes a hit in the back. The reason is obvious; he is too deep and created a different release point than the tackle has protected.

The shotgun presents a problem in the three-step game. If the quarterback catches the ball and throws it right away, the defensive backs do not back up. If we throw our three-step game from the shotgun, the quarterback still drops to get the defensive backs moving.

In our offense, we have some sprint-out passing game in our attack. You must practice throwing on the run to be effective at it. If the quarterback is throwing to a receiver while running, he does not have to run at the receiver to throw the ball. However, he does have to have his momentum going in the direction of the receiver. The key to throwing on the run is to relax. You have to point the shoulders at the receiver, but the quarterback has to relax. The quarterback has to overemphasize pushing the elbow up in the throw.

When the quarterback throws running to his left, he has to get his body around to deliver the ball. The elbow naturally gets higher for the right-handed quarterback throwing to the left on the run. Unless he has to throw the ball on a full sprint with someone chasing him, he throws it better going left than right.

On the footwork, the quarterback throws off his front foot while throwing on the run. If he is running right, he throws off his right foot. If he is running left, he throws off his left foot. It will happen naturally. If you do not let them slow down and look at their feet, it will happen without them thinking about it. Throwing the football on the run is like hitting the golf ball. If you can do the same thing every time, it makes it easier.

When we warm up, we move our feet or use some motion in the throw. We do not stand and throw the ball back and forth. It never happens like that in a game, so we do not warm up that way. After we warm up, we throw the ball at least 15 yards. By throwing an extra five yards, it improves your mechanics in the throw. If you want to become good at something, you have to do it. We want to work at throwing the ball hard on a rope at least 30 yards down the field. That is how you build arm strength.

I also believe an arm only has so many bullets in it. On some days, we throw very little in practice—especially in fall camp. We try to keep the arm as fresh as we can.

A coaching point that will help your delivery of a soft ball is in the foot movement. If you want to use touch and soften the throw, have the quarterback get on his toes as he throws the ball. It is helpful in throwing a fade, shallow cross, or a screen pass.

When throwing the fade pass, if the ball spins but never turns over, the quarterback is not finishing the throw. If the ball is thrown properly, the ball will spin and turn over as it comes down.

Question: What are the mechanics of the quarterback when he throws the bubble screen pass?

Answer: If I throw a bubble screen to the right, the quarterback steps with his off foot first. He steps with his left foot, his right foot, and throws the ball. There are times we throw the ball immediately to prevent it from being a backward pass. When we are in the shotgun, we catch and throw it immediately. We want to find the laces of the ball before we throw it because it is a more accurate throw. The way I teach them to find the laces is to see the ball in their hands. If they see the ball in their hands they know where to find the laces.

Question: What can you do to build leadership into the quarterback?

Answer: Leadership is something you have to teach and instill in a quarterback. Everyone is born with different degrees of natural leadership. When our quarterbacks see me, they know I am going to ask what they have done to be a leader this week. It is something you have to talk about and give them ideas of how to be a leader. One big thing to being a leader is to do things the right way. Leaders will back up the coach and not go against what he is being told. Leadership is a powerful thing. The most dangerous thing to have on your football team is a bad leader. If you have a bad leader, either the coach or the bad leader has to go. Either you get rid of him, or he will drag you down.

You have to coach them up and teach them how to become good leaders. More importantly, you have to expect those qualities. I am going to coach the quarterbacks hard. They know they will be coached hard, and the team knows it. As a coach, I want the team to hear me coaching the quarterbacks and at times get on them. However, I do not believe you can go wild on your leaders in front of the rest of the team or on the sidelines of a game. I think there is a fine line a coach has to be aware of in dressing down the team leader. You have to demand more from your leaders than anyone else. However, you cannot discriminate and look the other way when he is wrong. I think you have to coach them hard, but at the same time be smart in your reaction toward them.

Thanks for your attention.

16

Basic Quarterback Fundamentals

Mike Shula
University of Alabama
2004

First I want to let you know I am a little nervous today. It is only 60 miles from my home, so my wife decided to come with me today. She said she would go shopping while I could go to the clinic for the lecture. She has been out all day shopping, and I can assure you, that is why I am nervous.

I want to thank Nike and Rush Probst for having me on this clinic. It is an opportunity to get together and talk football. Hopefully, all of us will get better at what we are doing so we can help the kids get better. That has been one of the big things for me in coming from 15 years of experience in the NFL.

My first year in college coaching has been exciting in the personal relationships with individuals. In the NFL, you really do not have that individual relationship. I hate to say it, but in the NFL you have to treat the players as numbers. In college football, you get to know the parents of the players. In the NFL, you only see the players after their senior year, and that is only for about six weeks in training camp. A lot of the athletes are cut and they move on. You may never see them again. At the college level, we have so much more invested already in our recent recruiting class. I know a lot of their parents, and I know a lot of their coaches. So I am looking forward to working with the college players, parents, and coaches.

A lot of people outside of Alabama just do not realize what football means to people of this state. I thought I knew what football was all about when I came up here out of high school to play at the University of Alabama. After I got here, I found out I really did not know the true meaning of football to the people of this state.

What I would like to do now is to talk about basic quarterback fundamentals. I found my 1985 playbook about coaching the quarterback. These things were given to me by the head coach of the Miami Dolphins when I was in the eighth grade. I guess the thinking was this material would help me to get ahead of the game. These are things I was taught in high school and the same things I was taught in college. Also, I got the same information in my only year in the NFL.

I have told quarterbacks that I have coached the same information that was given to me by my dad when I was in the eighth grade. What I am saying is this: the method does not change, regardless of the level you are coaching. The basic fundamentals stay the same. We preach about all of the fundamentals, and we stress doing the little things right and being detailed. There are so many things involved with the quarterback position. It may be the mechanics, the fundamentals, the intangibles, the leadership, the way you must set examples and yet be your own self. You have to know how all of your teammates are going to look at you during crunch time and how you must respond. The quarterback must make quick decisions in three seconds.

I think the quarterback is a unique position. I am a little biased, of course. I am going to share some of these thoughts with you today. I will start with real basic fundamentals. After that, I will try to get into some of the intangibles. I want to stress gaining confidence for the quarterback, earning the respect of teammates, finding the winning edge, and doing what it takes to win. Some of this will sound a little repetitive. But again, that is the way we teach these fundamentals. The more the players can hear this information, the better chance they have of doing good things on Friday night and Saturday.

After we finish the fundamental session, I have some drills that I want to show you and I want to describe to you how they apply. If we have time, I will talk about some other things on tapes that involve other coaching points.

First, we start with the stance for the quarterback. With the quarterback under the center, we want the feet parallel, with a slight stager. Some coaches stress the stagger more than we do. We only want the opposite foot from the throwing hand to be slightly staggered. This is especially true when we are dropping back to throw the ball. At times, when you are handing the ball off, you may stagger the feet the other way. The thing we stress is getting the weight on the pivot foot so we can get an advantage without giving it away.

We want the knees slightly bent. The weight is over the instep, with the body slightly leaning forward. Any mechanics we teach, we want to really stress these points in the spring, more so than in the fall. We want our quarterback to be comfortable in his stance so he can look at the defense and study his keys. We do not want him worried about his stance in taking the snap.

The hands should be firmly pressed under the center's crotch. Basically, we want the quarterback to give the center a target to bring the ball up to on the snap. The second point is to have good hand pressure on the center's crotch so the ball does not come out when the center snaps the ball. We tell the quarterback to put his hands under the center's crotch, knuckles deep, and to apply pressure.

We want him to bend the elbows of the throwing hand slightly. We want the opposite thumb to be on the thumb of the throwing hand. The opposite thumb is where we want the pressure on the center's crotch. If the snap comes up a little deep and you have pressure on the crotch with the opposite hand, you have a chance of getting the snap so it does not split your hands.

The ball must fit into the crease of the throwing hand. We want the quarterback to trap the ball with the off hand. Once the ball is secure in the hands, we want to stomach the ball. In other words, we want him to "seed" the ball into his stomach. When he is handing off, he does not want the ball hanging outside of his body, or down low where he has to raise it up to get it to the ballcarrier. We want to make sure he gets the ball into his stomach as soon as he gets the snap.

Next we move to the pivot foot. It starts with the head and shoulders first. He must twist his body to look at the handoff spot. If he is handing the ball off, he must lock the ball into the mesh area. He must pivot on the foot with a little pressure on that foot. He comes out to the handoff area and he must look the ball into the handoff spot.

After the handoff, he fakes as if he has the ball, using proper footwork. The point we want to make here is this: we do not want the quarterback to get too excited about faking until he gets the ball handed off to the ballcarrier.

The handoff is the responsibility of the quarterback. For whatever reason, if the quarterback can not make the handoff, he tucks the ball and follows the back through the hole of the play called. He does not want to shovel the ball to the runner, and he does not want to be late getting the ball to the ballcarrier. If he misses the handoff, he follows the back into the hole and continues upfield. We do not want him to make the play worse by trying to get the ball to the ballcarrier when he is late or the back is too wide.

We use two types of fakes with the quarterback. First, we use a fake by showing the ball with two hands. If a quarterback is left- or right-handed, we do not ask him to take his throwing hand off the football. If we are going toward his throwing hand, he can give a one-hand fake with the open hand. He can give the open-hand fake and hide the ball on his hip.

If he is going away from his throwing hand, he will always use a two-hand ball fake and then set up in the pocket. We are never going to make an open-hand fake with our throwing hand. The reason for that is simple. If there is pressure and the throwing hand is late getting on the ball, the ball could come out and result in a fumble.

Next we move to the drop, where the quarterback gets to the passing spot. We use crossover footwork on the drop. It is a comfortable drop from the center to the set-up spot. Some coaches stress for the quarterback to keep the ball up near the open ear as they retreat on the drop. I am more interested in the quarterback being comfortable on the drop as far as the position of the ball is concerned. We do not want the ball down around the belt on the drop. As long as it is between the letters and the ear hole on the helmet, that is fine with me. It depends on the quarterback. He can use the momentum of the ball swinging back and forth as he sets up. That is what we teach them.

We talk about keeping the shoulders at a 45-degree angle on the drop. Not many quarterbacks can drop back where they can keep the shoulders straight down the field on the crossover dropback.

We use three drops. We do a three-step drop, a five-step drop, and a seven-step drop. We take the drop and set up, ready to throw.

There are a couple of ways we teach our quarterbacks as far as setting up. All of this is based on timing. On the three-step drop, the quarterback is going to take the third step, transfer his weight, and then thrown the ball. His action is not a hitch step.

On the five-step drop, we call it a quick five-step drop. Again, there is no hitch in the drop. He transfers his weight and throws the ball. When he does this, he must be under control. If he is taking five steps back, and his momentum and his weight are still on the back foot, it is going to be hard to transfer the weight in the throwing motion. It will be difficult to get much on the football He may be able to get something on the football, but he probably will not be accurate. The key is to keep the feet underneath you, transfer the weight on the fifth step, and then throw the football. This is one way we teach the five-step drop. This is used on a shorter route. These routes are very similar to the routes used on a three-step drop passing route.

Then we teach the five-step drop, which is a hitch and throw. The quarterback takes the five-step drop, takes a hitch step, and then throws the football. This is what most of our routes are set up on.

There will be some times when the quarterback has to hitch twice. Most times for us, the double hitch is on a seven-step drop. We try to time everything on the steps the quarterback has to drop to the pocket. Every now and then, it takes a little longer to run the route, or the defense is playing bump-and-run coverage and it takes a little more time to run the route. That forces the quarterback to take two hitches. He takes seven steps, hitch, hitch, and then throws.

On all the drops, we continue to stress the fundamentals. We check the feet to make sure he is balanced in his stance so he can make an accurate throw.

The last point here is play-action footwork. Basically, we are using the action on the running play. We want to get the feet and hips set up to throw the ball. He must get his feet set, and he must get the hips turned toward the target. These are the things we talk about in setting up before we throw the football.

Next is the throwing motion. I am no guru on throwing motion. I had the worst throwing motion in the world. But these are things that I have learned from people I had respect for when I was growing up around some good programs. These things made sense to me.

First is the motion of opening up the opposite hip. To do this, you must open up your opposite foot. A drill we use for this is having the quarterback drop on a line or yard strip with a receiver 10 yards away on that same line. The quarterback drops, and as he is ready to throw, we ask him to open his opposite foot This will help open the opposite hip, which will give him the power to get the ball to the receiver, and this will help him with the velocity on the throw.

If the quarterback is on the line and the receiver is on the line, the quarterback does not want to open the opposite foot too much. If he does, he will start throwing the ball across his body. He should open the foot on the line toward the receiver.

When the quarterback releases the football, the thumb on the throwing hand should be pointing toward the ground as the ball comes off the hand. He must snap the wrist to get the rotation on the ball. It is almost like throwing a screwball in baseball. You can take films of the quarterbacks and look at the thumb as they release the football. The thumb should be pointing down. To me this makes sense.

We teach our quarterbacks to visualize a four-pane window frame to throw the ball into on the pass pattern [Diagram 1]. He wants to release the ball through a window frame. That large window is divided into four panes. For a right-handed quarterback he wants to aim for the pane on the upper right-hand side of the window. This will give him the best chance to be accurate, and this also gives him a better chance for a higher release. We do not feel the low release is that bad, but we just feel the higher release gives the quarterback the best chance for accuracy and the opportunity to get more velocity on the ball.

The next point is the transferring of the weight from the throwing foot to the front foot. We have talked about setting up. We want to get the weight transferred from the back foot to the front foot. As far as the timing of it, some quarterbacks get the weight transferred too early, and that makes the arm come around too late. That is when the ball sails on them. Some quarterbacks have the arm going forward before they get the foot transferred. That is when the ball goes down low on them. The weight movement must transfer first, and the arm must come right behind it. Again, the key is to get the weight transferred.

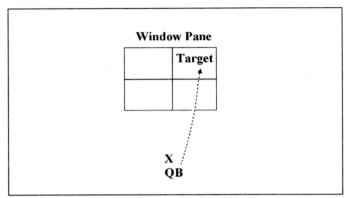

Diagram 1. Window frame

Now, I know there are some guys that can throw the ball off the back foot. A good example would be Brett Favre. Dan Marino and Jeff George were other quarterbacks that could throw off the back foot effectively. I do not see a lot of quarterbacks that can do this effectively. But as these guys released the ball, you could see the shoulder come forward as they came through the throw.

The last thing in this progression is the rotation that I talked about earlier. It starts with opening the foot and opening up the hips. Then the quarterback must rotate his shoulders. It is almost like a baseball player. The batter is sitting there, waiting on the pitch, and he is coiled. As the pitch comes to him, he uncoils. The quarterback wants the same type of motion. Dan Marino was one of the best ever at this.

Those are basic fundamentals that I have carried with me throughout my coaching career, and when I played quarterback. Again, this is technique. These things may be boring to quarterbacks but we still work hard on them in spring practice. We feel this is very important, and we start with page one of the fundamentals. We go through this each year. It may be boring to the older quarterbacks, but it is important enough that they can still pick up some important points.

Next I want to talk about some intangibles related to playing quarterback. I have been building on this for the last few years. These are little things that I think are important to quarterbacks. First is gaining confidence. The quarterback must know the play and the formation. He must know what to do. He must go into the huddle with confidence. The players can see if the quarterback has confidence or not when they get into the huddle. The players know if the quarterback knows what he is doing. At that position, he better know what he is doing. He better know what is going on before he gets into the huddle if he wants to be the leader.

The quarterback must step into the huddle and he must speak clearly. He must never assume the other players can hear him. For the college players, it is the freshmen coming into fall camp that have a problem with this. When I was coaching in the NFL it was the rookie quarterbacks that had this problem. They are real quiet and talk in a low whisper.

When the quarterback steps into that huddle, he must realize the wide receivers are winded from running the previous play, the linemen are breathing hard for an all-out effort, and he must speak up so they can hear him. He must be very precise in his annunciating, and he cannot take for granted what he is saying. He must be loud and clear.

When the quarterback gets to the line of scrimmage, it is the same thing. If he calls an audible, he must make sure he calls it loud and clear, and he must make sure everyone hears the calls. He cannot allow a penalty to occur because he was not loud enough on the audible.

He must always be himself. He cannot be a phony. The only way he can be himself is by knowing what to do as the quarterback. If he is not a rah-rah type player and all of a sudden he starts the rah-rah stuff, the players will see through this. He must show the team he knows what to do and he is in control. The quarterback must take charge in the huddle. He must demand respect in the huddle. To do this he must be able to perform.

We talk about leadership by the quarterback. To me, leadership is not getting on another player in the huddle. He cannot give the left tackle the devil because the quarterback got sacked by the defensive man the tackle was supposed to block. Leadership is not getting on a receiver in the huddle because he dropped a pass that could have been caught. To me, leadership is when the quarterback goes to the guard that was offside the play before and his head is down, and he tells him to forget that play and get ready for the next play. That, to me, is leadership. This will command more respect from teammates.

The quarterback is going to make mistakes as much as other players make mistakes. If he throws an interception, what can the quarterback expect the teammates to say to him if he is getting on them every time they make a mistake?

We want the quarterback to concentrate to avoid the silly mistakes. He can not be so concerned about the other positions that he makes a silly mistake. It may just be going the wrong way, but that is something that will not happen if he is concentrating.

He must always be positive in his support and in his commands. This is the same area I have just talked about. He does not have to get on the players. He should let the coaches get on the players. As the quarterback, he has a chance to be real positive in and out of the huddle and on the sidelines.

The quarterback must never criticize a player on or off the field. In college it is a little more involved with the media. In the NFL, it is a lot more involved with the media. There is always going to be a time when someone is going to say to the quarterback, "That receiver should have caught that pass. If he had caught that pass, you guys would have won the game." The media will bait you. This could even be your own teammates. This type of talk can spread. If you do get a chance to knock a player, don't do it. Leave the criticism up to the coaches. If you do not have anything good to say about another player, don't say anything.

The quarterback must be willing to take the responsibility for a poor play. If it is an interception and it is close as far as who was at fault, the quarterback must step up and say, "It was my fault, coach." If the ball does not hit the bottom hand and the snap is fumbled, he must step up and say, "It is my fault." He must take the blame for the snap even if the center did not get the ball up. This will go a long way in working with the centers. They know when the ball does not get up and they know when it is their fault. That goes a long way with them.

He must congratulate a teammate on a good play. So many times the quarterback will throw a touchdown pass and then just walk off to the sideline. He may come off the field with his fist high in the air and he may have a smile on his face. The rest of the team is down in the end zone congratulating the receiver that scored the touchdown. We want our quarterback to get his butt down to the end zone and congratulate his teammates.

He must congratulate his teammate when he makes a big block that leads to a big play. Again, it is showing leadership, and it is going to help him down the road.

The quarterback must never make excuses. This is the same thing we have just talked about. The last thing a coach wants to hear is a bunch of excuses. In the NFL, it is hard to change those kinds of players. They want to make excuses for everything. The coaches and the teammates do not want to hear excuses.

The quarterback must execute his position with precision on every play. It is obvious that his teammates are watching him on every move. He can not gain respect if the he does not know what to do.

The quarterback must do all of the little things. He must set the pace for the team. He must carry out all of his fakes on all plays. He must do the little things, such as changing up the snap count when necessary. These are little things that can help the quarterback gain the respect of his teammates.

I want to talk a few minutes about gaining an edge as a quarterback. He can watch film to see what the defense likes to do. Today, we are all seeing a lot more defenses than we use to see. By studying the film, he can pick up keys that will help him later in the game.

A key point here is for the quarterback to watch some film on his own. When the quarterback watches the film with the coaches, he is listening to the coaches. He watches what the coach is watching. If the quarterback can watch the film on his own, he can pick up some points without having to listen to the coaches.

Today we see all kinds of different coverages. We can pick those things up on the film. We know the safeties' alignment will always tell us what the coverage is going to be. These are things high school quarterbacks can view on their own. The more they can do this without the coach having to tell them, the better a quarterback they are going to be. If they only watch film when we tell them to look at them, they may be ok, but they will never be as good as they can be without doing those little extra things on their own.

Moving to the mechanical aspects, the quarterbacks can work on the things that give them the hardest time. It may be the drop, getting away from the line of scrimmage, or handing the ball off; they can work on their weaknesses. We all know we are only as good as our weakest part of our game. They must work on the mechanics so they do not have to think about them on Friday night. If they work on these points through the week, they should come natural to them in the games.

Here are some mental things we stress with our quarterbacks:

- Know the outlet receiver on every play.
- Be deceptive on the play fakes.
- Be prepared to mix up the snap count.
- Think about one play at a time. This is true on a good play and a bad play.
- Take what the defense gives you. As the saying goes, "You can't go broke taking a profit."
- Keep the chains moving by making first downs. Live to play another down.
- Be aware of all situations on the field. Be aware of the two minute situations.
- Know when not to take a sack.
- Be prepared to do extra study on your own.
- Have fun every day in practice. Go out with the attitude you are going to get better each day. See how many players will follow that lead.

Now I want to go to the drill tape to show these fundamentals. After the drills, we review these drills with our players to show them how the drills apply to the game.

I want to thank your for your attention. Good luck to everyone.

17

Quarterback and Receiver Reads

Cody Vanderford
Flower Md. Marcus High School (TX)
1998

I am going to talk about how we teach our quarterbacks to read defenses. What I am going to do is give you an overview and our progression that we use to teach our quarterbacks.

At Marcus we are not blessed with phenomenal athletes. We've got some good athletes. What we have to do is teach kids to run patterns and get open against superior athletes. What we have are hard workers who believe they can throw and catch the football with the best of them. I don't know if that is coaching or kids taking pride in what they do.

We have a good group of kids to work with. They are intelligent and we ask them to do a lot of things. That goes double for my quarterback. We put a lot of emphasis on the quarterback. We ask him to do a lot of things and know a lot of things. He is going to have to run the show. I am real fortunate because at Marcus, our head coach gives me the quarterbacks year-round. I'm going to take you through the year and show you the progression we use in developing our quarterback.

We start the progression in the off-season. Every single day that our quarterbacks come to our off-season program, they are with me. We do something every day that deals with playing quarterback at Marcus High School. While the other kids are working in the weight room or on agilities, the quarterbacks are in what I call a *quarterback school*. We spend about six weeks in this phase of our off-season. Every day that we can get outside we go. In a 30-minute period we work on footwork, drops, and mechanics skills. We work on throws, quick release, and throwing motion. We do anything that will help this kid to be a better quarterback.

We spend about 20 minutes a day doing some form of read and recognition. To begin with, we teach our kids to recognize and read coverage. We expect everyone on offense, except the linemen, to know what everyone on defense is doing. That helps us in the pre-snap read and reactions. If a defender aligns inside on one of our receivers, the quarterback and the receiver know what that defender's responsibilities are. When we teach our routes, we teach attacking certain areas of the field vs. certain coverages. We group all coverages into four things: cover 3, cover 2, man, or blitz.

When we started throwing the ball several years ago, we developed routes to beat specific coverages. We had a package for all coverages. What we found out was we had too much. What we did was to develop a package so that part of a route handled zone, part of it handled man, and we had an easy blitz adaptability.

We don't get caught up in the differences in zone coverages. We recognize zone. We teach our kids to recognize coverage and the responsibility of each individual in that coverage. We teach these things and expect our kids to know that. We practice them every single day.

As we develop during that 20-minute period, we start to teach combination reads. We work curl-flat combinations, two verticals, stop-corner combination, and things like that. I have 8 to 10 kids with me every day. We set up some form of drill that will work the quarterback making a read on a specific defender with two receivers. An example would be to have two guys running vertical against a free safety. I don't want the quarterback to hold the ball. We stress getting the ball out in a hurry.

After I get through the quarterback, I go to phase two of the off-season. During the off-season, each position coach takes his kids and does with them whatever he wants. We work on throwing every day that we can get outside. In phase two we are going to try to play 7-on-7 every day. We take our receivers, backs, and quarterbacks, and work against ends, linebackers, and defensive backs. My quarterback is going to learn how to run the offense through repetition. I want him to throw as many passes as he can and see as many situations that he can.

During these days if the need arises, we stop the 7-on-7 and work on technique and timing. If the receivers' coach or defensive coaches feel there is something they need to review, or some specific drill they need to work on, we use this time for that. But for the most part we work the 7-on-7 drill.

The focus with the quarterback is on recognizing the difference between zone, man, and blitz. We have taught those things, but now we are going to put it into a game-type setting and let them see it. All of our routes we have in our offense are designed to handle zone, man, and blitz. If it is zone, we work on a particular part of the route. If it is man, we work another part of the route. If it is blitz, we will make our blitz adjustment. This is when my quarterback begins to develop. I encourage my defensive coordinator to give me as many different looks as he possibly can. Our goal is to run each of our routes against all defenses, so my quarterback gets comfortable doing those things.

Once we get out of phase two, we go into spring football practice. That is not a great deal of change for us. The only difference is we add four defensive linemen and five offensive linemen to our drills. We have done all the individual drills and it should not be a big change when we go to team ball. The only change they go through is wearing the pads again. That should take them a day or two. The game doesn't change when you go 11-on-11, instead of 7-on-7. It is exactly the same thing they have been seeing for six or seven straight weeks.

The other aspect that spring ball brings is live scrimmages. We will scrimmage once a week with our best on best. Our 7-on-7 work is intense, but the live scrimmages really get intense. But all this time we are getting more reps at throwing. In scrimmages, the quarterback has to work under adverse conditions. In the 7-on-7 drill they see the blitz, but they are not feeling the pressure they get in live scrimmages. My JV team runs as the scout team for our defense. We don't take it easy on them. The JV's get a tremendous amount of experience by doing that.

Once spring ball is over we go to summer. Usually for the players the summer was fun time. It wasn't for me because I lived on a farm and had to work. The players got a break from football. But with the rule changes there are 7-on-7 tournaments all over the place. We get in them because it gives us another opportunity to play. Our quarterbacks get some of the best development during the summer that they can ever get. The reason is the 7-on-7 tournaments. The quarterback is totally in charge. He is responsible for getting his team together. He is responsible for making sure they show up at where they are going to play. He calls his own plays. He must match up formations with plays, down, and distance. All the things the coaches do on Friday nights he has to do by himself. During this process he is learning several things. He is learning why we call the plays we do. When they start to make those decisions, they start to see what you have been coaching. When I talk to the quarterback, he understands what I am talking about, because he has been in the situation and has experienced it. Working the down and distance becomes apparent to him. His calls need to match the down and distance.

The biggest thing that is developed is leadership. He has taken his team members with him all summer and organized everything. When we come back in the fall, those kids have confidence that he knows what he is doing. He has been calling the shots for the last two months. Also, they get to compete during the summer.

After the summer we get ready for the start of the season. Once we get to the season it is time to apply everything we have been doing over the course of the year. Instead of putting the red-mesh jersey on, they put the nice game jersey on and go out and do it against somebody else. The quarterback has been preparing for seven straight months. During the season we get our extensive film work. We don't do a whole lot of filming in the off-season. Our film sessions during the season are very intense and extensive. Throughout all this process, the quarterback has taken thousands of snaps against most possible looks and situations.

A lot of what I've said so far has been philosophy. I want to take a play and show you how we teach it. Keep in mind we have already taught coverage recognition. When the kid comes to the line he knows what he is seeing. We are going to stick a play in there and tell him how to apply it. In our offense we name our plays. That particular name tells everyone what he is doing. We are not going to tell each individual receiver his route plus tag a route on for the backs. We give it a name. The route I'm going to talk about is called *double curl*. We are going to run this from a trips set. In our trips set with the ball in the middle of the field, the wide receivers are at the bottom of the numbers. The 2 receiver splits the different between the tackle and wide receiver, and the third receiver splits that distance. If the ball is on the hash mark, the wide-side receiver moves in toward the ball so that his distance is the same. When you hear the word double, you probably think there are two curls in the pattern. There is only one curl and I'll explain the name as we go through the adjustments.

The base pattern with no defense is a 15-yard curl by the number 1 receiver. The first inside receiver, or number 2, runs what we call a slice, working to a depth of 15 yards. The slice route is a crossing route into the middle over the ball at 15 yards. The second inside receiver, or number 3, runs what we call a chair. The chair is a fade move up the sideline. The single receiver on the backside runs a post. Remember, a part of this pattern is good against zone and man coverage.

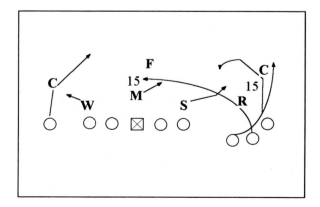

When we first start to teach this we talk about zone. Let's look at it against a base-cover 3. My kids all know that the rover is a flat player, the corner is the deep third player, and the strong linebacker is responsible for curl. We think the curl is the best part of the route for that type of zone. My quarterback from the pre-snap read knows he is keying the corner. On the snap of the ball his eyes go to the key. If the corner sinks, he works the curl. If the corner sits down on the curl, we throw the chair behind him.

If we are working against cover 2, the read is still the corner. It is still zone coverage so we work the curl-chair read. The only problem is the safety trying to rob the curl. If that happens, we like the matchup on the chair route. The outside receiver has an option if he sees the robber coverage coming. We'll talk about that later. We give our receivers a little flexibility as to where he goes in the route.

Let's look at the same play with a man-free look. When I draw these things up I use the R for rover. It doesn't matter who that is. We see him as a flat player even though he may be a linebacker, safety, or rover. When we see the man coverage we no longer work the curl-chair combination. We take a peek at the chair route. We have a cross between the slice and chair routes on release. If we get a rub off where the chair comes open, we'll take it. We don't like to throw that route if it is not an obvious completion. We work the slice all the way. We have one of our most agile receivers in that position. We have him running across the formation with somebody chasing him. The backside post clears that area of the field.

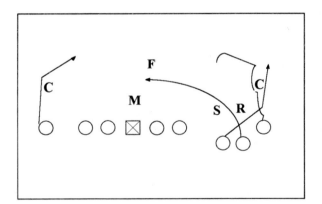

As I said earlier, we spend a lot of time on blitz. When we saw blitz in the early days we changed the play. In those days if people showed you the blitz, they came. Now they fake the blitz and don't come. What we do now is post-snap-read everything. If we see the blitz we convert the most apt part of the route to two areas of the field. We want someone coming over the middle and someone vertical. Let's say we see a free safety blitz coming. In this pattern the single receiver would be the vertical route.

He runs the skinny post and keeps going. The curl is normally run at 10 yards. With the blitz read we shorten it to six yards. But he is going to work vertical and try to get down the field. He knows there is no help in the middle of the field. He gets inside leverage and works in. That gives the quarterback the field to throw into. The chair continues to run that pattern. The slice, which was working to a depth of 15 yards, flattens off the route and brings it down to six yards. We tell the quarterback if he gets away from the center clean, on the third step he is going for the home run. If everything caves in on him, he has someone coming right in front of him at six yards.

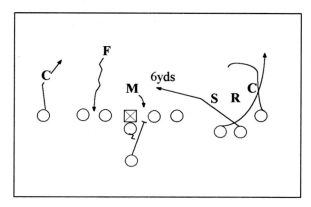

We have taken this one pattern and have handled zone, man, and adapted it to the blitz. We get the reps on all these defenses. The biggest thing is recognition of coverages. You have to see what they are in and what they are doing and adjust accordingly.

I'm going to turn the program over to Bob Bounds and he will talk about the receivers.

COACH BOB BOUNDS—RECEIVER READS

We have gotten away from pre-snap reads. The defense is not going to be in the defense they show you before you snap anyway. We had to figure out a way to read the coverage on the fly.

Cover 3 is the most basic coverage you can get in football. When we come out of the huddle as receivers, we look to the middle of the field. We are looking for the safety situation. If we see one free safety, we know we are going to get one of two looks. We generally are going to get a base cover 3 or a man free. If the safety starts to vacate the middle of the field, there is a chance of blitz.

If we see two safeties in the middle of the field 8 to 10 yards deep, we can get cover 2 or cover-2 man coverage. They could, however, roll out of that look into a cover-3 look.

The next thing we could see is the cover-4 look. That is all four defensive backs spread across the field in quarters. They can do a lot of things from that look. They can get into cover 2 or 3 easily. They can play straight or blitz from that look.

We have gone to the post-snap read of the secondary coverage. New receivers who have not been on the varsity level have to be taught some new things. The first thing they like to do is look at the ground. That is a tendency of a young receiver. He is out there trying to impress someone with his route running. What he is doing is running blind. I tell them the ground is going to be there the whole time and he doesn't have to check it. The receiver has to have his eyes up. Playing receiver is like driving a car. We have to look ahead down the field, not just what is in front of us.

Let's go to the zone read. There are several keys. The first one is the defensive back in front of us. If the defensive back goes to a hard backpedal, that is probably zone. If the eyes go inside that is probably zone. They are coached to get a key off the quarterback. It is hard to tell if the receiver is running a 10-yard stop pattern, but if he is running a crossing route, it is easy. If the defensive back lets us go inside, it is zone.

We have to understand route setup. If the receiver has an inside-breaking route in a zone coverage, he needs to be on the inside of the defender. We don't want to get caught up. We don't want to let the defensive back blow his coverage and still be in position to make a play. I may tell the defensive back I'm going inside, but it doesn't tell him what I am going to do. The same is true if we are going to run an outside route. We want to stem to the outside shoulder of the defensive back.

The man read is next. As we come off the ball, we look at the defensive back's eyes. If his eyes are on us and nowhere else, he is probably in man coverage. If the defensive back jumps inside trying to maintain inside leverage, that is man coverage. Of course, if we break inside on a crossing route and the defensive back stays with us, it is man coverage.

The route step up on man coverage is a little bit different. When you play against man press coverage, or bump and run, the defender is trying to wall the receiver to the outside. We have to make a move to get inside if we have an inside-breaking route. We get upfield and at the break point of our route, we make a good move to get separation. At the good- move point, we accelerate away from the defender.

Let me cover this *plain-Jane* pattern. We have a curl and double curl. I'll show you this from a wing set. That is two receivers to each side. The outside receiver fires off the ball. At 10 yards he makes a post cut like he is going deep. We want to threaten the corner with depth. Once we make the post break we are headed to another zone in the field. That is another player. We want to focus on that player.

We have to threaten the safety also. We try to make eye contact with the safety. We drive three to five steps to the inside and shut the pattern down. Our best receiver was this receiver. A lot of teams would take a defender out of deep coverage and try to double him on the curl. If he reads the robber coverage coming out of the inside, he has the option to try to run by that coverage into the middle of the field. The whole time we are driving downfield we have to find out what the curl player is doing. There are different windows in the field depending on who is taking the curl. We have to get in the proper window right now. When we come out of the last break we can't be standing behind the rover. We have to know where the window is going to be. There is usually a 20-square area to run this route.

I train for this type of route running in the off-season workout. We run the routes and I stand where the rover is going to be. I give them finger numbers. They have to yell out the numbers I give them as they run their route. They are running their route and concentrating on what numbers I am flashing.

The inside receiver on the curl is running a chair, which is a deep fade-type pattern. To the backside they are running what is called a middle and a post. We are trying to work the front side of this route, but we are not afraid to come back to the backside. The back runs the middle route. It is a 15-yard route down the middle of the field. He has a lot of freedom with this route. If he sees man coverage he continues to run. If the free safety sits down on this route, we hit the post.

When we recognize blitz, we make adjustments to the routes. We can signal the quarterback to what we are going to do. We draw the coverage up by running shortstop hitches. We hit the deep route behind the safeties.

18

Quarterbacks and the One-Back Passing Game

Ed Zaunbrecher
University of Florida
2002

From that introduction, you can see I have coached at several schools. I enjoyed the years at Marshall University. I am looking forward to working at the University of Florida. I know it has been interesting the last six weeks.

In today's world, coaching football requires motivational techniques. To motivate, you must be able to communicate. When I was a young boy, my dad used to make me speak with marbles in my mouth. As I got better at speaking, I was allowed to take out the marbles one at a time. When I lost all of my marbles, I went into the coaching profession. I am sure we all can appreciate this point of view.

As coaches we can have a lot of good ideas of what we want to do and how we are going to do those things. But you must be careful you do not try to do too much. What you know is great, but the key is how much your players know and what can they do. That is more important than anything you know. I can draw up the best pass pattern in the game of football, but if my quarterback cannot make that throw, it is not a good play. The same analogy applies in coaching quarterbacks. There are a lot of coaching points you can get into. I tried to keep things as simple as possible without cluttering the quarterback's mind with a lot of coaching points. It is different for me at the college level because we recruit players. If a player cannot throw the ball, he should not be in the program as a quarterback. We recruit good players, but we still have to put them on the right page to do certain things.

In working with young kids in camps, I do the same things. To me, the important thing in working with quarterbacks is to *keep it simple*. There are two basic drills for working on the mechanics of throwing the football. They need to set the ball in the drill. They get tired of doing this but they need to learn how to set the ball. They do not want any wasted motion or any dipping of the ball. If you have a quarterback that is having problems, have them work on setting the ball in the throwing stance. Have them work on holding the ball where they want it.

After they learn to set the ball, they must learn to *step and throw*. Next, they practice a few motions, and then you put the actions together. That is how you want them to throw the football. Everything else is extra. Any other motions are wasted. If you can get them to do the basic things upstairs, you have a chance. Spend most of your time where it is important. That is down on the feet. That may sound crazy because you are throwing with the motion of the upper body. Watch the quarterback when he plays *catch*. If he can be accurate in that drill, he has a chance to be successful. He knows he can make the throw. It is the job of the coach to put him into that position after he has dropped. It may be a play-action pass, a bootleg, or whatever type of pass it is, but you need to put him in that same position so he can make the same throw. You have to put him in that position over and over again. That is the whole purpose of the pass drop. We want to put the quarterback in a position where he can repeat the throw.

The basic things we tell the quarterback in throwing the ball is to start with the weight on the inside of the rear foot. *The gun is loaded.* If the ball is up in the set position, the gun is loaded. If he is sprinting out, he must have the weight on the rear foot, so he can step and throw the ball. Everything moves toward the target and he must follow through. It sounds simple. I know guys are different, but any coaching you do should be to smooth that procedure out and to make him consistent.

When I went to Marshall University and went to practice that first day, I met Chad Pennington. Actually, I had met him the day before spring practice started. I got there the night before and we practiced at 6:30 a.m. I introduced myself to Chad. "I am your new coach," I said. I told him I did not know the plays and that he could coach the plays. I told him I was going to work on the techniques. I watched him for about five seconds and decided that Chad could throw the football. Even my wife could tell this guy could throw the football. I could see he did not need a whole lot of coaching. Everything from the shoulders up was as good as you could get. The only thing we needed to work on was balance.

When a quarterback can set and throw without pressure, most of them are pretty good. When they have to move around they get off balance, and this is when they have a problem. They are not consistent. This is what I work on with them.

If the weight is on the inside of the rear foot and the quarterback moves, he must get the weight on the rear foot to throw the football. We work on this over and over again. We are concerned about being consistent in throwing the football. We are interested in the quarterback being a high-efficiency quarterback as far as completion percentage is concerned. This does not mean just dumping the ball off. I want them to be consistent down the field as well as on the short routes. The only way to do that is to have him do the right things over and over again.

At the same time, we work on some of the off-balance throws. We do that because the quarterbacks are going to throw off balance at some point in time. So we work on them doing drills where they have to set their feet and throw the ball. After a few throws while they are warming up, I want them to start moving their feet. We do not want them to stand in one spot and throw for very long. We are going to be moving. It does not have to be a long throw. We want them to move for four or five yards and set their feet. The weight is on the inside of the rear foot every time. We do not want them to get off balance. That will happen sometimes. We do not want them to throw off balance if they do not have to. We repeat this process over and over.

I can live with the quarterbacks releasing the ball from different spots. As long as the elbow is shoulder-high so everything is moving in the same direction, he should be fine. I have had some quarterbacks that threw the ball with the ball a foot outside the shoulder. But they knew where the ball was going. When the elbow starts dropping down, you get a lot of rotary action, and the ball is going to take off in different places. As long as the ball is set, and the ball is above the shoulder, he should be able to throw the ball.

We do a lot of work on the abs with the quarterbacks. They are important for the quarterback. But the point I make to them all of the time is this: the strongest muscles they have are in the middle of the body. The abductors are very strong muscles. There are very few players that have a *strong arm*. Not many of them can stand flat-footed and throw the ball 70 yards. I have only had one quarterback that could do that. I have been lucky. Most coaches never have a quarterback with an arm that strong.

Most people have a connection with the ground. A lot of you play golf. If you did not use your legs you would not hit the ball very far. It is the same with the quarterback. He must get in a good position with the weight on the inside of the rear foot, step, and throw. I keep repeating this because that is how I coach it. We keep running the basic drills over and over again. I do not want the quarterbacks thinking about the mechanics of throwing the football.

When we practice, we go through sequence just like most teams do. The first part of practice is the individual phase. This is when I want the quarterbacks to think about mechanics. Then we go into other phases where we are working with other players. Now we are thinking timing, spots on the field, and other related aspects on the passing game. When we get into the pass-skeleton drills, we start thinking keys in the secondary. The last phase is when we get into teamwork. This is where we tie all of the passing game together. This includes protection and the keys.

When you get into teamwork, you cannot spend a lot of time on technique. If you do this, you are losing focus on the most important things you are working on at that time. If you need to get him out after practice and work on techniques, don't dilute what you are trying to get done by spending all of your time working on correcting techniques. If there is something that is a real flaw, you may want to make a correction, but you really try to minimize what you are doing. You can make a note of it and work on it later. With young players, you may have to do more along those lines.

There have been a lot of coaches that do more on details related to the quarterbacks. I like to recruit good quarterbacks and teach them where to throw the ball. It may be more than this and we may have to be a little more specific, but when we have camp with eight-year-old kids, I still get them doing the five-step drop with no wasted motion. I get them stepping and throwing with the weight on the inside of the rear foot. They get the ball up and turn the palm down and the ball comes out in a spiral for them. The body falls in line. To get the bottom line done, the body will adjust.

If you are the quarterback coach, or any other position coach as far as that goes, and you cannot give the player enough detail about the position and put it in writing for him, then you do not know enough about the position. For example, you must be able to give him the details on how to read different defensive coverages. He must be able to determine where to go with the ball. You must be able to give him the details on how to do those things.

Once you have given him the details on those things, you can ask him for feedback. That is very important. If he can't tell you what you want to know, then he does not know the system. If you cannot tell him, then you do not know. The first thing you must know when you put in a new pass play are the details related to that play. What does the quarterback do if something goes wrong? If the receiver falls down, what do I do? If the defense is not in the coverage we expected, what do I do? Is the play still a good play? You better know the details, and you better be able to communicate the details clearly.

I do not think coaches get enough feedback in the classroom setting. I am not talking about on the field. Coaches get in such a big hurry they do not give the players the opportunity to provide feedback in the classroom setting. I want our quarterbacks to be able to get up in a meeting and draw up a formation and what the receivers are doing on a play. I want them to be able to draw up the protection and I want them to be able to draw up the defensive fronts and coverages. I want them to be able to show me how the defense lines up to disguise their coverages. I want them to be able to draw up everything about the play. We have to spend time with the quarterback teaching this information if we expect him to know all of it. The front end is really loaded for the young quarterback coming in for the first time. We spend a lot of time teaching defensive concepts and what we want the quarterback to do against those concepts. How do you attack defenses? What are the good plays to run against each of the defenses we face? If the defense lines up wide, we run inside. If the defense lines up tight, we run outside. If the defense lines up in two deep, we attack the corners. If the defense lines up in three deep, we attack the seams. We work on those things over and over again, so they can attack what they see on defense. The more the quarterback knows and the more they can use, the better coach you become.

If you saw Marshall University play this past year, you know our quarterback had a lot of freedom in the offense. We gave him a lot of choices in the concepts we gave him. I would call the formations and tell him to watch for certain things from the defense. "The first time we see three deep, we want to run four verticals." He knew what to do when the defense gave us that look.

If you sit down and study a game, you will find there are 6 to 10 times per game when you have the right offensive look against the defensive look that gives you a chance for a big play. Not very often do you have a chance for a big play in the game. You do not want to waste those opportunities. If you concentrate on this point just one more time per game it will result in an additional touchdown. If you can communicate this to the quarterback, now you have a chance to do it.

We put it down on paper for the quarterbacks. We teach them defensive theory. Things have gotten a lot more complicated in college football in coaching quarterbacks than they were when I first started coaching. When I first started coaching, the defense lined up in three deep or two deep. The defense played zone or man. Then the defense started playing quarter coverages. Now we see brackets, combos, keys, and cross-keying is the thing with the defense.

All of this makes it tougher to coach the quarterback. In some ways, this has changed how I coach the quarterback about defenses. We teach him basic alignments, but once the ball is snapped, we teach him concepts. Is there a safety in the middle of the field? Are they playing the deep secondary with two half safeties or not? We want them to know our plays, but we also want them to know what to expect on defense. By the time the quarterback takes that first step, he has a good idea of what is happening by the flow of that middle safety. By the time the quarterback gets to his second step, he knows if a blitz is coming or not. If the blitz is not coming, he knows he has a zone or man coverage, and any other factor that he needs to know about the play.

We use drills that apply to game movements. I will line up as the free safety in front of the quarterback. I will take two steps and the quarterback must tell me what the concept is. We want him to tell me right now what the defensive concept is that the free safety is executing. We want to teach him what is good and what is not good.

Another example of what we are trying to get across to the quarterbacks would be this. Let's say you have a real good play to the backside. If the defense has four defenders sitting over on the backside, it is not a good play. The quarterback has to know that is not a good play and he has to be able to change the play. We do not want to waste a play.

We use visualization with our quarterbacks. We want them to see themselves making plays. We want them to go through the keys on the play. Today I was talking to some coaches about working on drills with the quarterback with his eyes closed. Some of you may say I am crazy. How can a quarterback work with his eyes closed? When we are working on fundamentals it has nothing to do with seeing the defense. We tell him to close his eyes and take a pass drop. The quarterback comes back and sits up. He may be off balance but he will be aware of it. There is no reason he cannot set and be balanced with his eyes closed.

Then we go to the next step. We have a man that runs for four steps and we throw him the ball. He takes a balanced step and throws the ball to the receiver at five yards. There is no reason he cannot do this. We do this drill until they can hit about every pass. I make a point to them. "Use your eyes to watch the defense. It has nothing to do with passing the ball." I make them go through the sequence.

It is important to make the players give you feedback. I have to know if they understand what we are trying to accomplish. Make sure they know the details. Make them draw it up on the board. Give them a study sheet to take home. If they can't put it down on paper, they do not know it yet. You may have to find another way to teach them. Do what you have to do to teach them the concepts. That is why you have coach in front of your name. Figure out a way to get it done.

I have gone to a lot of practices from grade school to high school, from college to the NFL. Over the years I have seen a lot of great drills. The thing that struck me about some of these drills is that they did not have anything to do with football. They were creative but they did not have much to do with what takes place in a game. To make a point, make sure your drills improve a specific skill.

We want our quarterbacks to practice all of the different kinds of passes. If you have a quarterback that wants to practice in the summer, but does not have his receivers available, here is what he can do. He can put up a net and throw toward the net. He can get a bucket or trashcan, and throw at them. He can just throw to that spot. When we throw the corner routes, this is about where the ball should be. Tell him this in an outline that he can take home with him. The corner route for us is 26 yards deep and two yards from the sideline. If we are working the seam route, it is going to be 18 to 20 yards deep and two yards outside the hash mark. He can go through all the motions of throwing to the sideline on a flat route.

While the quarterback is working on this in the summer, I want him to visualize the whole pass route. He can practice all of the throws in the passing game without his receivers.

Let me cover one point about teaching quarterbacks. How you say things is more important than what you are saying. Most of you teach the curl-flat combination in some form. Most teams teach the quarterback to read the strong safety or the flat defender, or whomever it is, to decide where to throw the football. You teach them to read the defender and throw the ball opposite that man.

Defensive coaches know this as well. They will screw the quarterback up by having the safety hang around on the curl until the linebacker can get depth, and then the safety will cover the flat. The quarterback is sitting back in the pocket trying to figure out what to do with the ball. He is making snowballs. He wonders why the curl-flat pattern is no good.

Try telling the quarterback something like this on the play. "Here is what I want. Run the curl-flat route. You throw the ball to the flat unless you cannot throw it there." Now he comes back on the drop, looks at the receivers, and throws the ball to the flat. Next play he does it again. No one covers the play. Now the defensive coach gets on the safety to get outside and cover the flat route. The next time he drops back, he runs the ball. We want him to make the defense define what they are going to do quicker. Make them commit quicker than they want to. We do not want them to call the route unless you are satisfied with the flat route.

The next point I want to cover is how to teach the quarterback to throw the ball over the head of the linebackers, and in front of the safeties in the hole. It is the same area on cover 2 on the fade route between the corner and safety. We want to work on improving the throw down the field. We take a receiver and place him behind the goalpost at about seven to eight yards deep. We have the quarterback and a center set up inside the 10-yard line. We want the quarterback to take the snap and throw the ball to the receiver behind the goalpost. If he is making the correct throw, the ball will skim the crossbar. If he floats the ball, there will be air under it. If he tries to muscle the ball to the receiver, it will go underneath the crossbar. He has to put the touch on the ball. We tell him to hit the receiver in the mouth with the ball. Players love this drill. We throw the ball at an angle. We can change the angles up and have him throw four or five times from each side. We do not let the quarterback look at the crossbar. Once they get the feel of it, they will take it over the ball and in front of the safety. The player does not have to be a pro to make that throw. You have to let them get a feel for the throw and a sense of dumping the ball over the rushing linemen, and dropping it to a back. The goalpost drill can be a good instructional tool. You can use different angles with this play.

We do a lot of timing with our receivers. We want the quarterback to be able to let the ball go when he hits on his fifth step. He wants to set up and get the weight on the inside of the rear foot.

I am not going to spend much time talking about teaching the drop. I teach it the same way as I did when I first started coaching. We teach the drop with no hitches so we can throw the ball on time. Hitches will come when you need them. We work on this. When they finish on the drop, I want the weight on the inside of their rear foot. If the weight is on the front foot when they finish the drop, they cannot throw the ball on time.

We encourage our quarterbacks to stand up and throw the ball. Some quarterbacks want to get bent over and throw the ball bent forward. We want the spine up so everything is normal. If we are throwing the ball deep, we may tell them to tilt the spine back a little. This will help them get a little more air under the ball.

On the five-step drop timing, we teach it like this: one-two-three, four, and five. On the first two steps we are getting depth. On the last couple of numbers we are not getting depth anymore. This is how it goes; one-two-three, four, and five, and then you can get into the throw.

I am going to touch on the one-back passing game. There are a lot of different forms of the one-back offense. There are a lot of different ways to do things. The one-back passing game is a game where you can use the concepts that you have been taught since you were in junior high school. You can have different combinations of passing routes. You can have curl-flat routes, corner routes, vertical routes, hook routes, and three-step routes. It is all the same stuff. You do not have to come up with a lot of different combinations. You have the ability to put in a few plays here and a few things there. You do not have to be the most creative quarterback in the world to complete a pass. It helps to have an extra receiver out on the play. It is not against the rules to have the curl-flat route on one side and the curl-flat route on the other side. It is a lot simpler for the quarterback. We say *less is better; less is more.*

Have some things in the offense that you know they can run. Then you can go to the quarterback and tell him because the defense is playing in such a way we are going to put in three plays for them. It could be something we know the quarterback can do. I have our receiving coach make sure we did not put in too many running plays. We had our five base running plays and three additional plays we just put in. Now if we wanted to put in another play, that receiver coach would ask what play are we going to take out if we are going to add another play? It is the same thing in the passing game. The offensive line coach is in charge of that aspect of the game. If we want to add five new routes, the line coach wants to know which five routes are coming out. If you keep adding five plays each week, at the end of the year you have a list of plays that is a mile long. You have plays so you can attack any defense in football. The problem is the players can't run the plays because they have not practiced them enough. If you have an experienced group, you can do more things. Make sure the lowest common denominator does not get wiped out. Make sure you put people in position for success.

One thing I like about the one-back passing game is that you can spread the field out. Obviously, that helps in the running game as well. The mentality of most defenses today is to stop the run first. This is true with teams that throw the football. Teams still line up to stop the run first against us at Marshall. We obliged them by throwing the ball. We threw more in some games than we did in others. When we sit down at the end of the year and take a look at the balance between the run and the pass, it comes out that we pass about 55 percent of the time. Some people think we throw the ball 80 percent of the time, but we don't.

In the one-back passing game, if you have some athletic players, it gives you a chance to take advantage of their skills. You can put players in a 1-on-1 situation where you can be successful. If you do not have better players than what you are playing against, it still gives you a chance to utilize the skills they have by taking advantage of matchups.

You can go away from the one-back set and run the empty set. You can get four receivers to one side, three receivers to one side, or two receivers on each side. If the defense keeps too many players inside, you have them outflanked. When you have them outflanked, there are not many defenders to make the play. You always want to have something on offense that can take advantage of the defense when you use the different formations. You may use the sprint-out game, the three-step screen game, or anything that takes care of the defense when they do not have enough players in a certain area. The quarterback must be schooled on what he is looking for in each situation. If the defense is spread out all over the field, then we should be able to run the football.

Just because you are in the one back does not mean you cannot use play-action passes. Sometimes it is even better from the one-back set. It does not matter if you run it from the shotgun or from under the center. It is hard for the defense to see the ball when you are in the shotgun. The pop pass to the tight end is better out of the one-back set than it ever was out of the two-back set. In the one-back set, there are more defenders out of the picture. They are not in the way like they are in the two-back set.

The theory of the one-back offense is that you have taken the fullback out of the picture and you are putting him in different places. It may be that you have a receiver playing for the fullback or you have a more skilled player at the fullback position. Sometimes it is easier to find another receiver than it is to find another fullback.

It helps the quarterback to see the blitz from the one-back set. When everyone is bunched up on the two-back set, it is hard to tell who is going to blitz.

A lot of teams like to disguise their coverages. At Marshall, that was the reason we went to the no-huddle offense. After 10 or 12 plays into the game, that disguise in the secondary is gone. We snap the ball fast before the defense can change up. Now the defense is out of position, and they are sitting there looking at their wristbands looking for the call and the ball is snapped. They are out of position when they get to the sideline. Now the defense has to play us honest and the quarterback can see this and take advantage of the situation.

Some offenses attack everywhere along the line of scrimmage with the run. They only attack the passing game in a few areas. In the one-back passing game, you can attack the entire field. You can make the defense cover the entire field. You can get more people into more protection even though it appears that you are in a wide-open formation. You can still get six- or seven-man protection from the one-back set.

At different times in my career, this has been a big factor. You do not have the big linemen up front, and you cannot knock them off the line as well as you would like to. A lot more linemen can learn to get in front of a man and try to keep him out of the way than can knock them off the ball. The defenses have such good athletes today it is hard to knock them off the line. You have a better chance of preventing the defensive line from overpowering you in the one-back set than you have trying to knock them off the ball in the two-back set. If you have linemen that can knock them off the ball, it is even better. Now you can spread them out and still run the passes as well.

I like to move the pocket around. You can run bootleg, spring-out, or stop-out behind the tackle. If the defense knows where you are going to set up all the time, they attack that spot. If it is six or seven yards behind the center, they are going to go for that area. They attack that spot. They can get good at it because they know that is where the quarterback is going to be. But if you are there 60 percent of the time and somewhere else 40 percent of the time, it is a lot tougher. Even if you just move around 20 percent of the time it makes it tougher for the defense.

We like to run our basic routes and a lot of different combinations. One of my favorite routes is a 10-yard hook route. You run down the field 10 yards and turn around and look for the ball. We can be in four wide receiver and all four receivers run the hook route. We can be in all combinations and still run the same route. It does not matter what formation we are in, we can run that route. The quarterback takes his five-step drop and throws the ball. It puts a receiver against a linebacker. We run it over and over. Then the defense thinks they have us figured out. Now we run four verticals on the same path. Zoom, we are gone. We run four verticals.

The one-back set lets you use your strength. You can find a way for one of your receivers to take advantage of someone on the defense. You must use your strengths to take advantage of the defense.

I do not have time to go over everything we do in the one-back set. I want to talk about some different concepts that you already have in your offense that you can use.

You can get into your three-step drop game. Run the hitch routes. You can run the hitch or the quick-out routes. Not every quarterback can throw the quick-out routes. At Marshall, we had a quarterback that could throw the quick-out route.

The slant route is very important. Make sure the receivers run the correct angle when they run the slant route. Depth is important to a certain point where you are not being jammed. The receivers must know when it is time to break. They must break on the right angle. The quarterback can adjust to the depth of the route. Basically we are going to take three steps and cut at a 45-degree angle inside and separate. The big problem is when the receivers do not take a good angle and the defender is too close to them. You must have a way to account for him to clear, or you must have another receiver inside. The receiver has to beat the corner and then run at the angle.

We want to be able to throw the fade route on the deep outside. We want to be able to throw the ball in a hurry. We do not just throw this pass on the goal line. It may be when we have a tall receiver and the defense is covering him with a short player. Find out who the best receiver is to run the fade and use him for that route. Not all receivers can run the fade. Even the good players cannot always run the fade route. When you find a receiver that can run the fade, you must take advantage of him.

We have routes that go to certain spots on the field. We talked about the hook route. We send the receiver down 10 yards and have him come back toward the quarterback. That is a simple concept. It has been effective for a long time. You can use different combinations on these routes. The receivers get good at running them. All positions for us learn how to run a hook route. We can split the running backs outside and have them run the hook.

We talked about the curl-flat route. Teach them to run that pattern. I have run the curl 12 to 16 yards. What determines the depth? It depends on how fast the receivers are. If your receivers run 5.0 for the 40-yard dash, then you are running them 16 yards deep. I would speed up something because you cannot protect the quarterback that long. The curl route is not a route that you throw on time. On the hook route it is a five-step drop, and set the foot, and then throw the ball. The curl is not thrown on time. There is an extra count in there. If you take the five steps and set and throw the curl, it will not set up. It takes a hitch step first before throwing the ball. There are more routes than those, but these are examples of the ones we use the most.

Here are some routes we use on movement. First is the out-cut. Some coaches are afraid to throw the out-cut. If the defense picks it off, it is a touchdown. It is not a problem if your quarterback learns to throw the route properly. If the defense is covering him, the quarterback should not throw it over there. The quarterback must have confidence in the throw because you were confident enough to call the play. When you are working with the quarterback in the preseason and you are in pass skeleton drills, I want him to take chances with the football. I want him to see if he can fit the ball in on a route. Otherwise, he will never know if he can make that throw or not. If he gets it intercepted in practice, you can work with him to improve his throw. Until he tries the throw, he will not know. I want him to be aggressive. We can always back him off a little. We can go over his mistakes and make corrections after he makes the mistakes in practice. We do not want to wait until the game to make the mistakes and the corrections.

The out and comeback routes fall in the same category. The question is how deep the receivers run on the route. On the comeback, we go 18 yards deep and come back to 15 yards. If we have a fast receiver, we may send him 20 yards deep and back to 17 yards on the comeback. Also, it depends on the quarterback action. If we do a bootleg, we will send the receivers a little deeper. That gives us more time to run the deep route.

If you are scared to throw the out route, you can move the pocket for the quarterback over toward the side of the pass. You do not have to run a full sprint out for the quarterback. You can run half-sprints on the out-cut to get the quarterback close to the receiver.

The one thing teams do not do enough of is to attack down the field. You do not just have to throw streak routes or post routes. There are a lot of different routes you can use.

We like to run deep-crossing routes. The defense tends to lose the receivers on crossing routes. You will need some time, but you can run bootlegs and other actions.

We love corner routes. We run these routes against two deep and against man coverage. We do not run them against three-deep coverage. We are gong to throw the ball away from trouble against the man coverage.

On the streak route, we like to run four vertical receivers down the field. We try to find out who can run the best vertical routes and who can catch the long ball. The man that can play the ball in the air is the man you want to throw the ball to. Throw it to the man that can make the catch. How do you find these things out? You have to try it, and you have to practice it. You can find out if you can run that play or not. We run a couple of post routes. We have a skinny post that we throw on time. On the deep post, we are going to throw the ball deep down the field.

There are two basic concepts on the play-action pass. First is the quick series. This includes the plays where you are attacking linebackers. If the linebackers step up into the hole, the quarterback throws the ball to the tight end on the pop pass. We want the high-percentage and high-efficiency passes on this throw. These are not touchdown plays. They are efficiency plays. These plays slow the blitz people down.

When you go deep on play-action, you want to work on the safeties. Corners should not bite on play-action plays. The safeties are the defenders that come up to stop the run to quick.

We like to run the screen play. In the one-back, that is the way we run a sweep. I like to get the ball outside. If we get five yards on the play, we are happy. If we get the all-out blitz, we want the big play. One of the hard things about practicing screens is getting a good look on defense. Scouting teams do not run the right defense. So we practice them on air most of the time. We put the bags outside where the defenders are supposed to be, and we go block on the bags. If you do takeoff drills at the beginning of practice, it is a great time to work on your screen plays. If you put the ball on the 10-yard line and you are running plays into the end zone on goal-line drives, you can run the screens on the calls. You can get a sense of rhythm on screen plays.

I hope this gives you a concept of what we are trying to do in the one-back offense. We repeat those concepts over and over. We run a few crossing routes, a few corner routes, a few hooks and curl routes, and we throw the ball down the field. We keep putting our quarterbacks and receivers in those situations over and over again.

I appreciate your attention. Thank you very much.

About the Editor

Earl Browning is a native of Logan, West Virginia. He currently serves as president of Telecoach, Inc.—an organization that conducts the Nike Coach of the Year Clinics (www.nikecoyfootball.com) and produces the annual *Coach of the Year Clinics Football Manuals*. A 1958 graduate of Marshall University, he earned his M.Ed. and Rank I education certification from the University of Louisville. From 1958 to 1975, he coached football at various Louisville-area high schools. Among the honors he has been accorded are his appointments to the National Football Foundation and to the College Hall of Fame Advisory Committee on moving the museum to South Bend, Indiana. He was named to the Greater Louisville Football Coaches Association Hall of Legends in 1998. From 1992 to the present, he has served as a radio and television color analyst for Kentucky high school football games, including the Kentucky High School Athletic Association State Championship games.